T0048239

SCHIRMER'S LIBRARY
OF MUSICAL CLASSICS

JOHANN SEBASTIAN BACH

The Well-Tempered Clavier

Forty-Eight Preludes and Fugues

For the Piano

Edited by
CARL CZERNY

With a Biographical Sketch of the Author by
PHILIP HALE

IN TWO BOOKS

Book I — Library Vol. 13
→ Book II — Library Vol. 14

G. SCHIRMER, *Inc.*

DISTRIBUTED BY
HAL•LEONARD®
CORPORATION
7777 W. BLUEMOUND RD. P.O. BOX 13819 MILWAUKEE, WI 53213

Copyright, 1893, by G. Schirmer, Inc.

Printed in the U. S. A.

Preface.

The principal object in issuing this new edition of J. S. Bach's "Well-tempered Clavichord" has been to make it as correct and complete as possible, both by means of comparison with all preceding editions, and by collating with some earlier manuscripts. In marking the fingering, which renders this issue far more generally useful, two points have been steadily kept in view:

First, to keep the hands as quiet as may be, even in extremely complicated passages;
Secondly, to enable the player to bring out each separate part independently, with perfect smoothness, and with due regard to the phrasing.

Patient study, either on the pianoforte or on the organ, will be rewarded by the rich and full effect produced by a smooth and flowing polyphonic rendering.

It has been my endeavor to indicate tempo and interpretation;

First, according to the unmistakable character of each movement;
Secondly, according to the well-remembered impression made on me by Beethoven's rendering of a great number of these fugues;
Thirdly, according to convictions matured by more than thirty years' study of this work.

Wherever an extremely rapid tempo is indicated, this is, of course, meant only for the pianoforte. When playing passages so marked on the organ, the tempo must be moderated very decidedly.

Those who have no Maelzel's Metronome at hand are reminded, that the Allegro in these old compositions is to be taken, as a rule, much more tranquilly and slowly than in modern works.

Vorwort.

Bei dieser neuen Ausgabe von J. S. Bach's wohltemperirtem Clavier hat man vor Allem gestrebt, durch Vergleichung aller frühern Ausgaben so wie einiger ältern Handschriften, die möglichste Correctheit und Vollständigkeit zu erlangen. In der Angabe des Fingersatzes, wodurch dieses Werk eine weit grössere Gemeinnützlichkeit erhält, wurde stets der zweifache Gesichtspunkt beachtet:

Erstens, die Hände, auch in den verwickeltesten Fällen möglichst ruhig zu halten;
Zweitens, jede einzelne Stimme von den Andern unabhängig, streng gebunden und folgerecht ausführen zu können.

Der Spieler wird die daran zu verwendende Mühe, sowohl auf dem Pianoforte wie auf der Orgel, durch die gehaltreiche Wirkung belohnt finden, die mit einem vollstimmigen und fliessenden Spiele hervorgebracht wird.

Das Zeitmass und den Vortrag habe ich:

Erstens, nach dem unzweifelhaften Character eines jeden Satzes;
Zweitens, nach der wohlbewahrten Erinnerung wie ich eine grosse Anzahl dieser Fugen einst von Beethoven vortragen hörte;
Drittens, endlich nach den Ideen aufzuzeichnen und zu bewahren gesucht, welche ich selbst durch ein mehr als dreissigjähriges Studium dieses Werkes in mir festsetzte.

Wo ein bedeutend schnelles Zeitmass vorgeschrieben wurde, ist es natürlicher Weise nur für das Pianoforte berechnet. Wollte man jedoch die so bezeichneten Sätze auch auf der Orgel vortragen, dann müsste allerdings das Tempo bedeutend langsamer genommen werden.

Für diejenigen, denen kein Maelzel'scher Metronom zu Gebote steht, wird noch erinnert, dass das Allegro bei diesen ältern Compositionen in der Regel viel ruhiger und langsamer zu nehmen ist, als bei modernen Tonstücken.

CARL CZERNY.

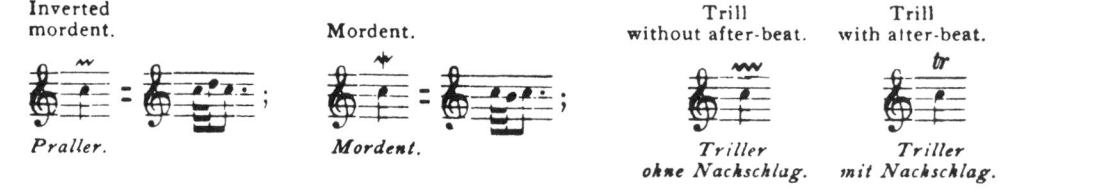

Inverted mordent.

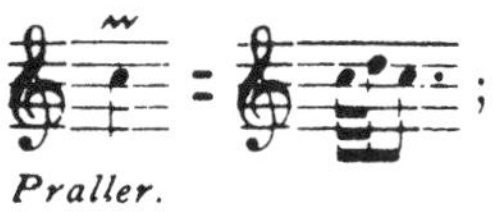

Praller.

Mordent.

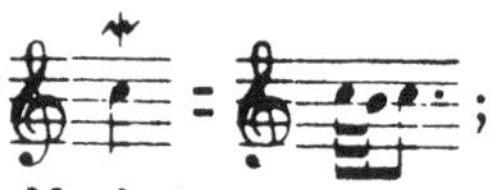

Mordent.

Trill without after-beat.

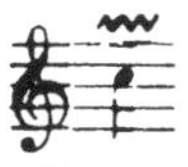

Triller ohne Nachschlag.

Trill with after-beat.

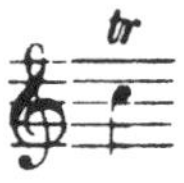

Triller mit Nachschlag.

Contents

Vol. II

Part Second.

Preludio I.

J. S. BACH.

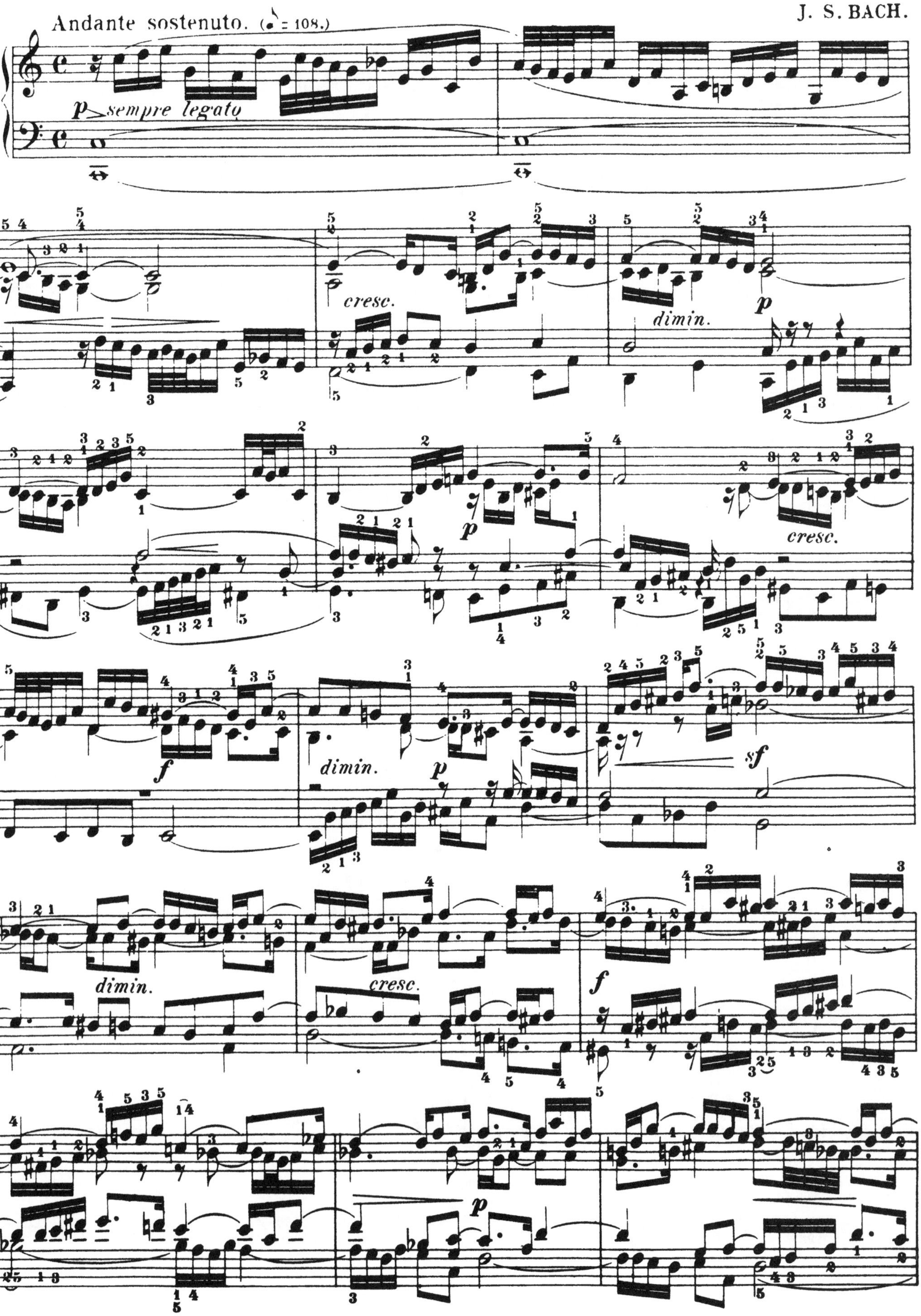

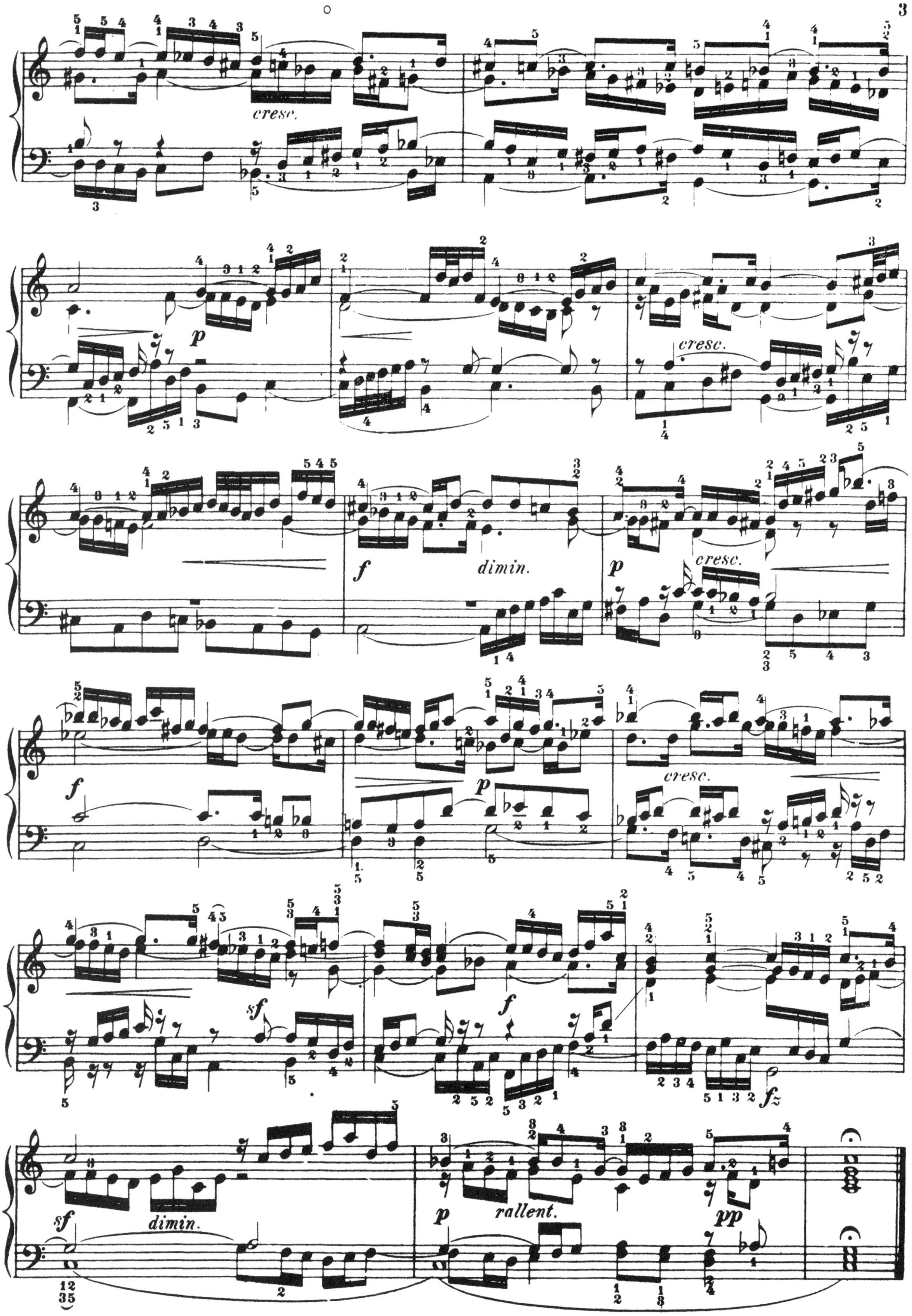
cresc.
p
cresc.
f
dimin.
p
cresc.
f
p
cresc.
sf
f
fz
sf
dimin.
p
rallent.
pp

Fuga I.

a 3 Voci.

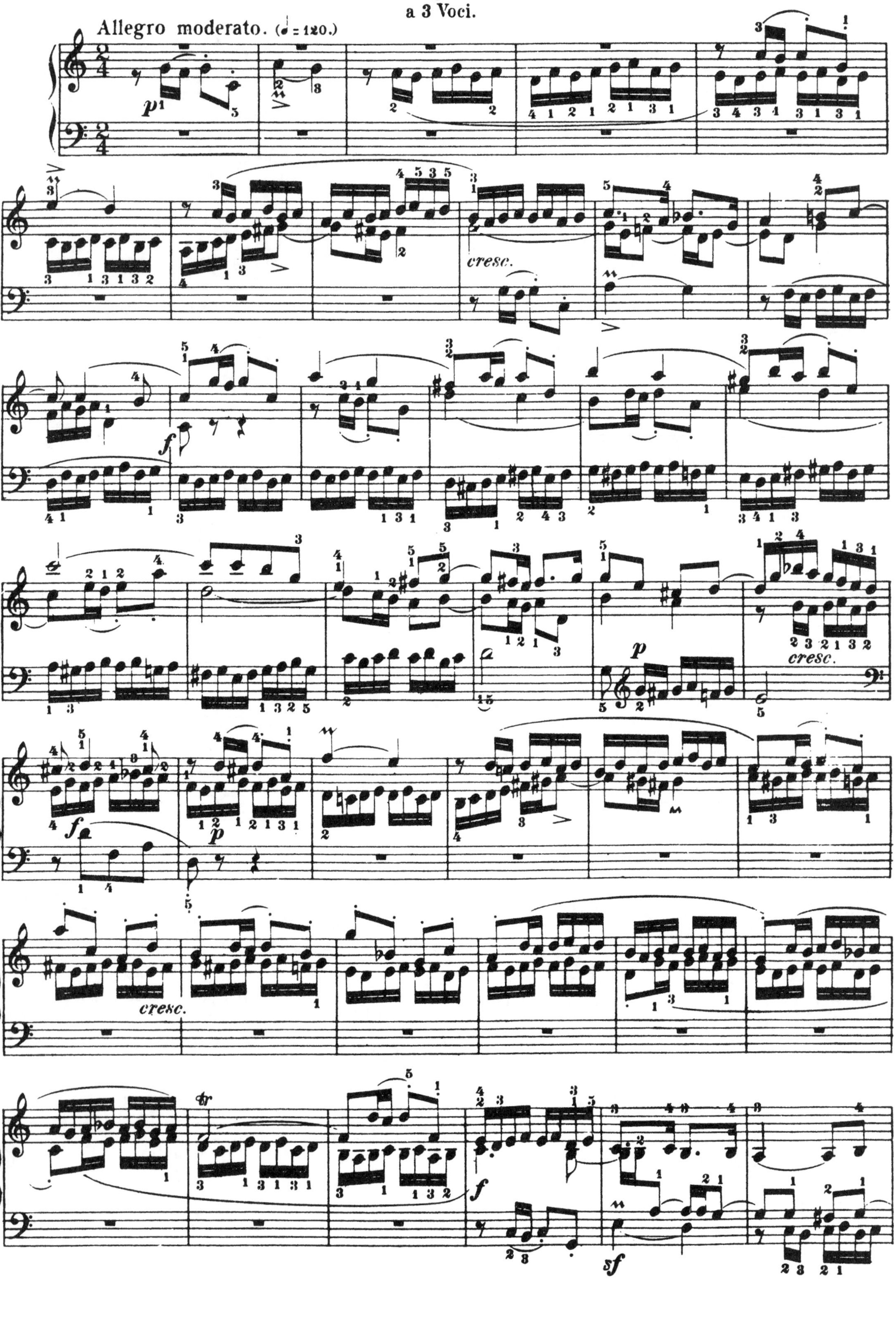

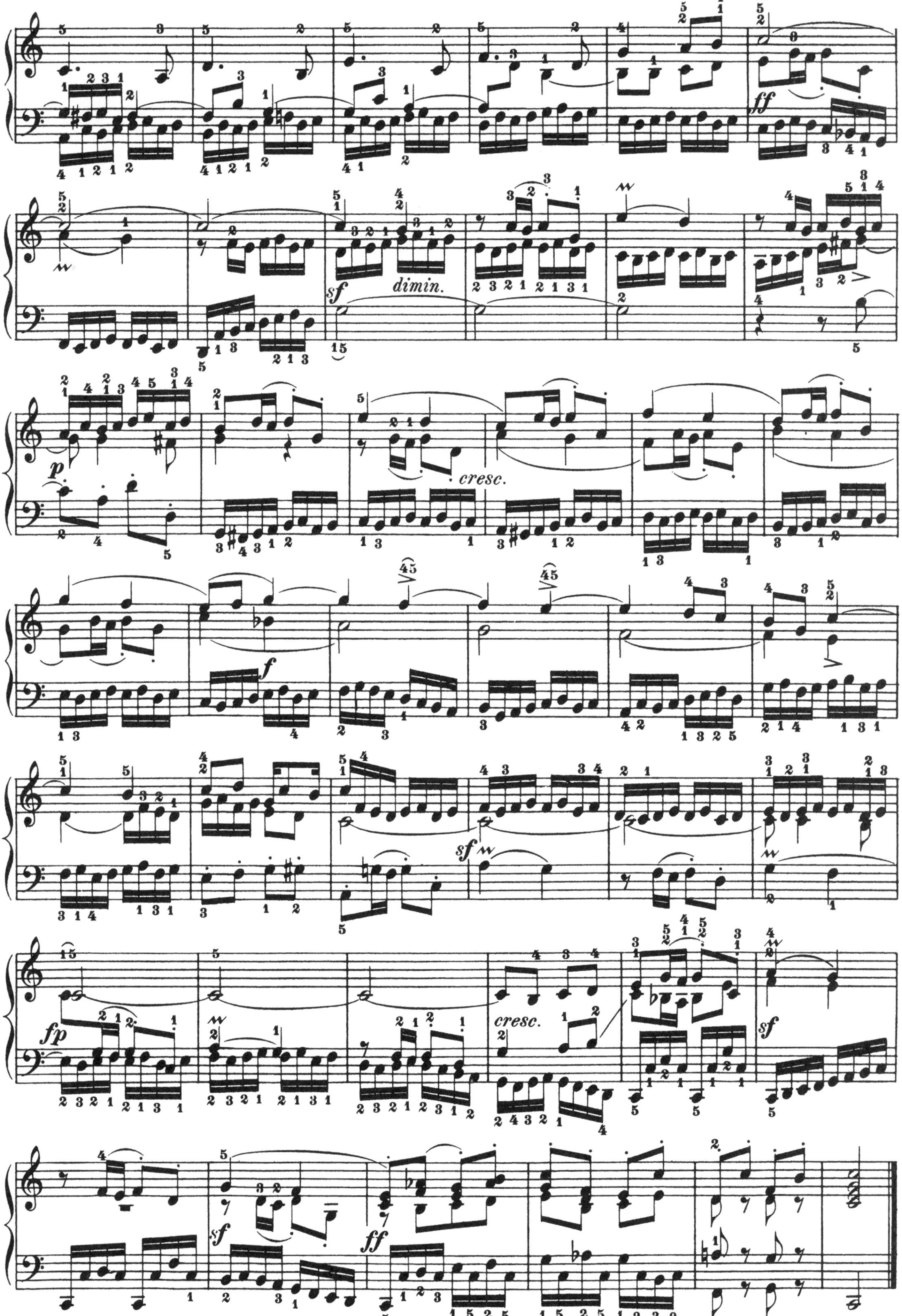
dimin.
cresc.
cresc.

Preludio II.

Allegro. (♩= 132.)

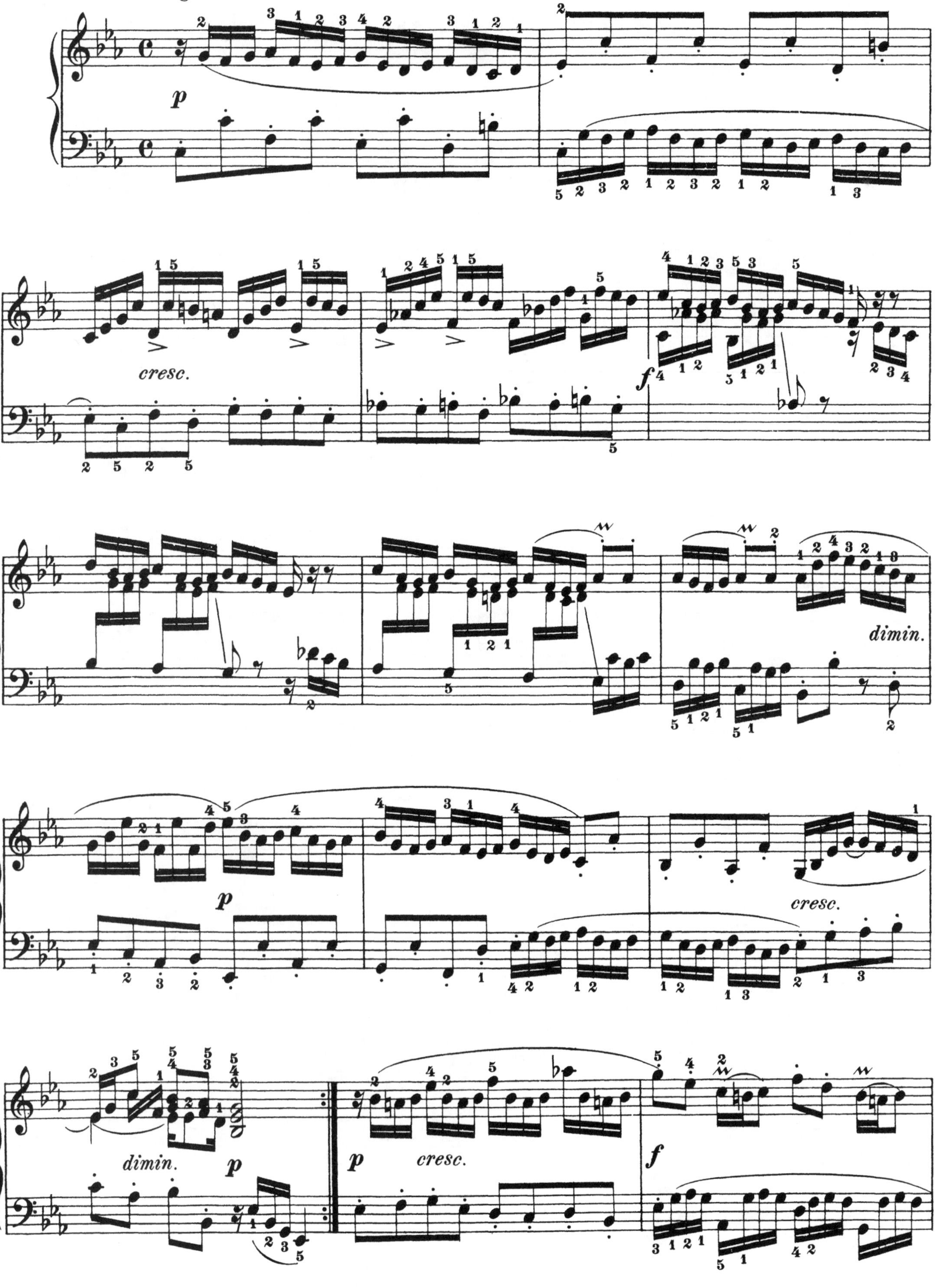

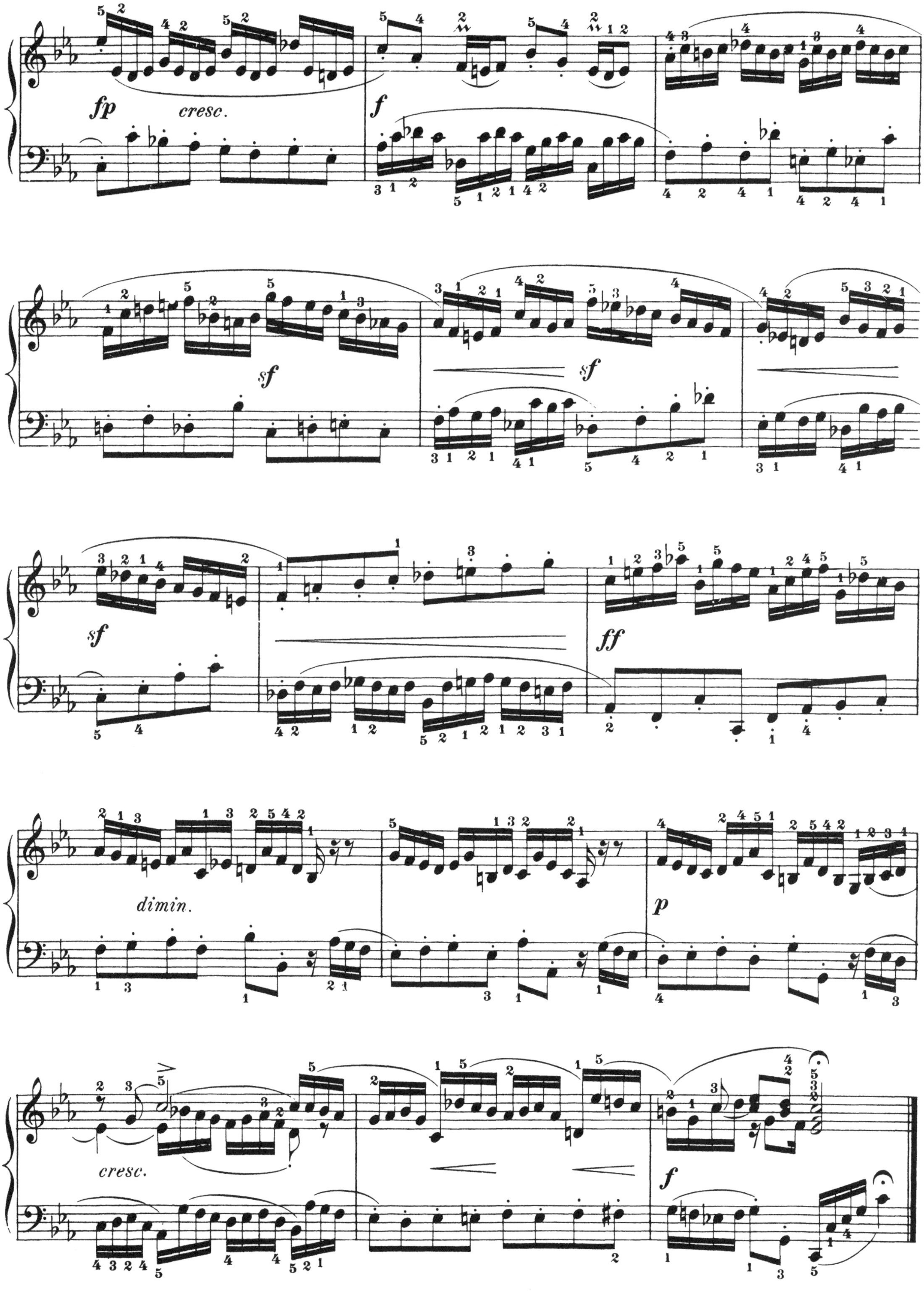
fp
cresc.
f
sf
sf
sf
ff
dimin.
p
cresc.
f

Fuga II.

a 4 Voci.

Moderato quasi Andante. (♩= 69.)

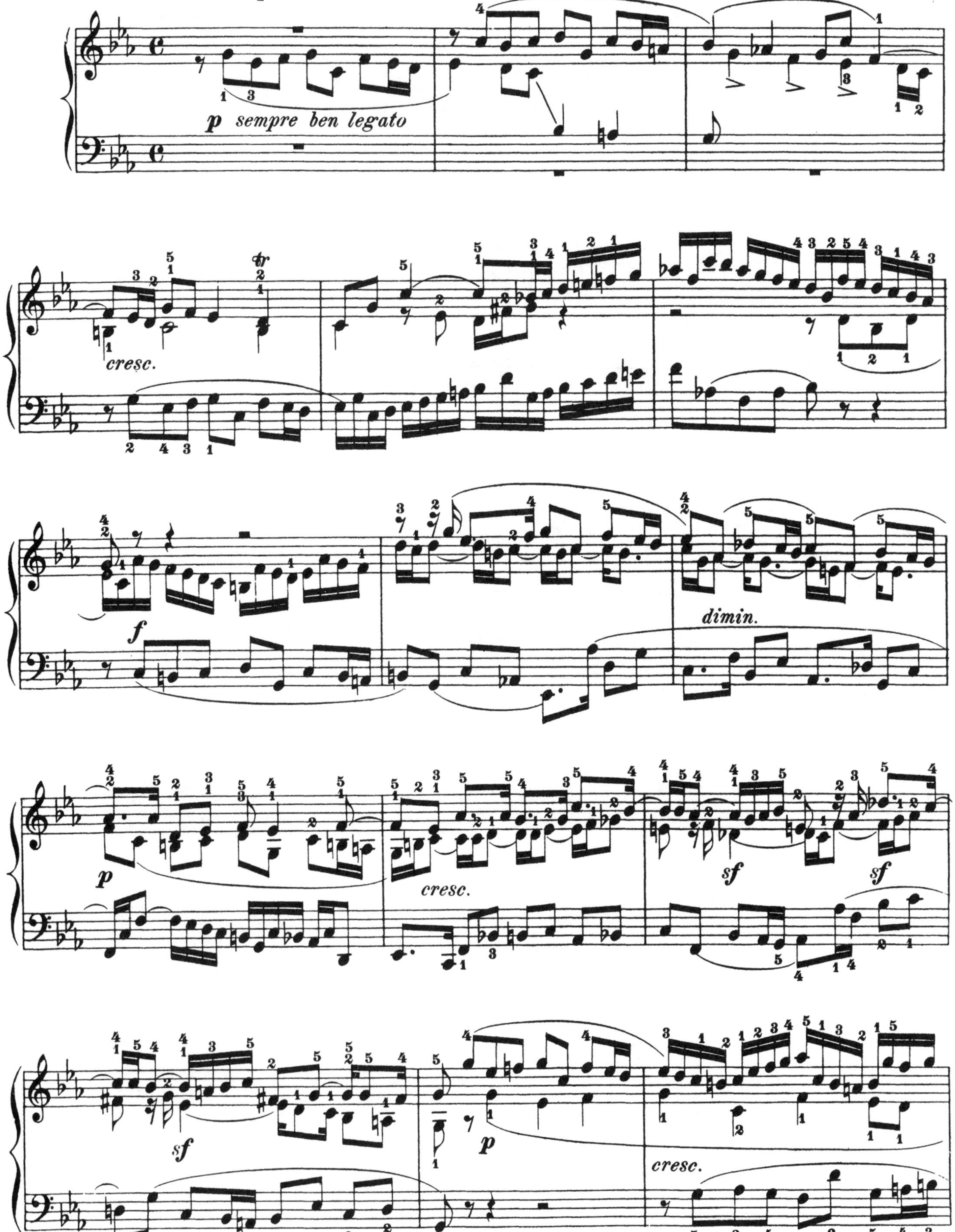

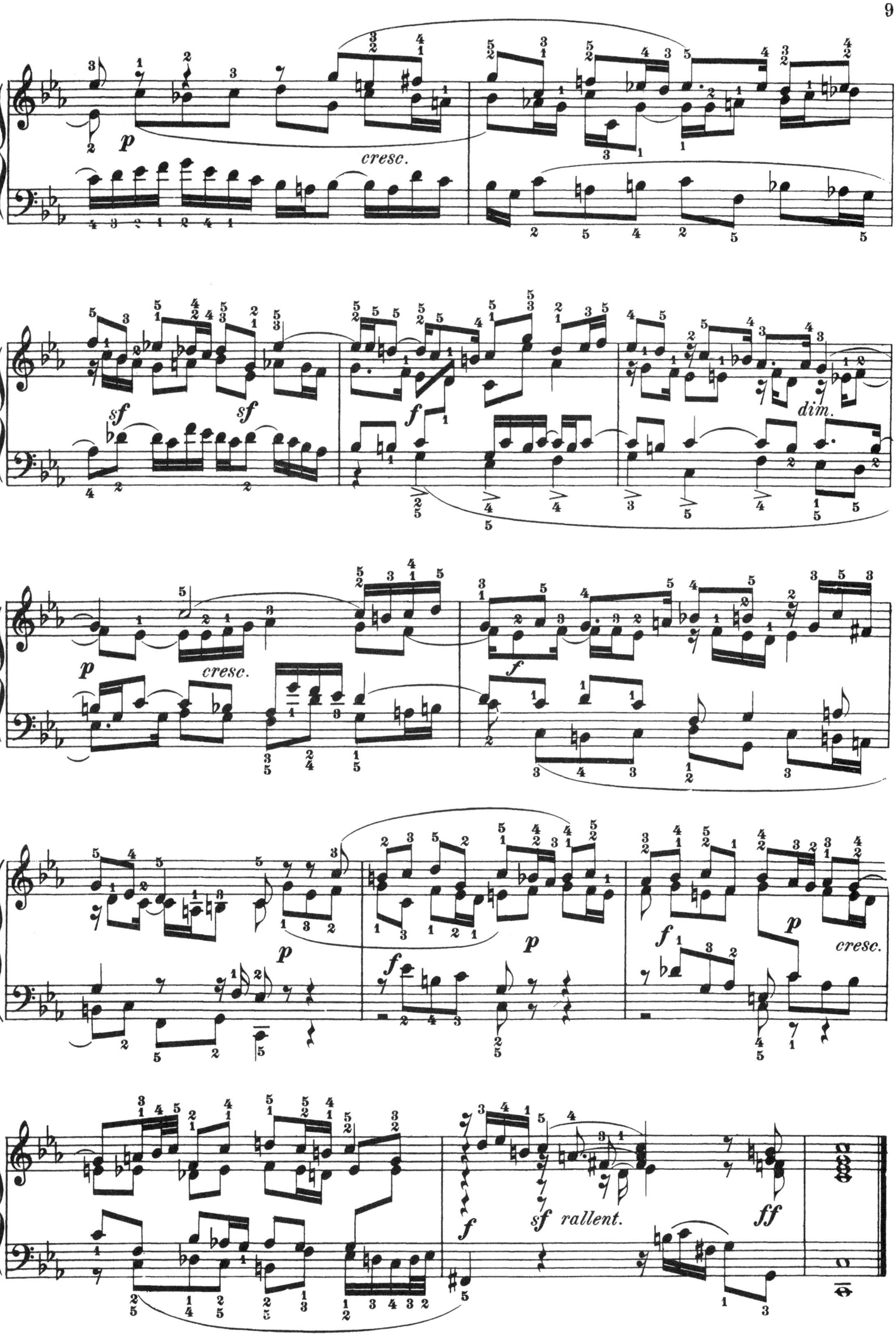
cresc.
sf
sf
dim.
cresc.
cresc.
sf rallent.

Preludio III.

Moderato. (♩=80.)

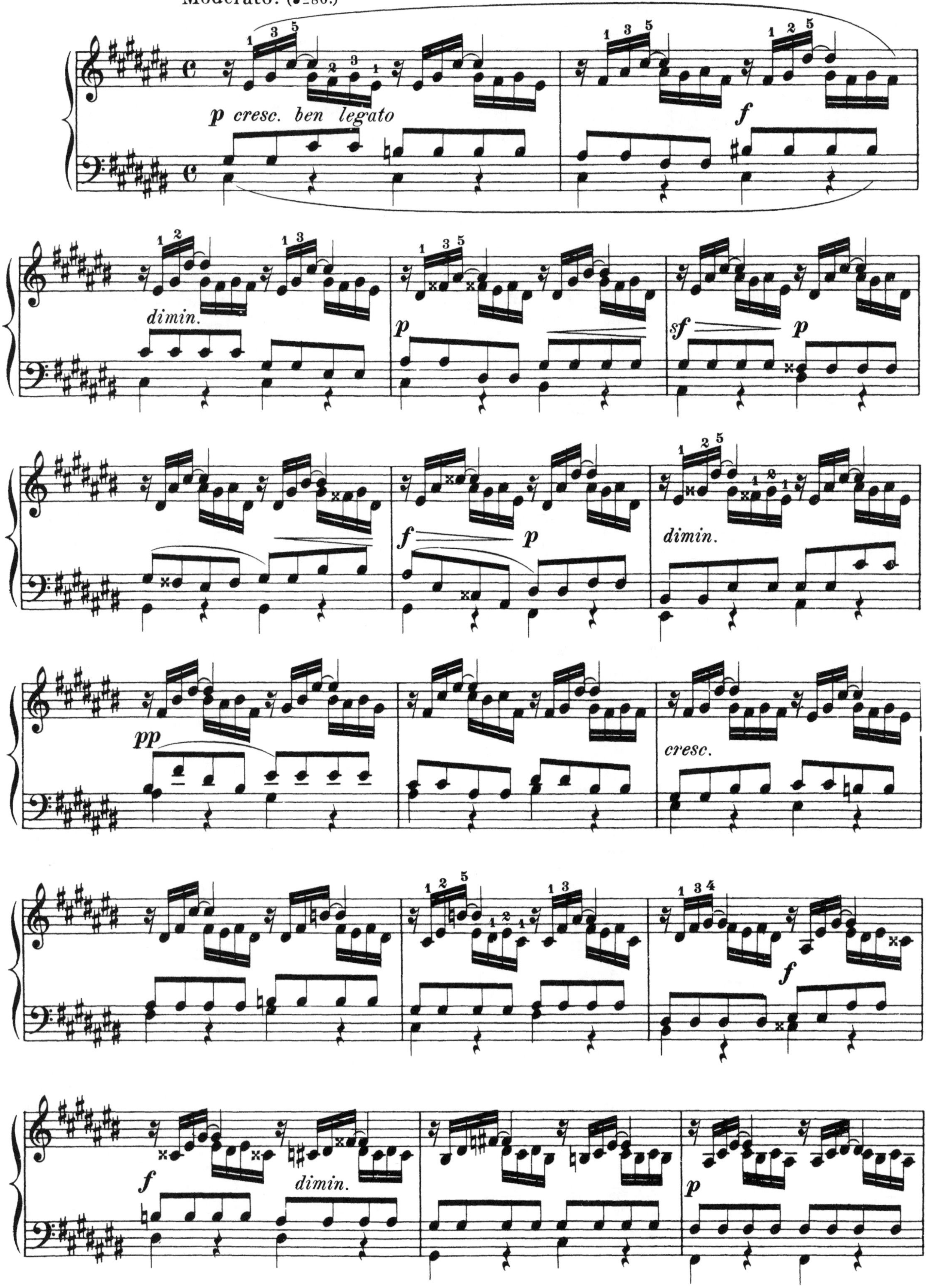

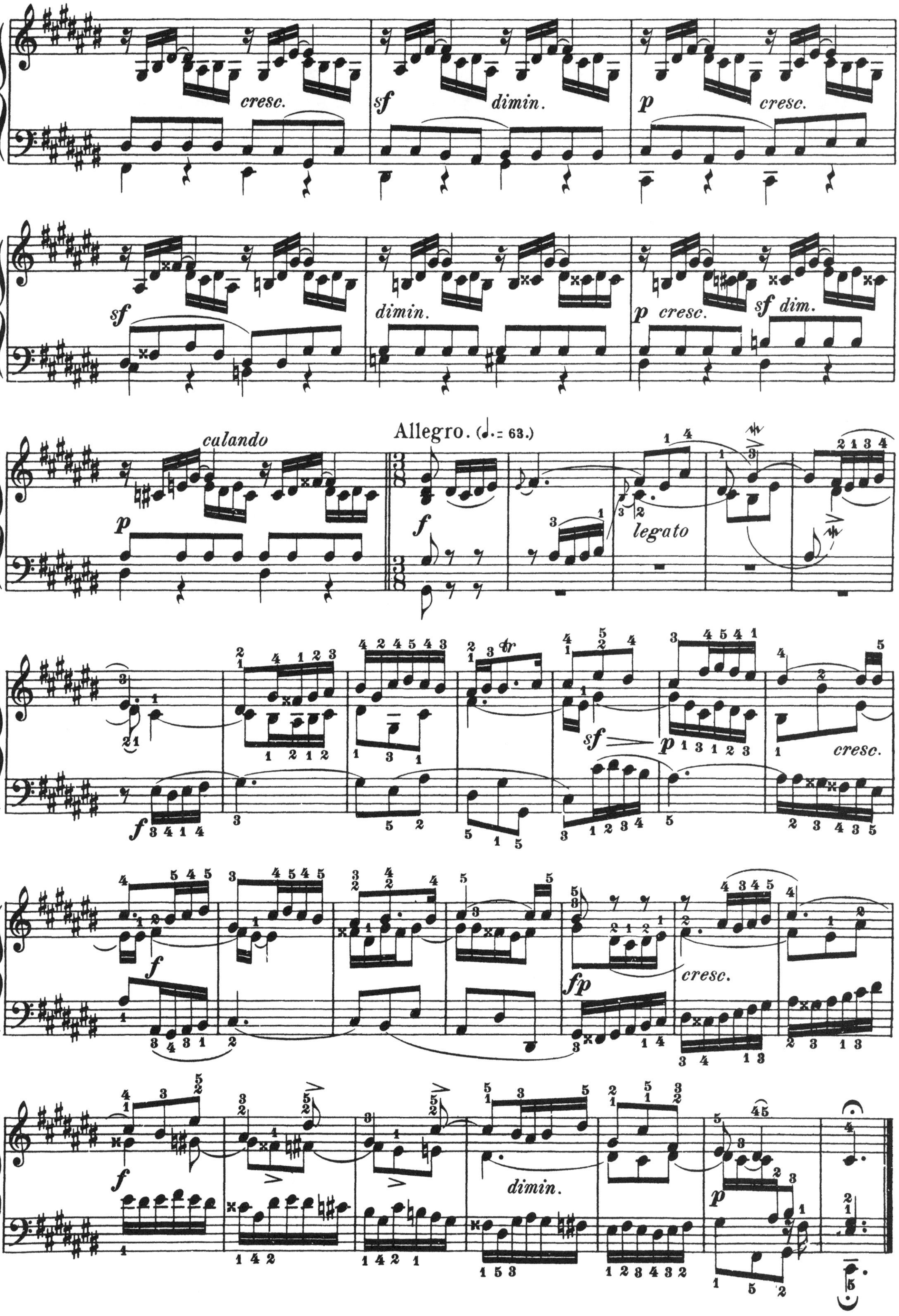
cresc.
sf
dimin.
p
cresc.
sf
dimin.
p cresc.
sf dim.
calando
p
Allegro. (♩. = 63.)
f
legato
f
sf
p
cresc.
f
fp
cresc.
f
dimin.
p

Fuga III.

a 3 Voci.

Molto moderato e maestoso. (𝅗𝅥 = 76.)

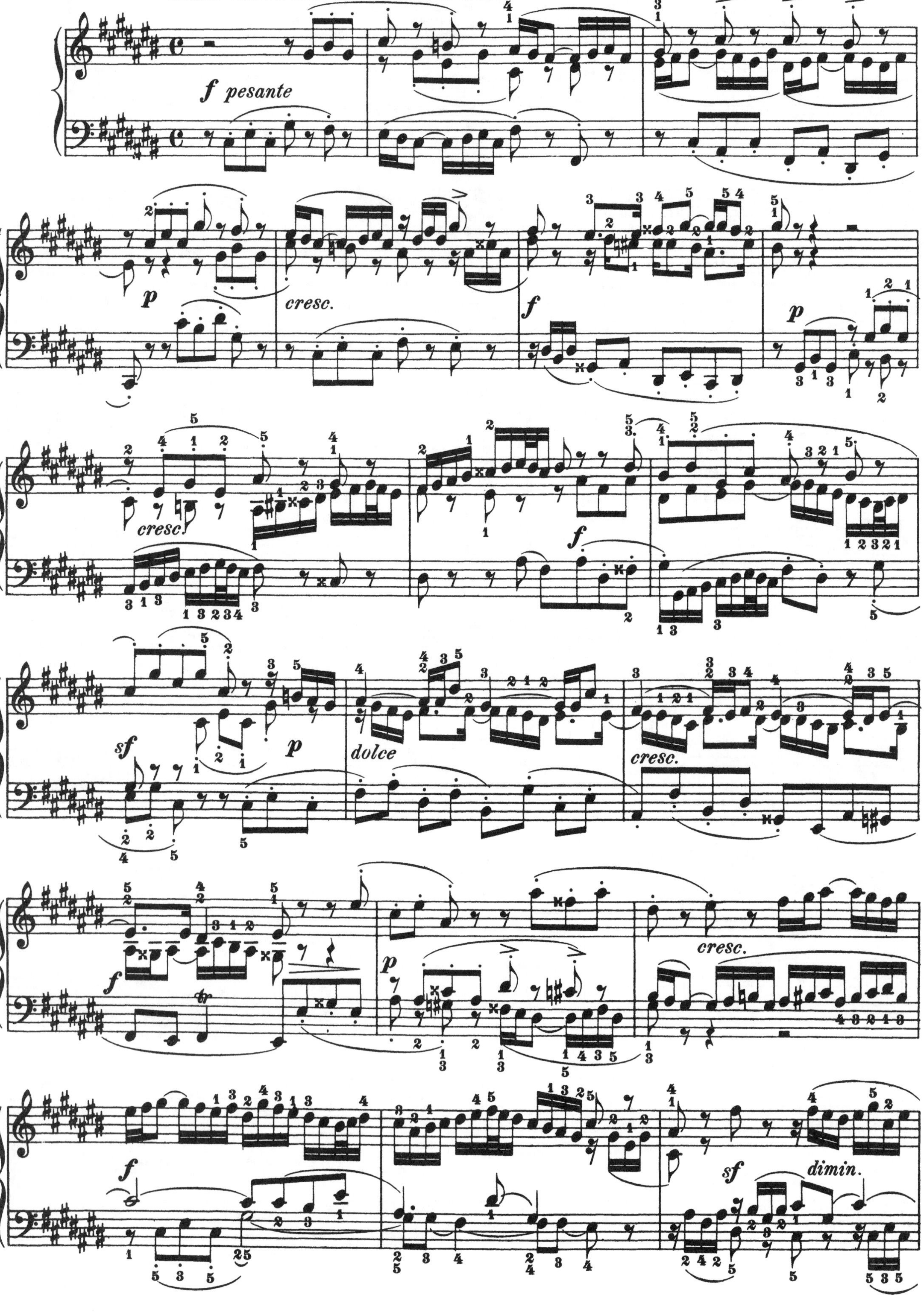

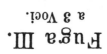

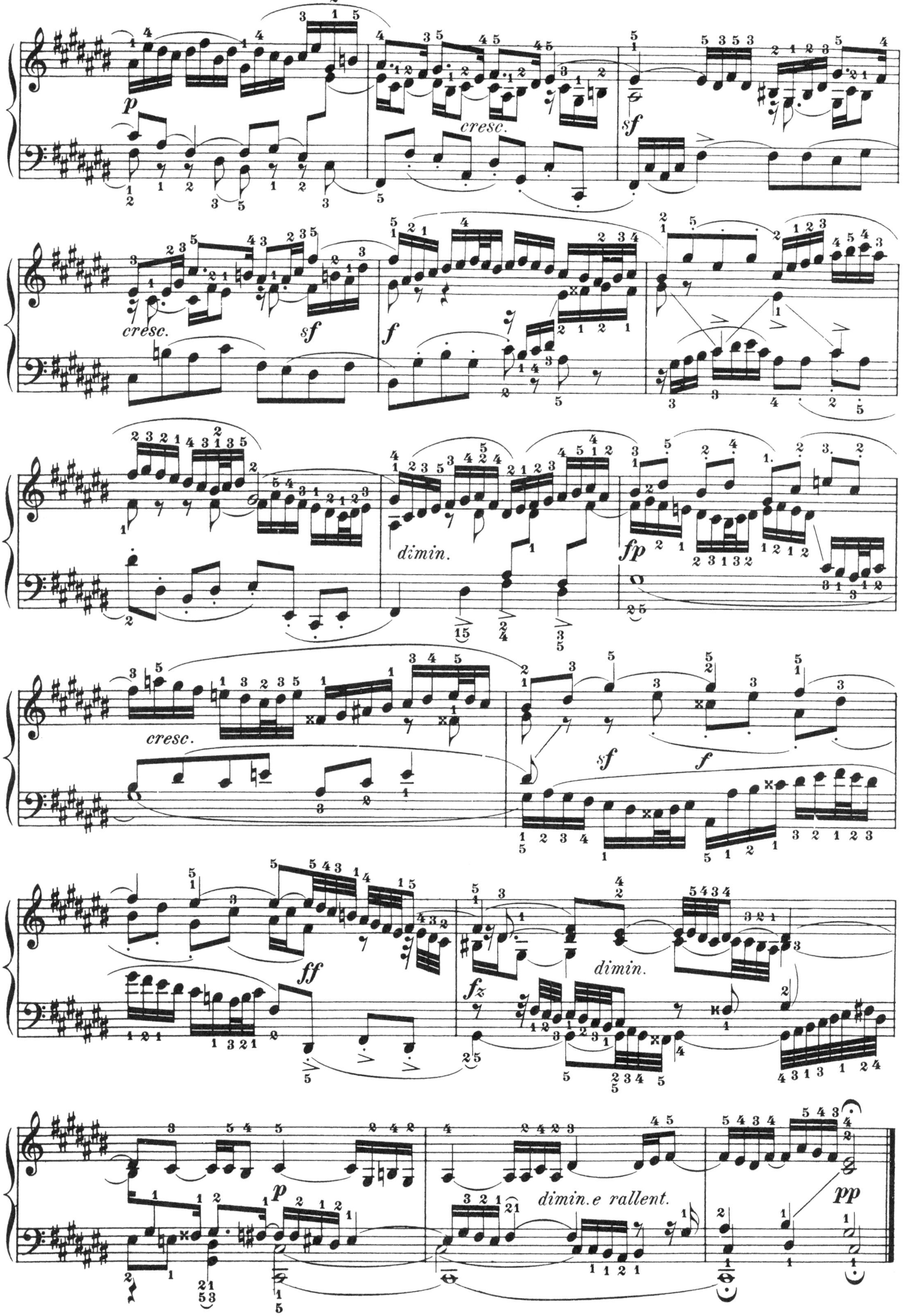
p
cresc.
sf
cresc.
sf
f
dimin.
fp
cresc.
sf
f
ff
fz
dimin.
p
dimin. e rallent.
pp

Preludio IV.

Allegretto moderato. (♩.=58.)

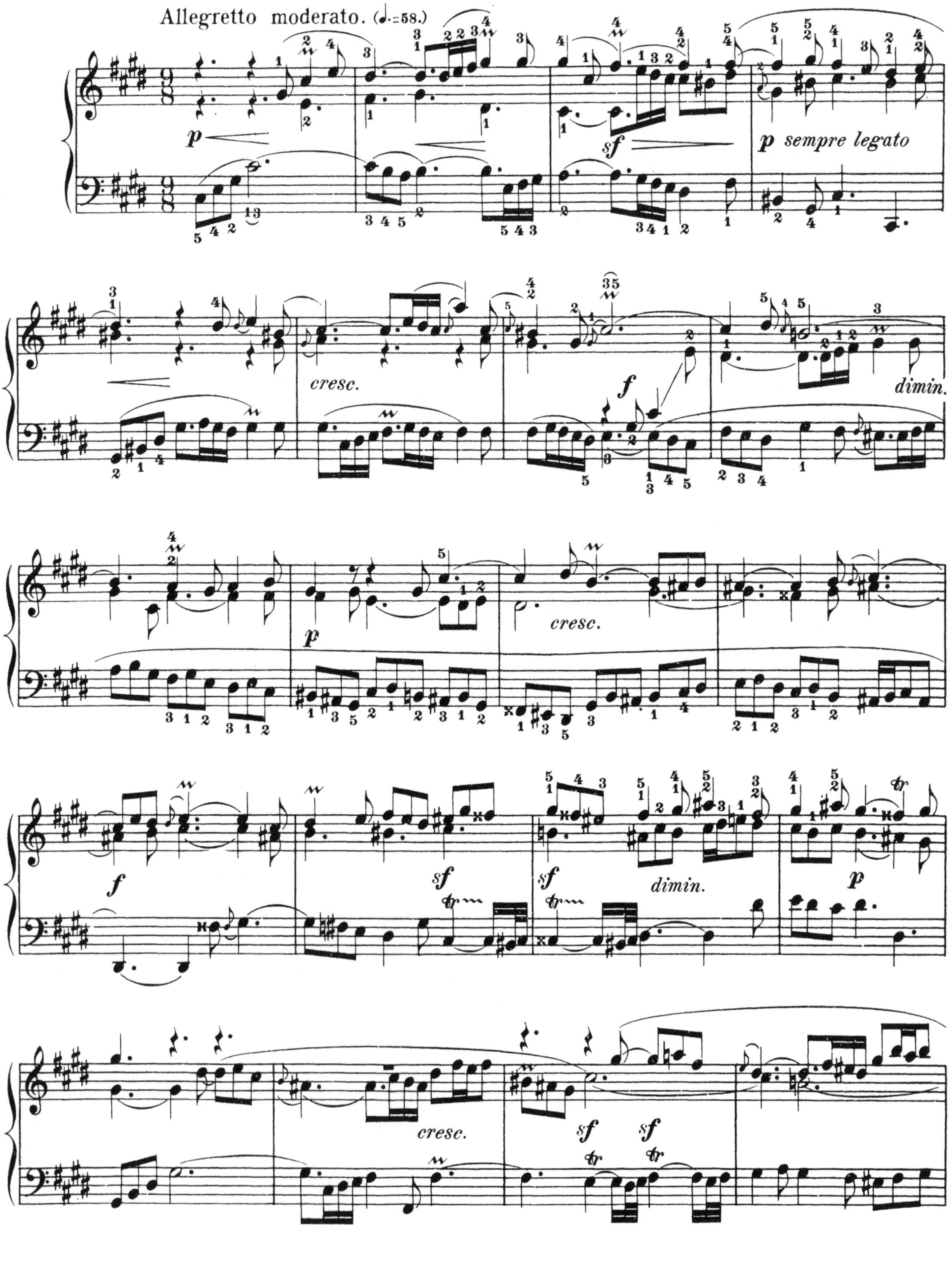

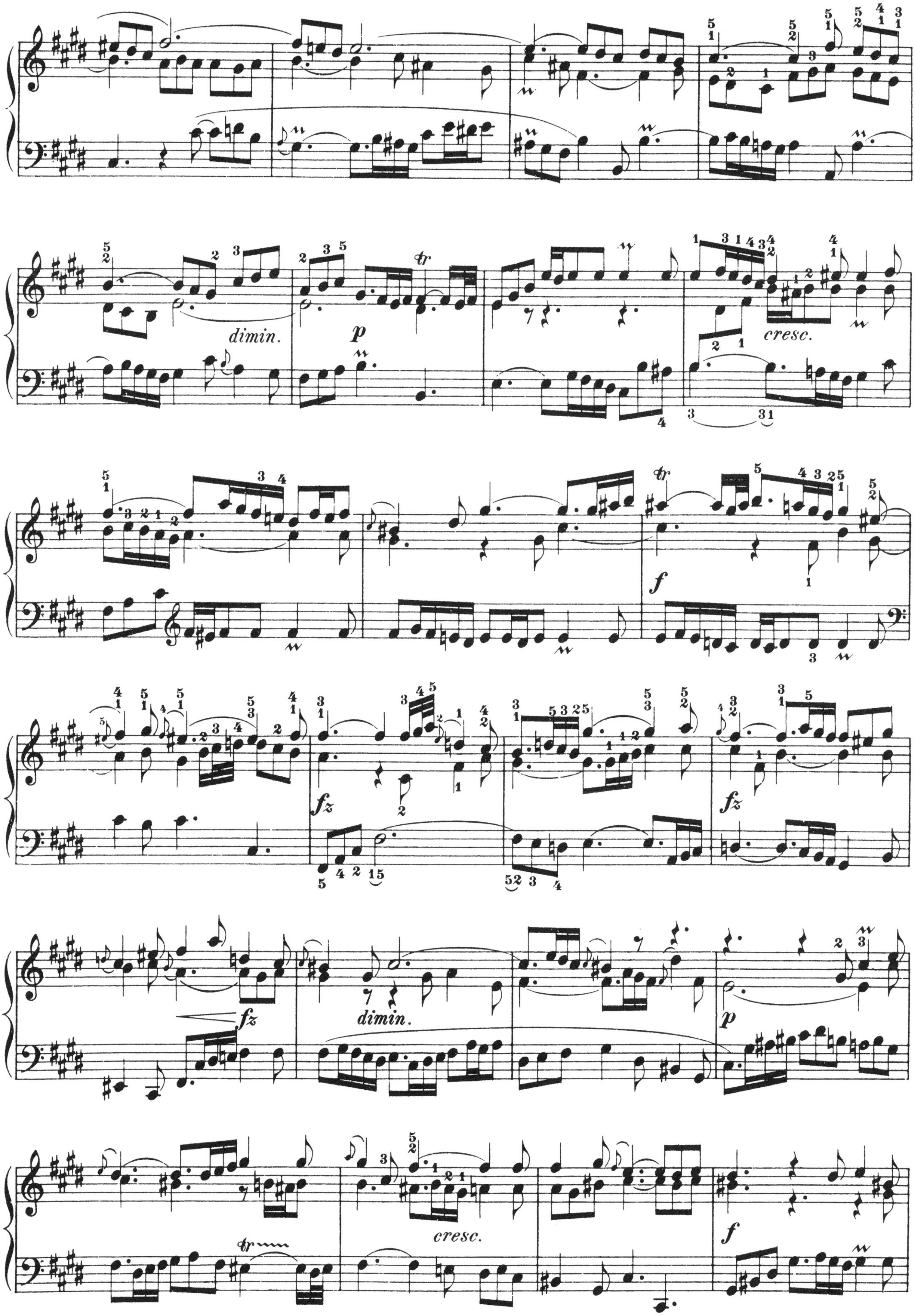
dimin.
p
cresc.
f
fz
dimin.
p
fz
f
cresc.

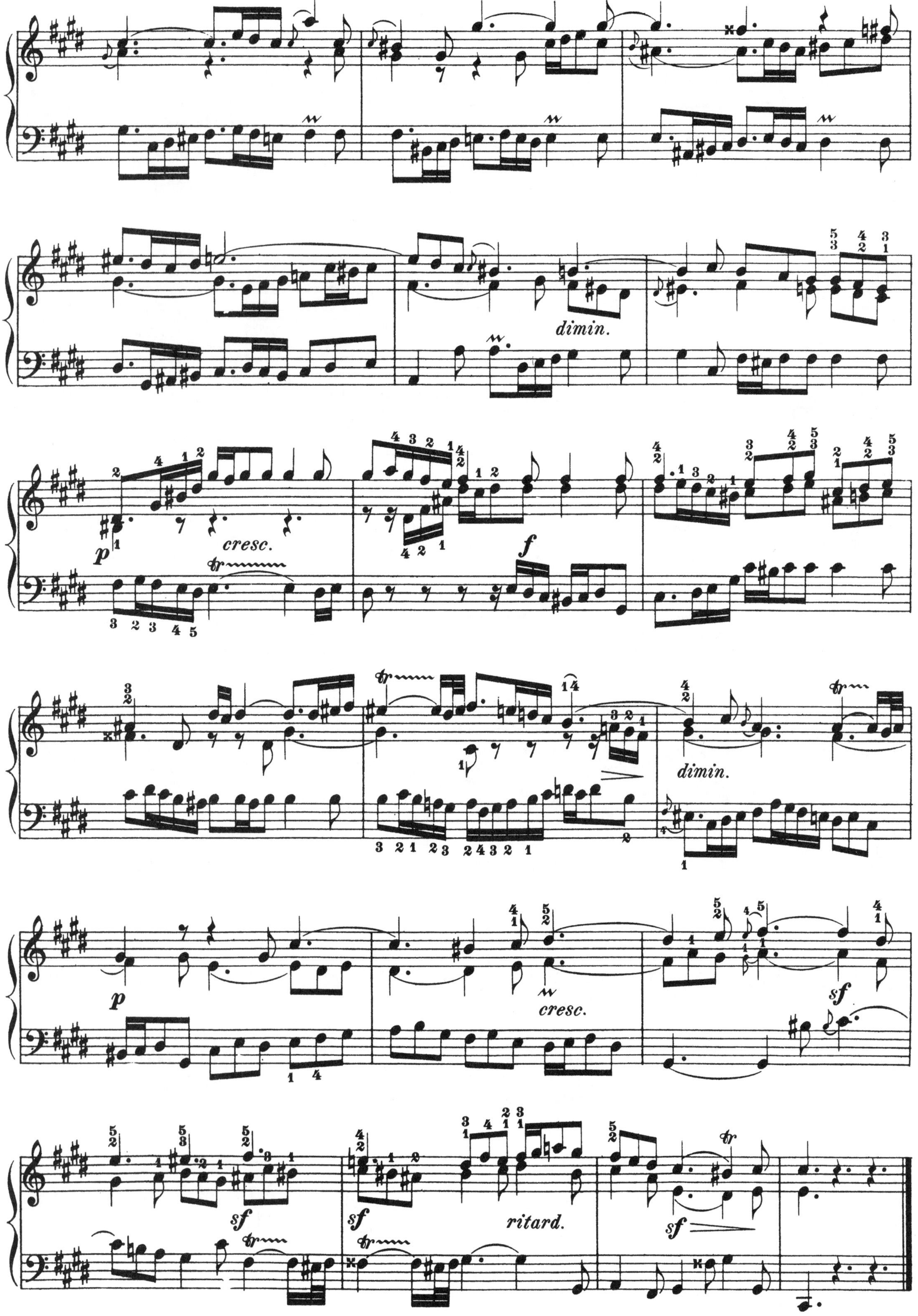
dimin.
p
cresc.
f
dimin.
p
cresc.
sf
sf
sf
ritard.
sf

Fuga IV.

a 3 Voci.

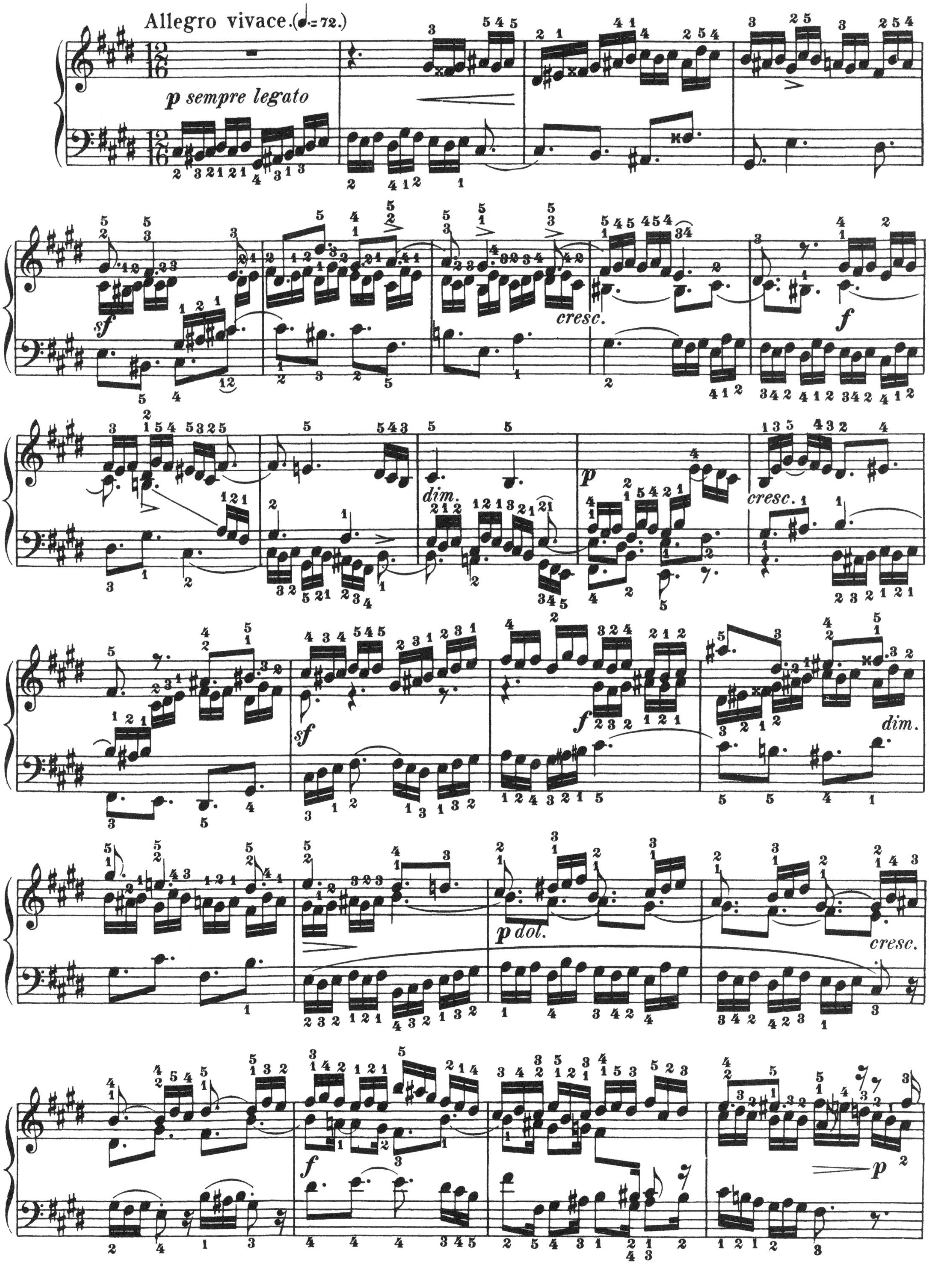

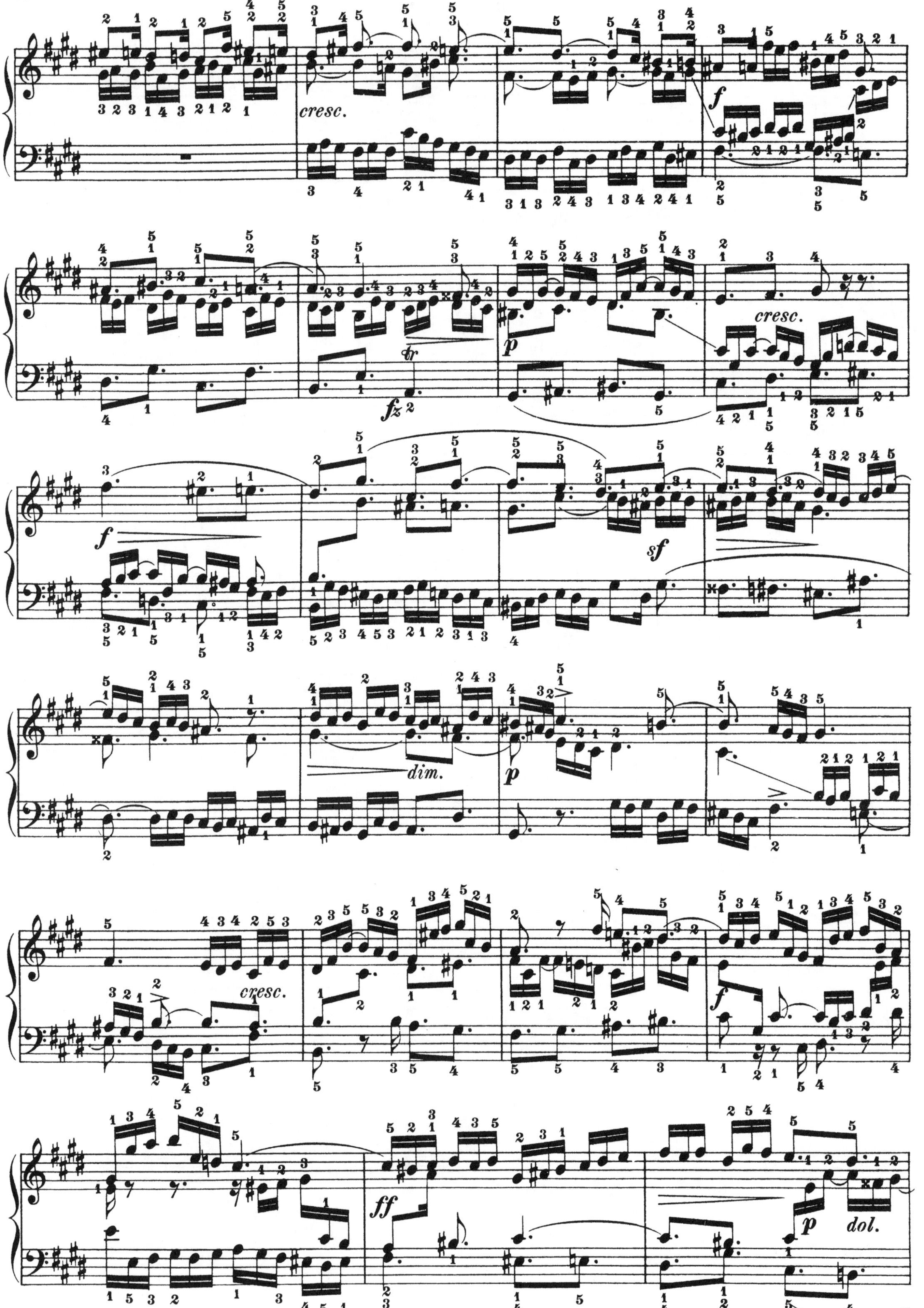
cresc.
f
fz
p
cresc.
f
sf
dim.
p
cresc.
f
ff
p
dol.

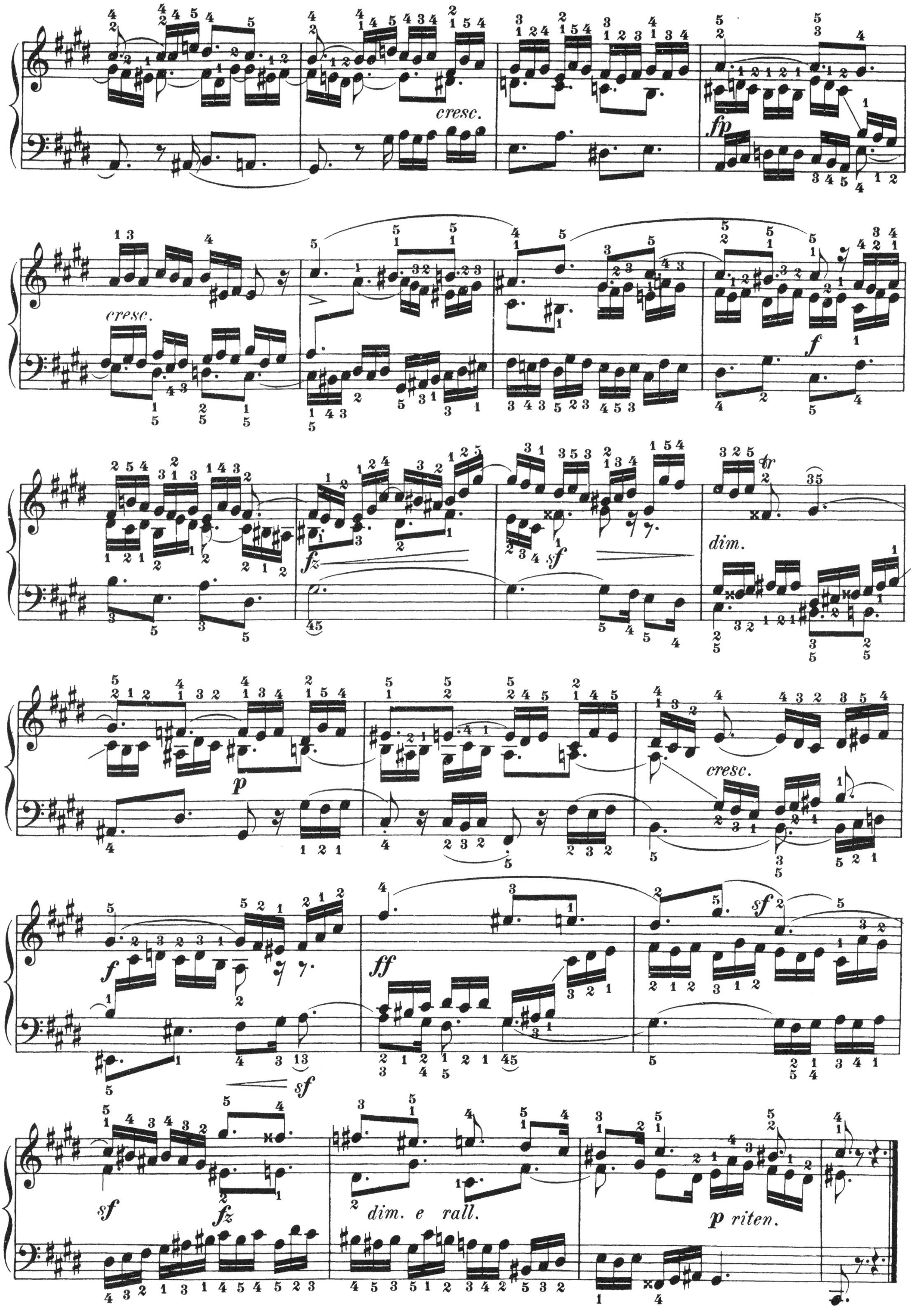
cresc.
fp
cresc.
f
fz
sf
dim.
p
cresc.
f
ff
sf
sf
fz
dim. e rall.
p riten.

Preludio V.

Allegretto vivace. (♩. = 96.)

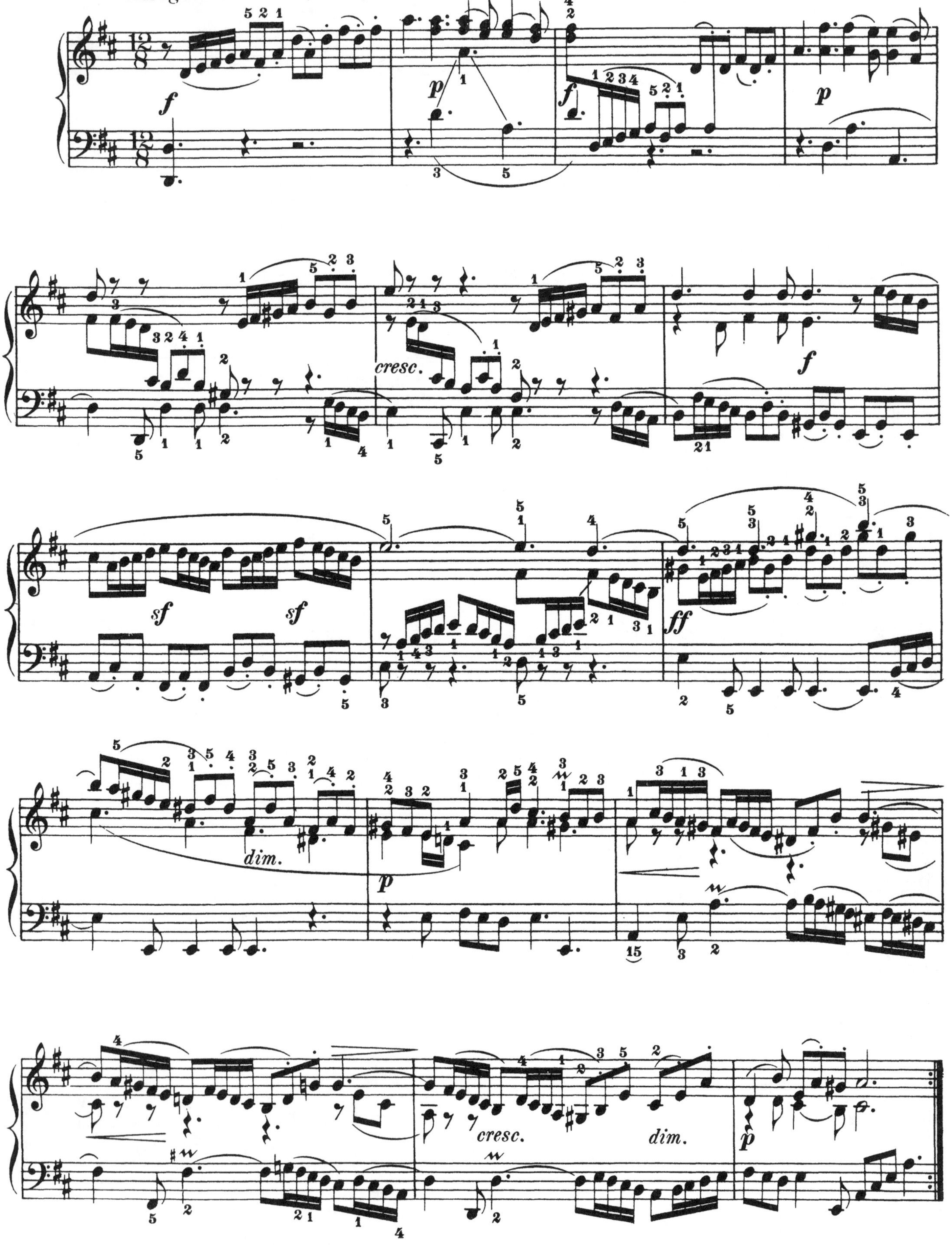

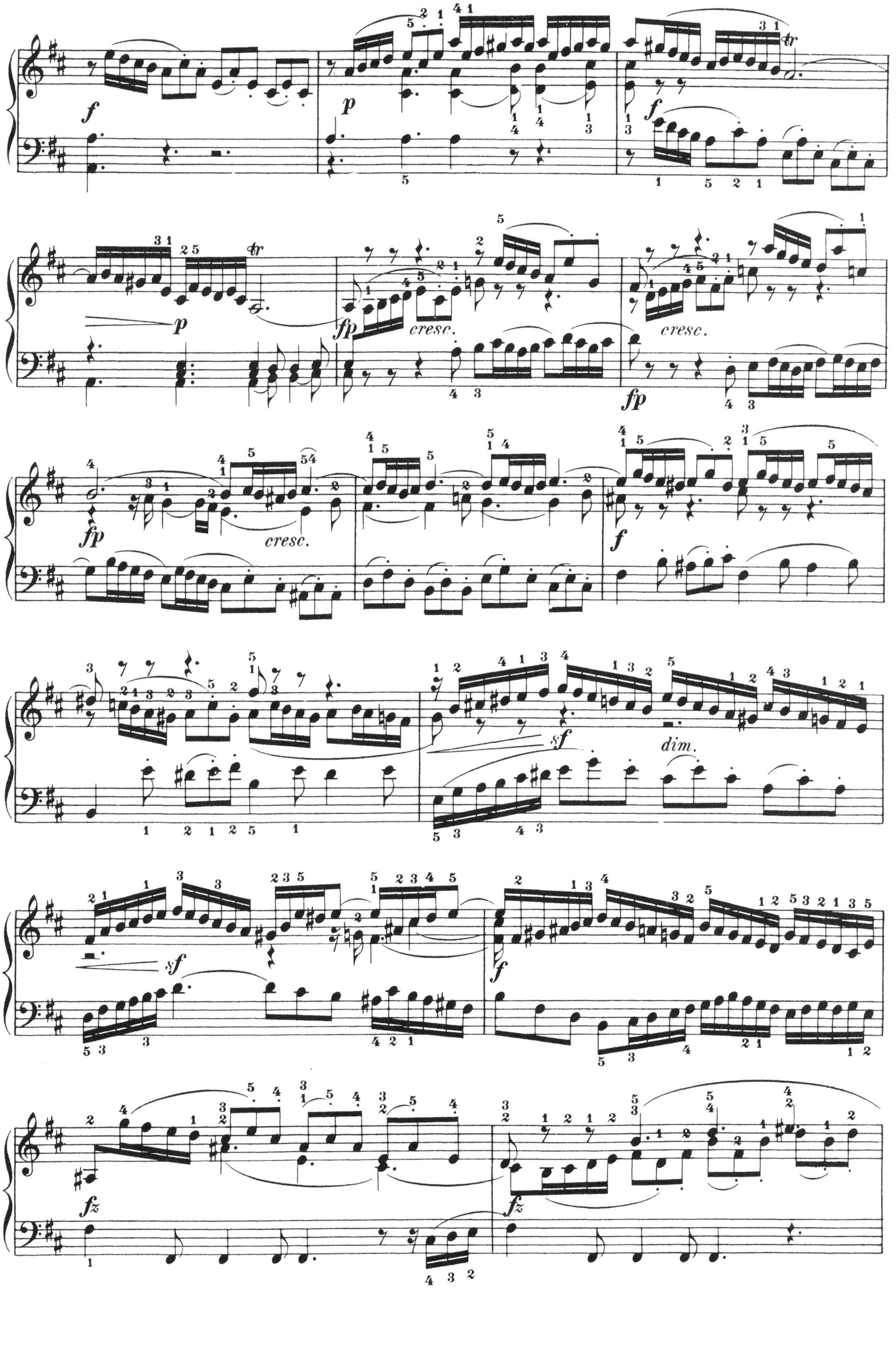
cresc.
cresc.
cresc.
dim.

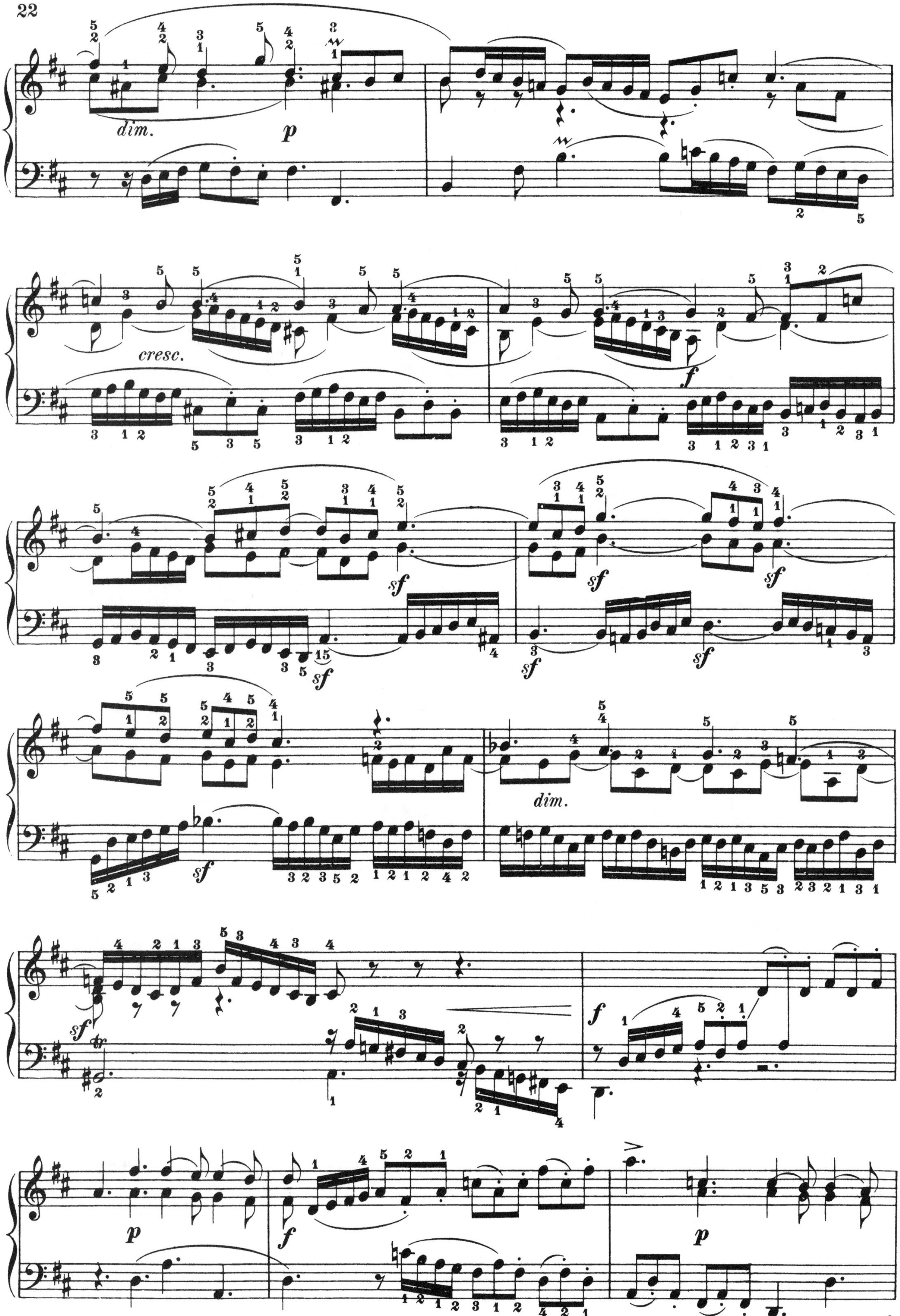
dim.
p
cresc.
f
sf
dim.
tr

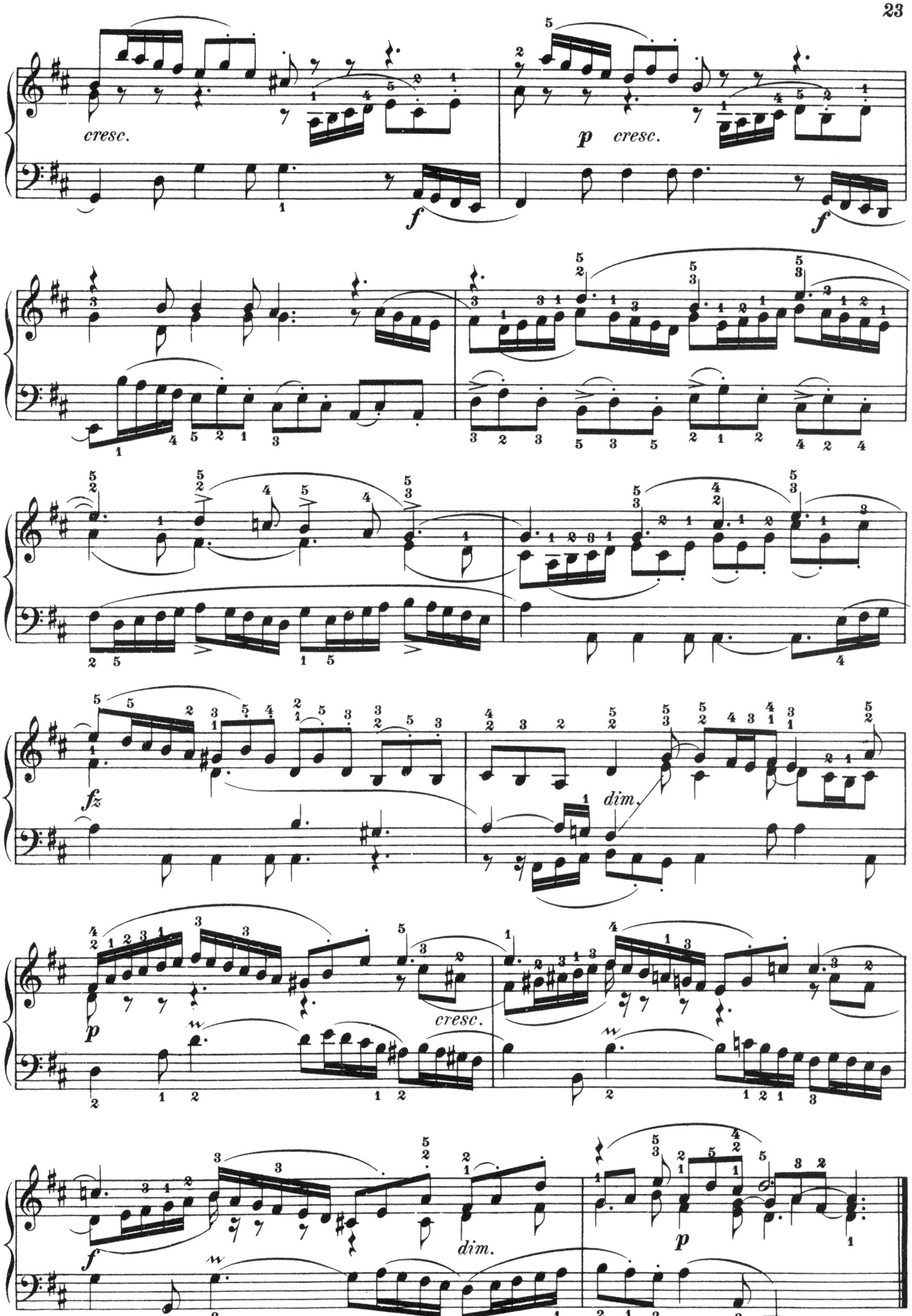
cresc.
p
cresc.
f
f
fz
dim.
p
cresc.
f
dim.
p

Fuga V.

a 4 Voci.

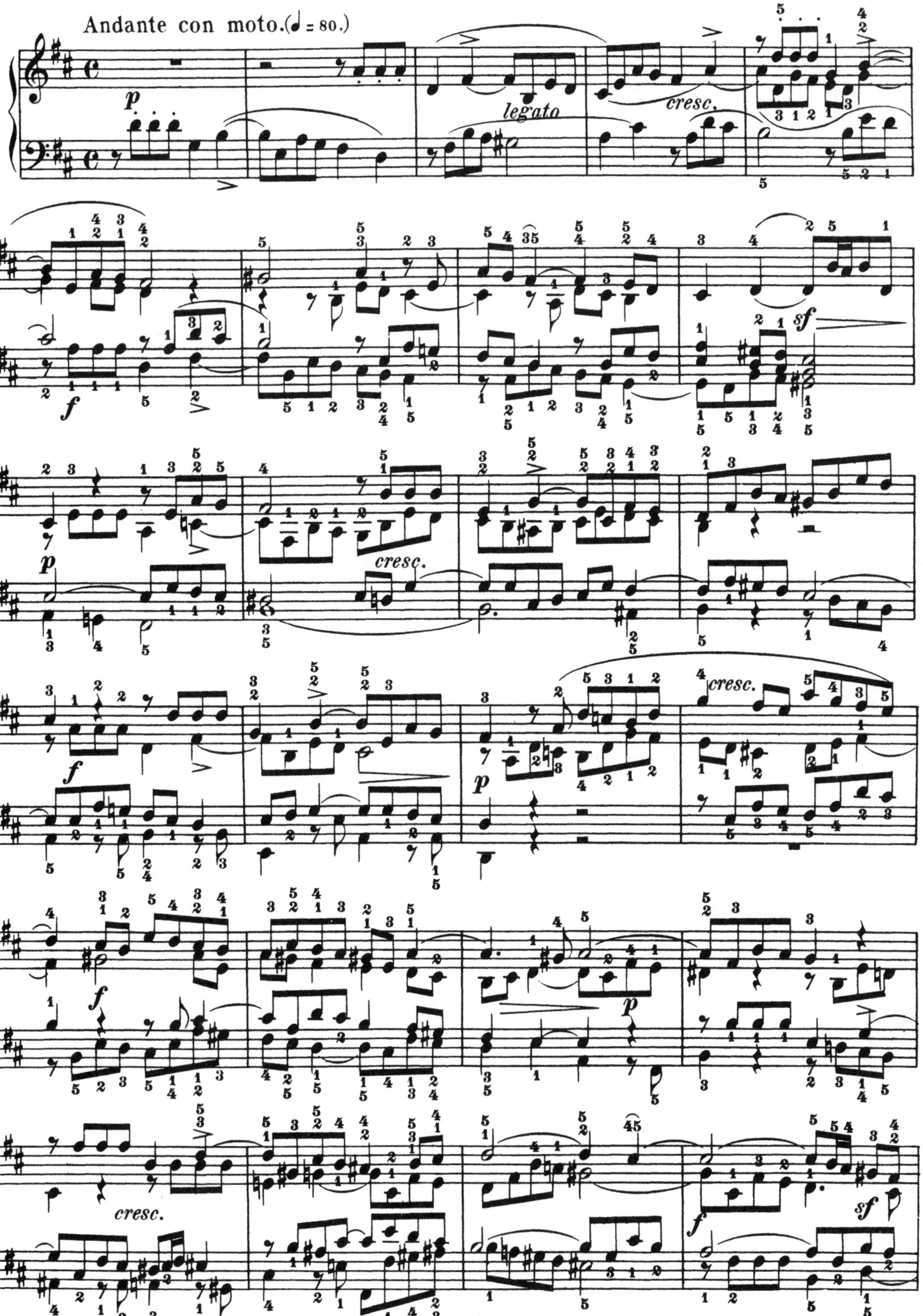

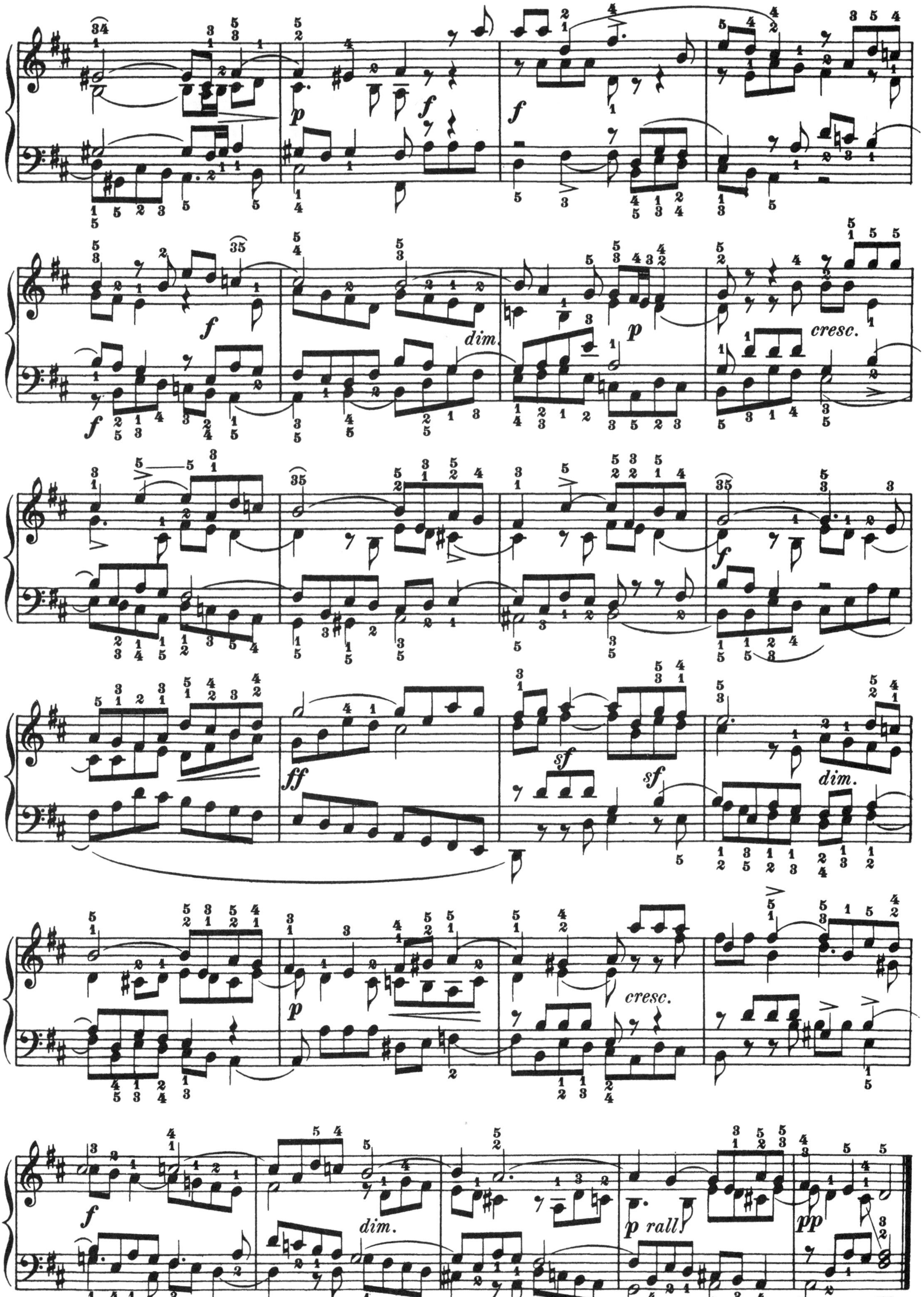
p
f
f
f
f
dim.
p
cresc.
ff
sf
sf
dim.
p
cresc.
f
dim.
p rall.
pp

Preludio VI.

Allegro vivace. (♩ = 126.)

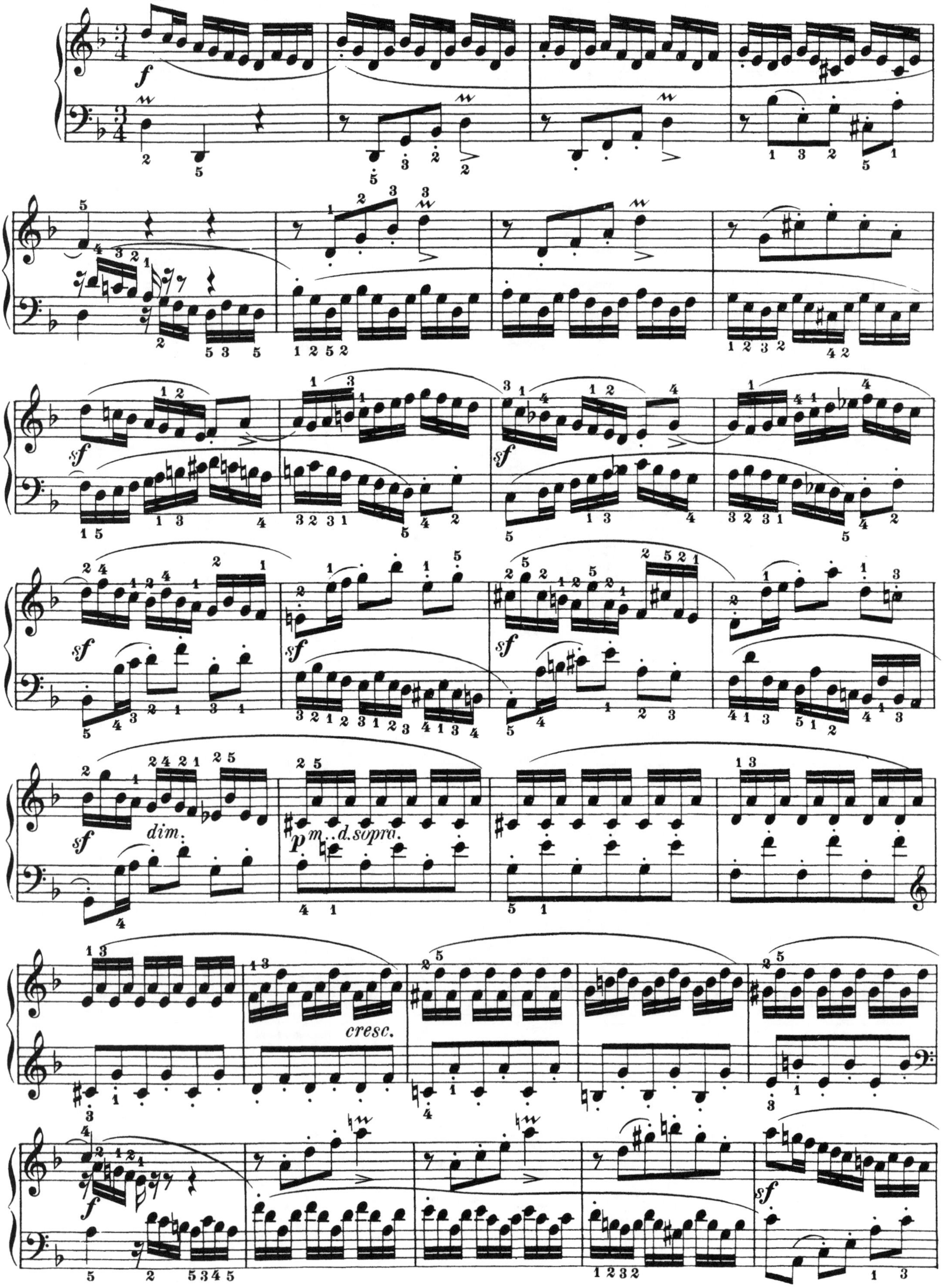

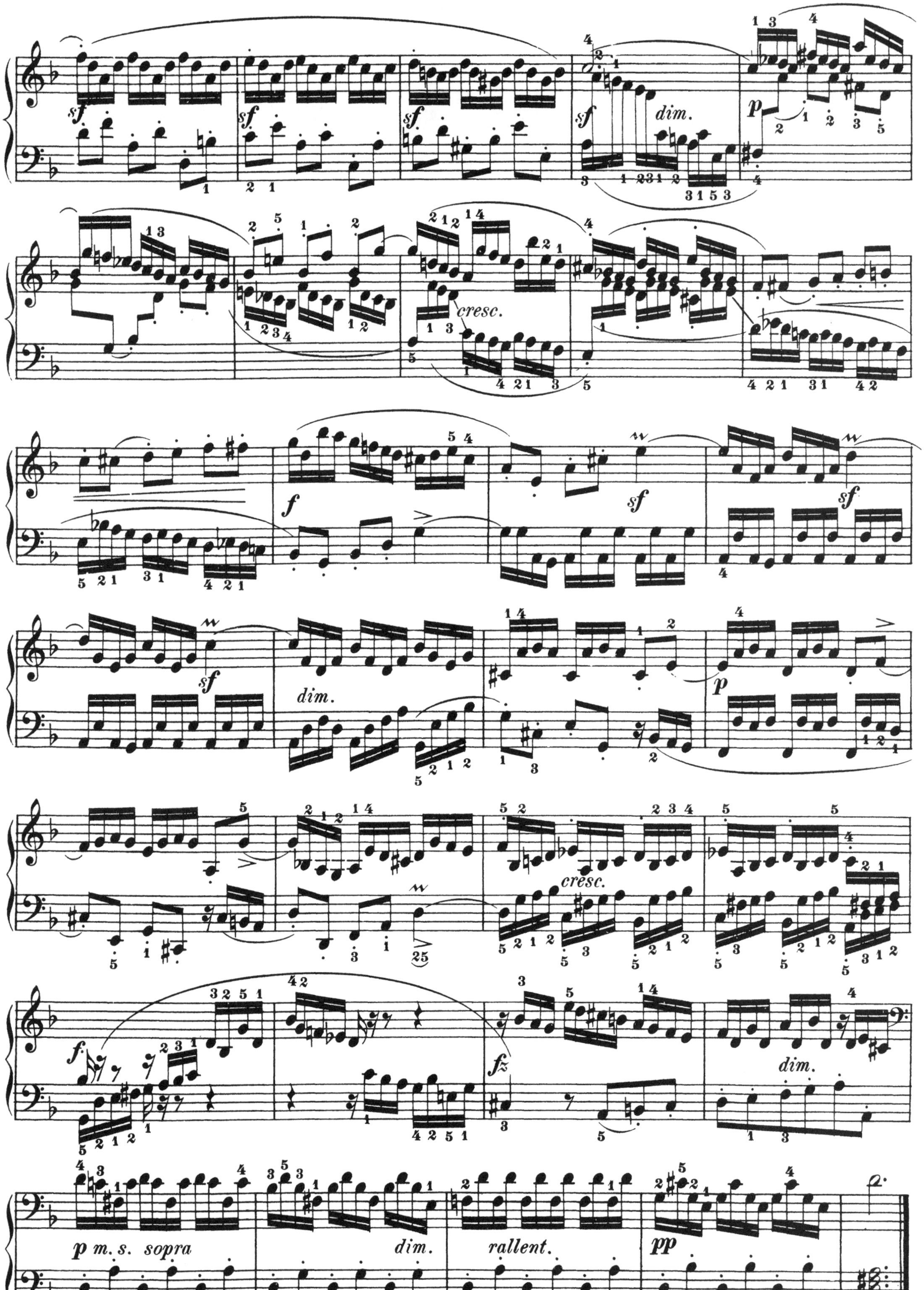
sf
sf
sf
sf
dim.
p
cresc.
f
sf
sf
sf
dim.
p
cresc.
f
fz
dim.
p m. s. sopra
dim.
rallent.
pp

Fuga VI.

a 3 Voci.

Vivace. (𝅗𝅥 = 80.)

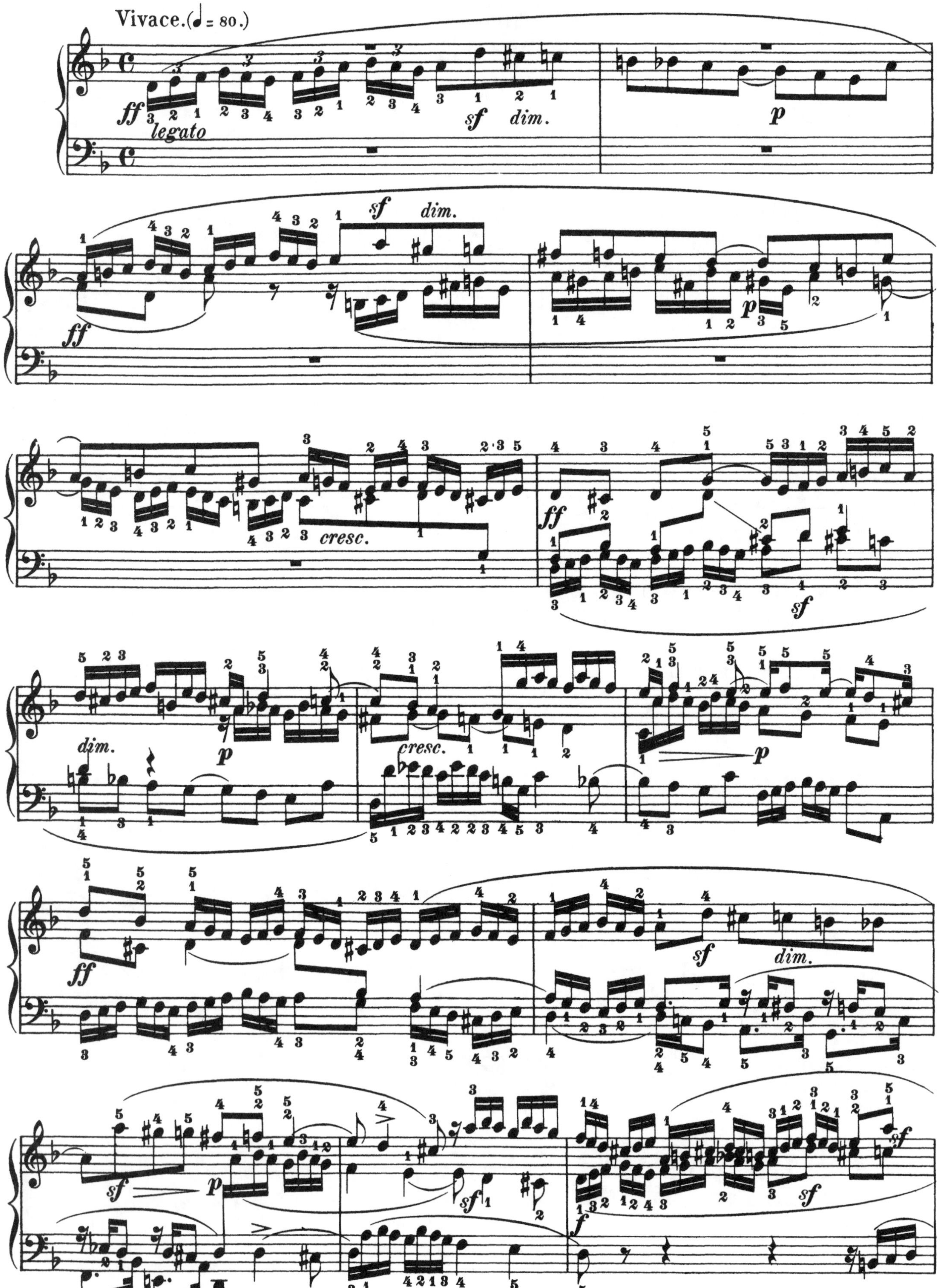

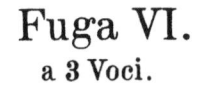

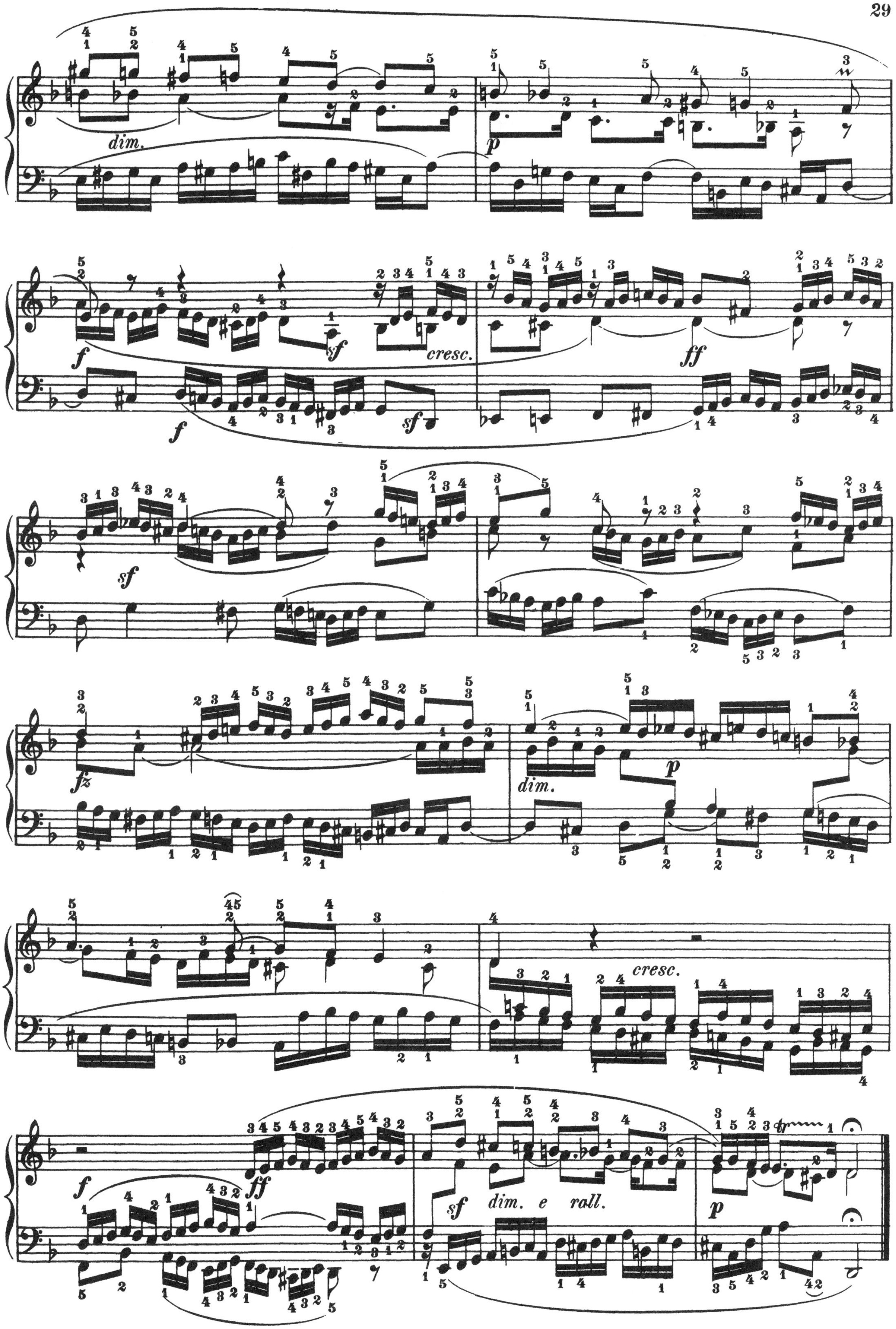
dim.
p
f
cresc.
ff
sf
fz
f
ff
dim. e rall.
p

Preludio VII.

Allegretto moderato (♩. = 84)

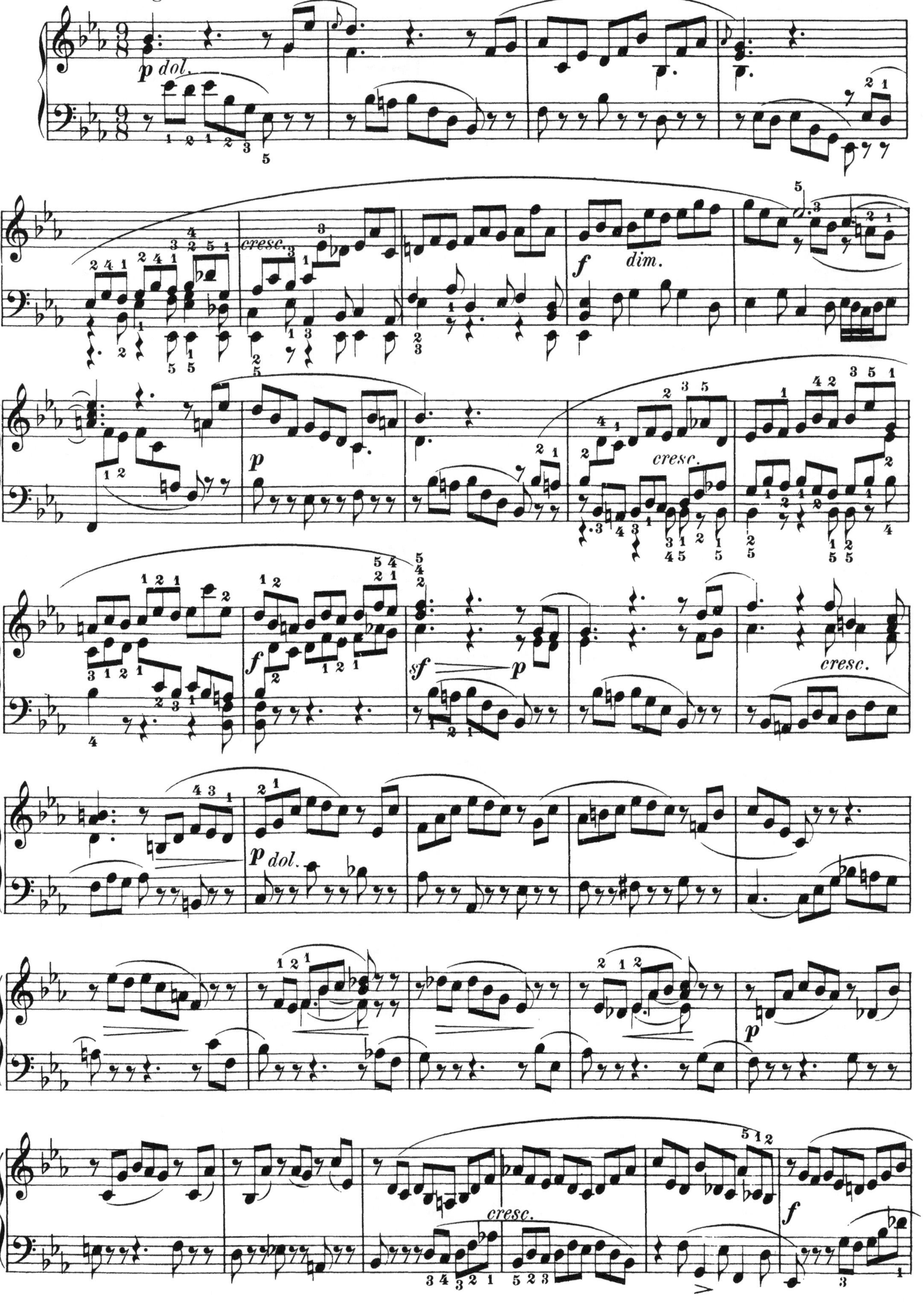

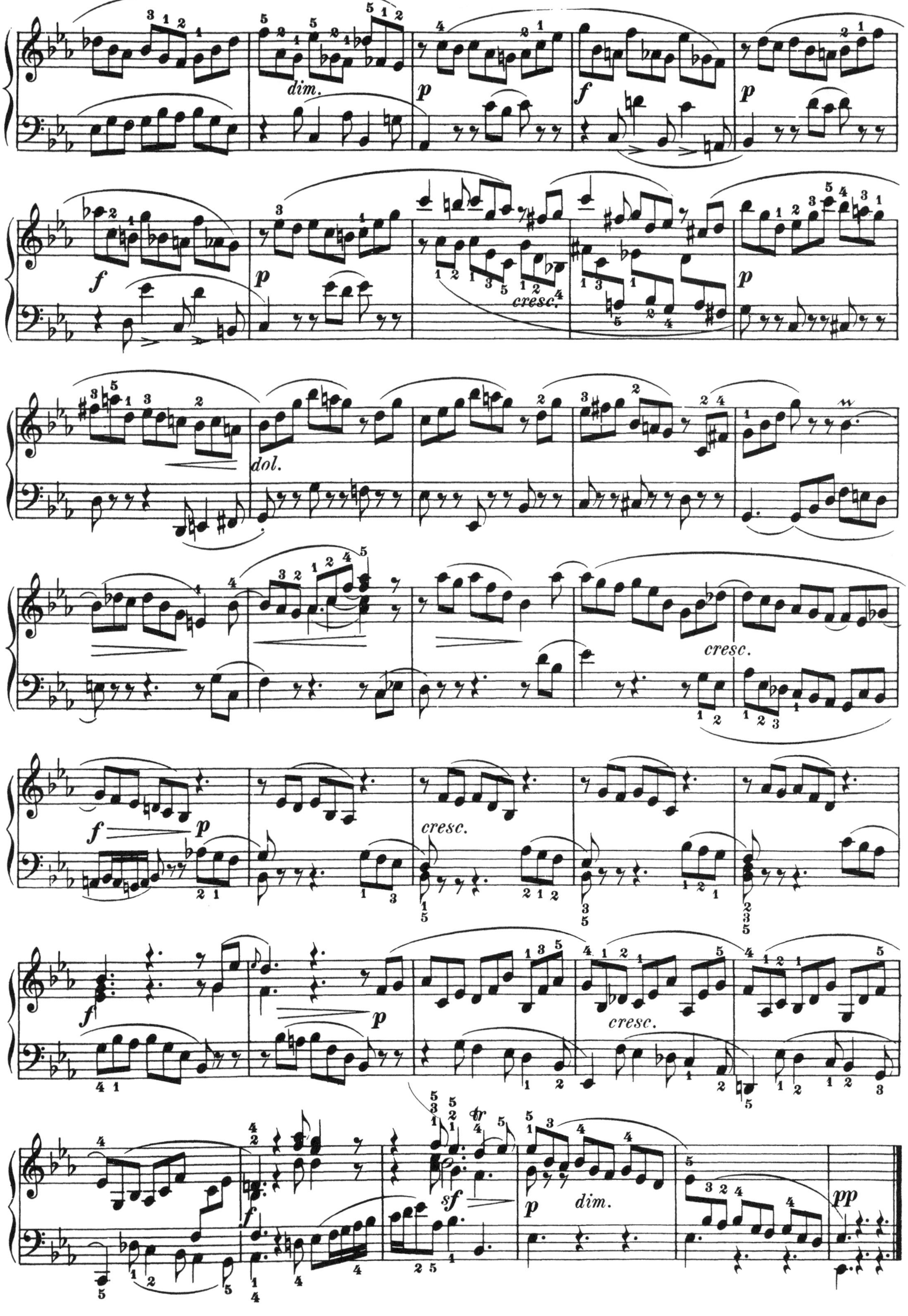
dim.
p
f
p
f
p
cresc.
p
dol.
cresc.
f
p
cresc.
f
p
cresc.
f
sf
p
dim.
pp

Fuga VII.

a 4 Voci.

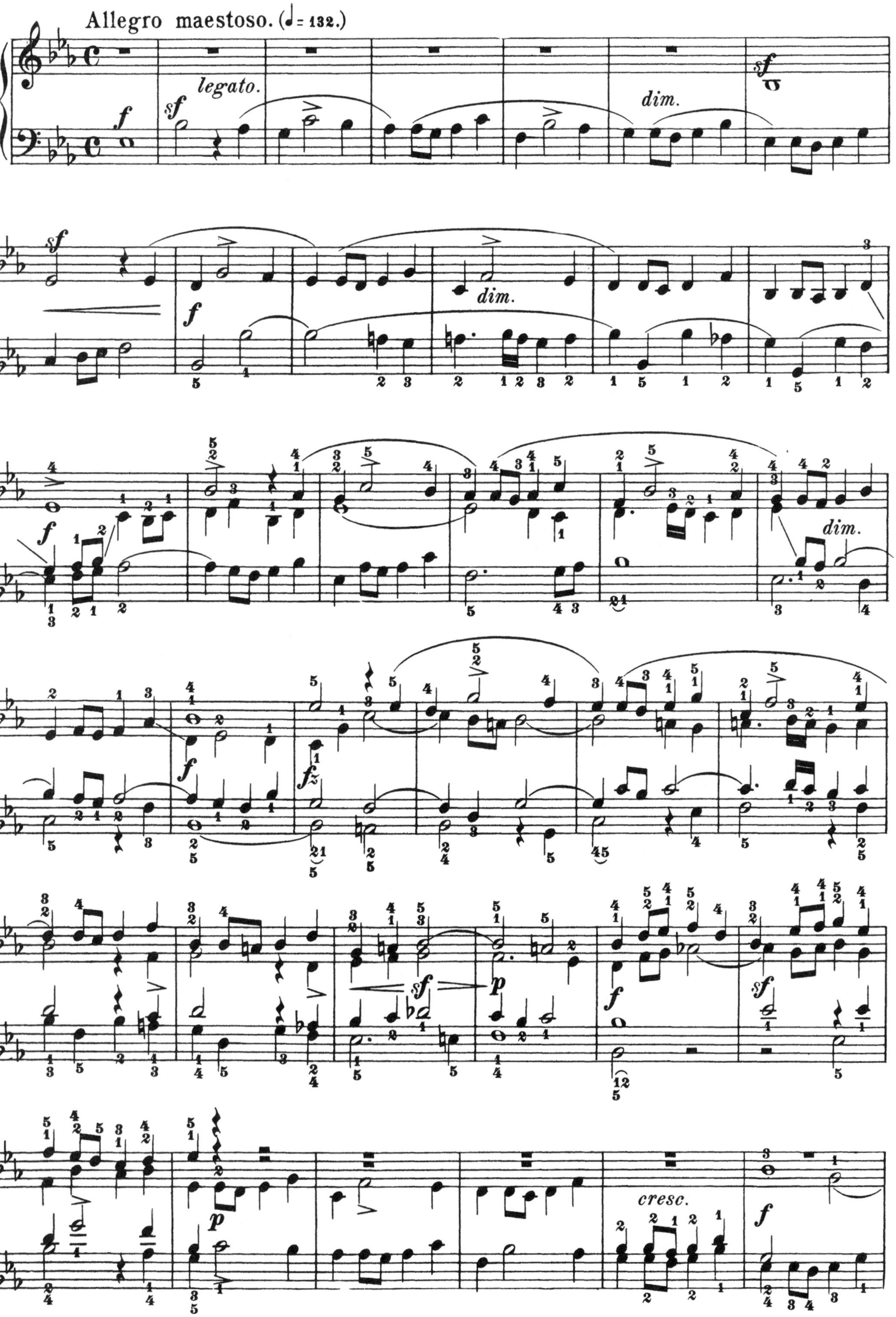

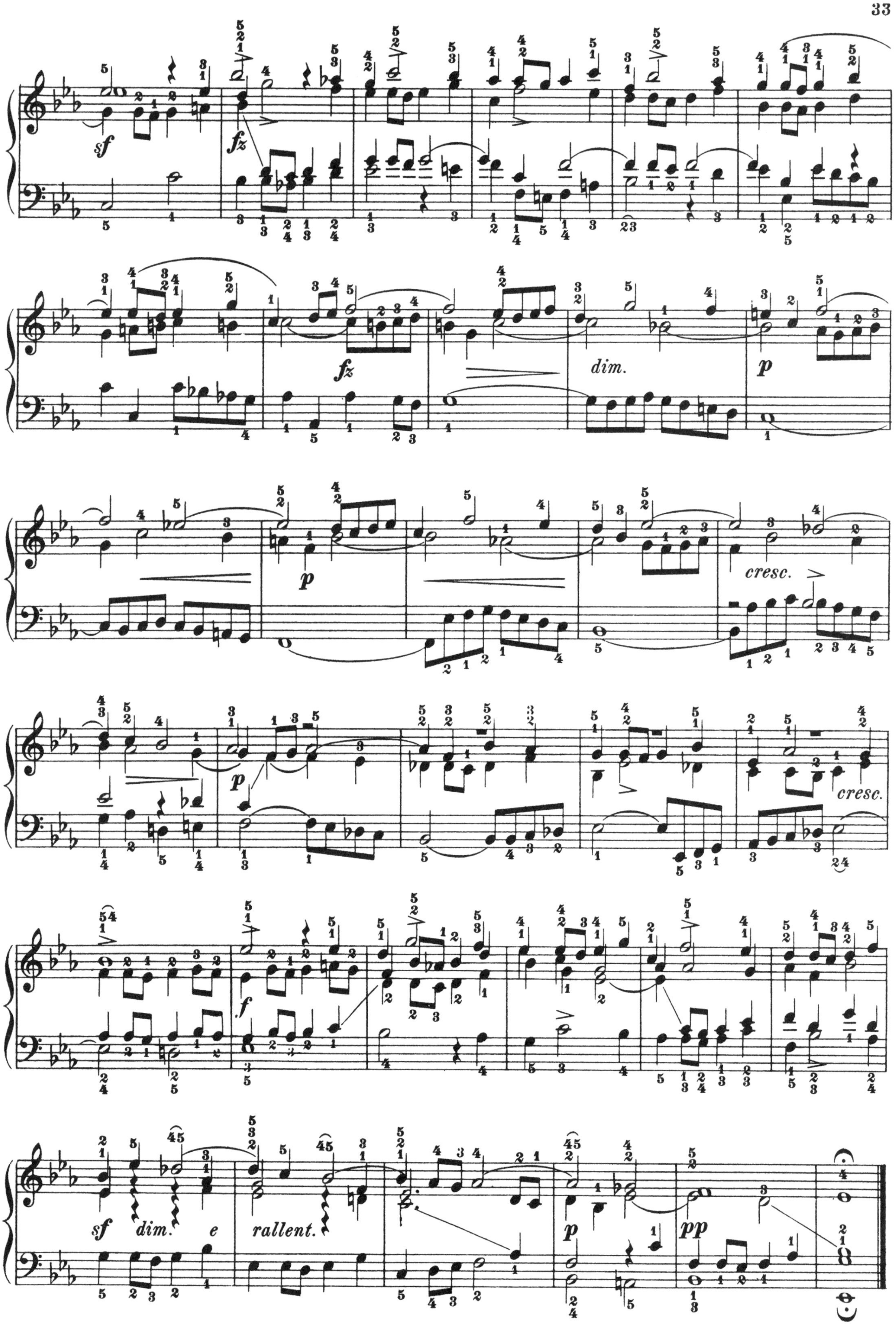
sf
fz
fz
dim.
p
p
cresc.
p
cresc.
f
sf
dim.
e
rallent.
p
pp

Preludio VIII.

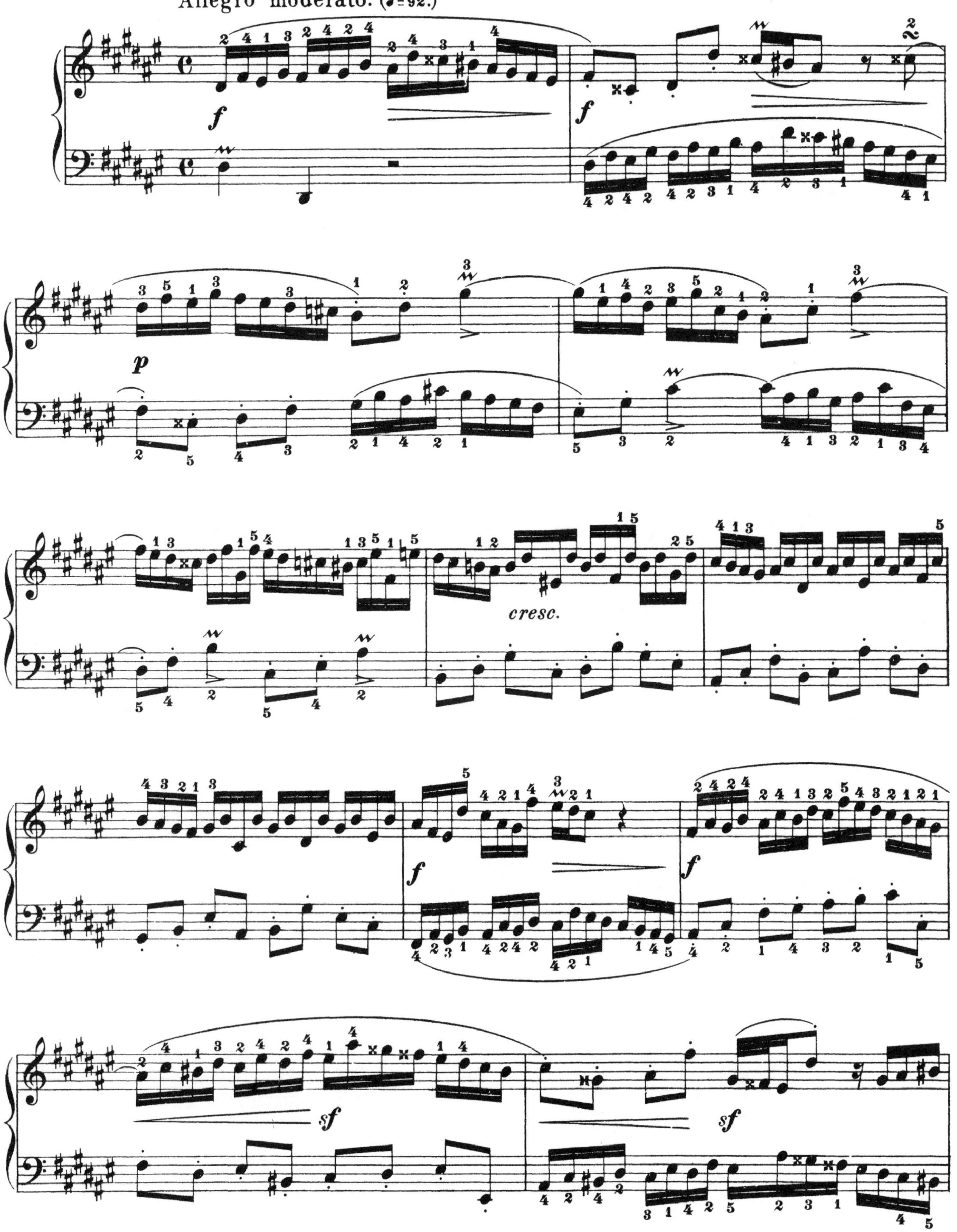

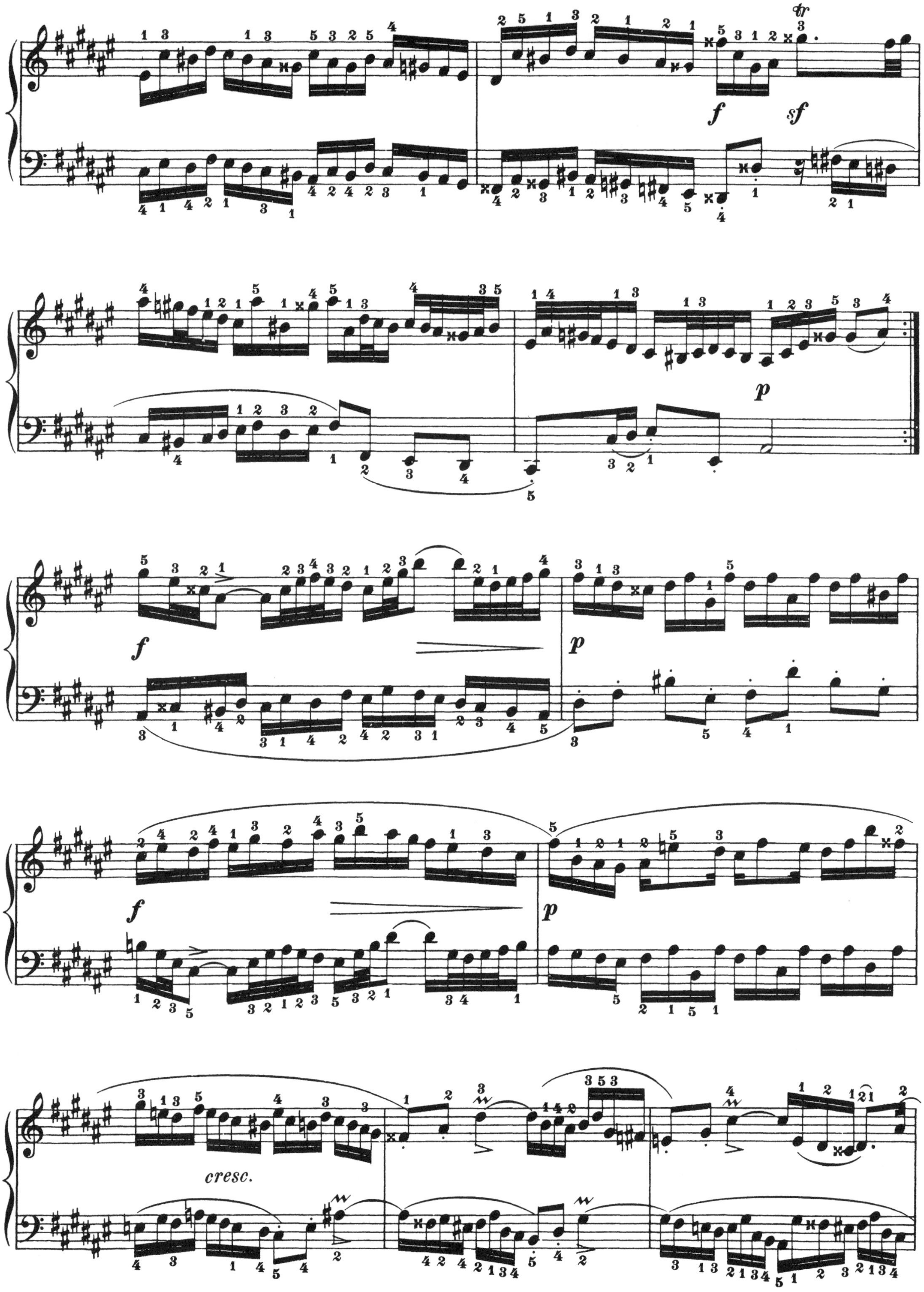
cresc.

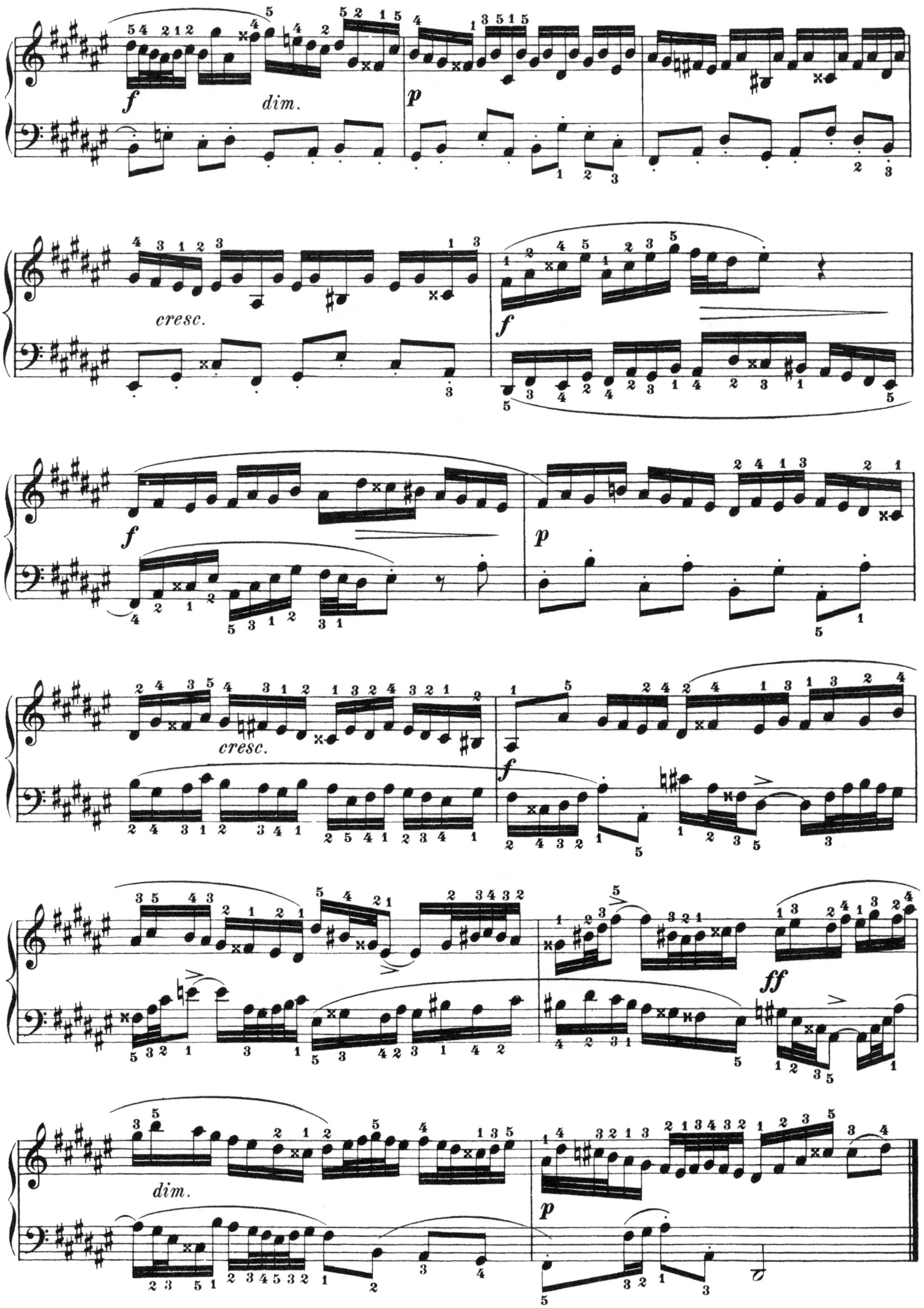
f
dim.
p
cresc.
f
f
p
cresc.
f
ff
dim.
p

Fuga VIII.

a 4 Voci.

Andante serioso ed espressivo. (♩= 56.)

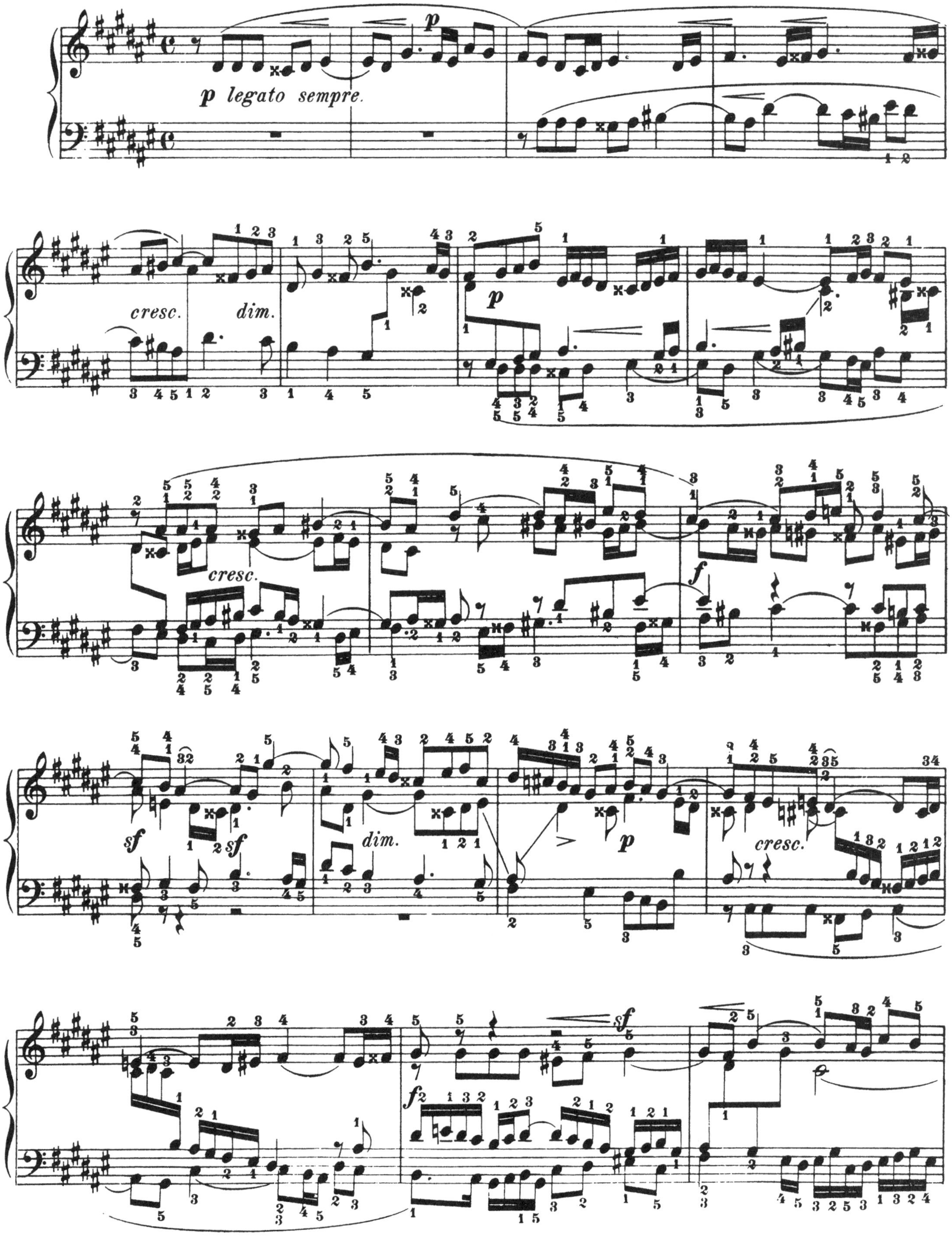

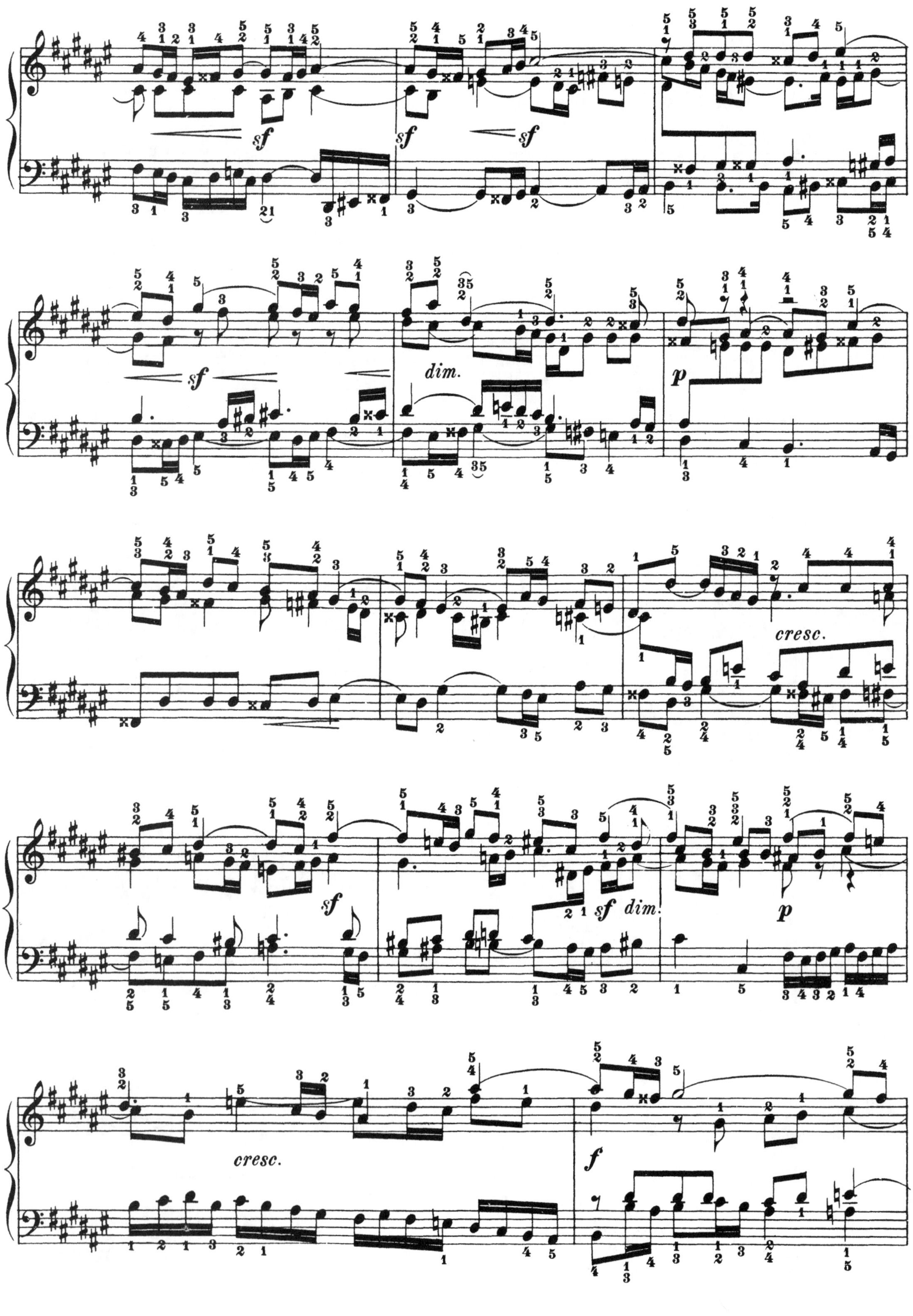
sf
sf
sf
sf
dim.
p
cresc.
sf
sf dim.
p
cresc.
f

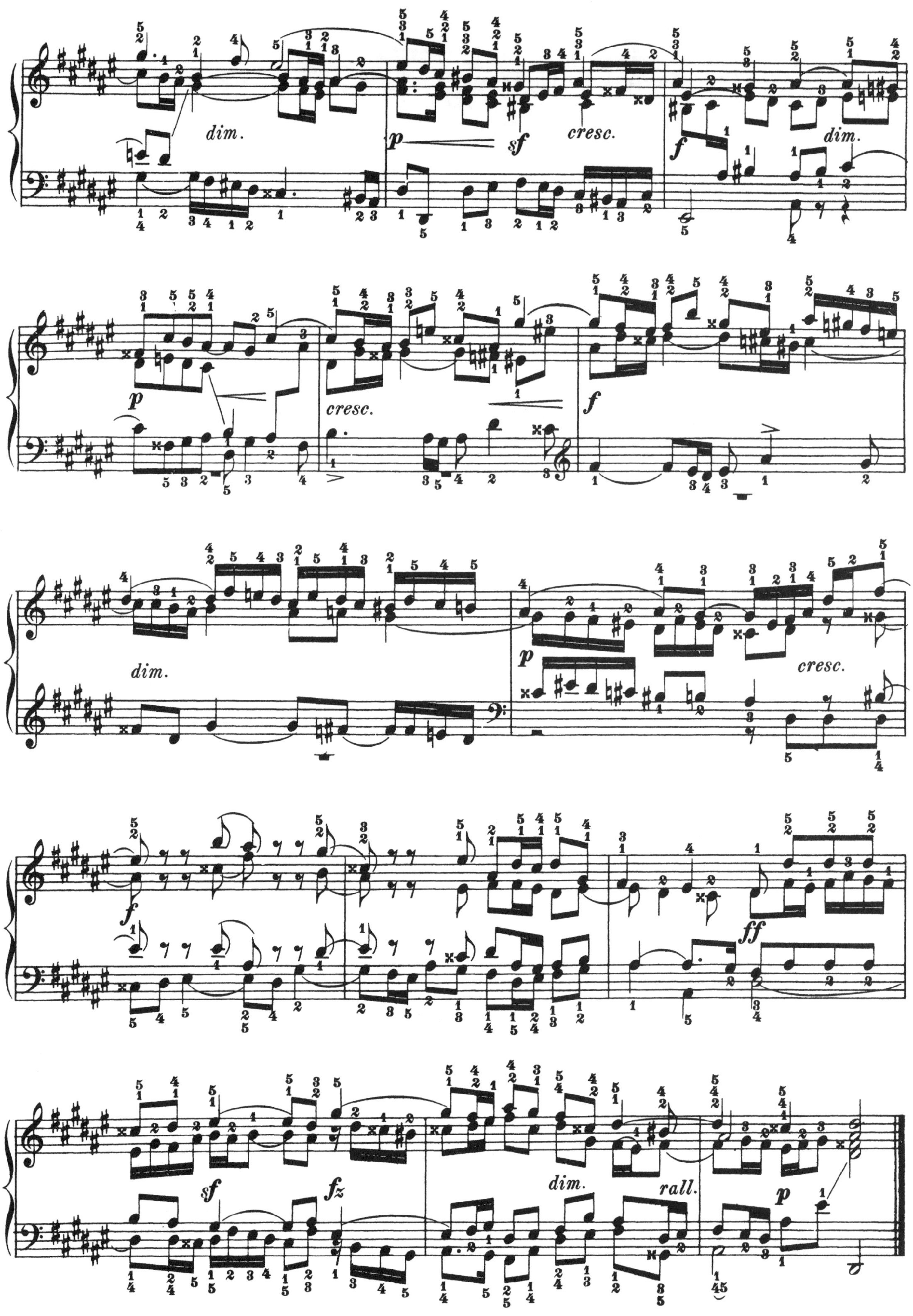
dim.
p
sf
cresc.
f
dim.
p
cresc.
f
dim.
p
cresc.
f
ff
sf
fz
dim.
rall.
p

Preludio IX.

Lento moderato. (♩= 80.)

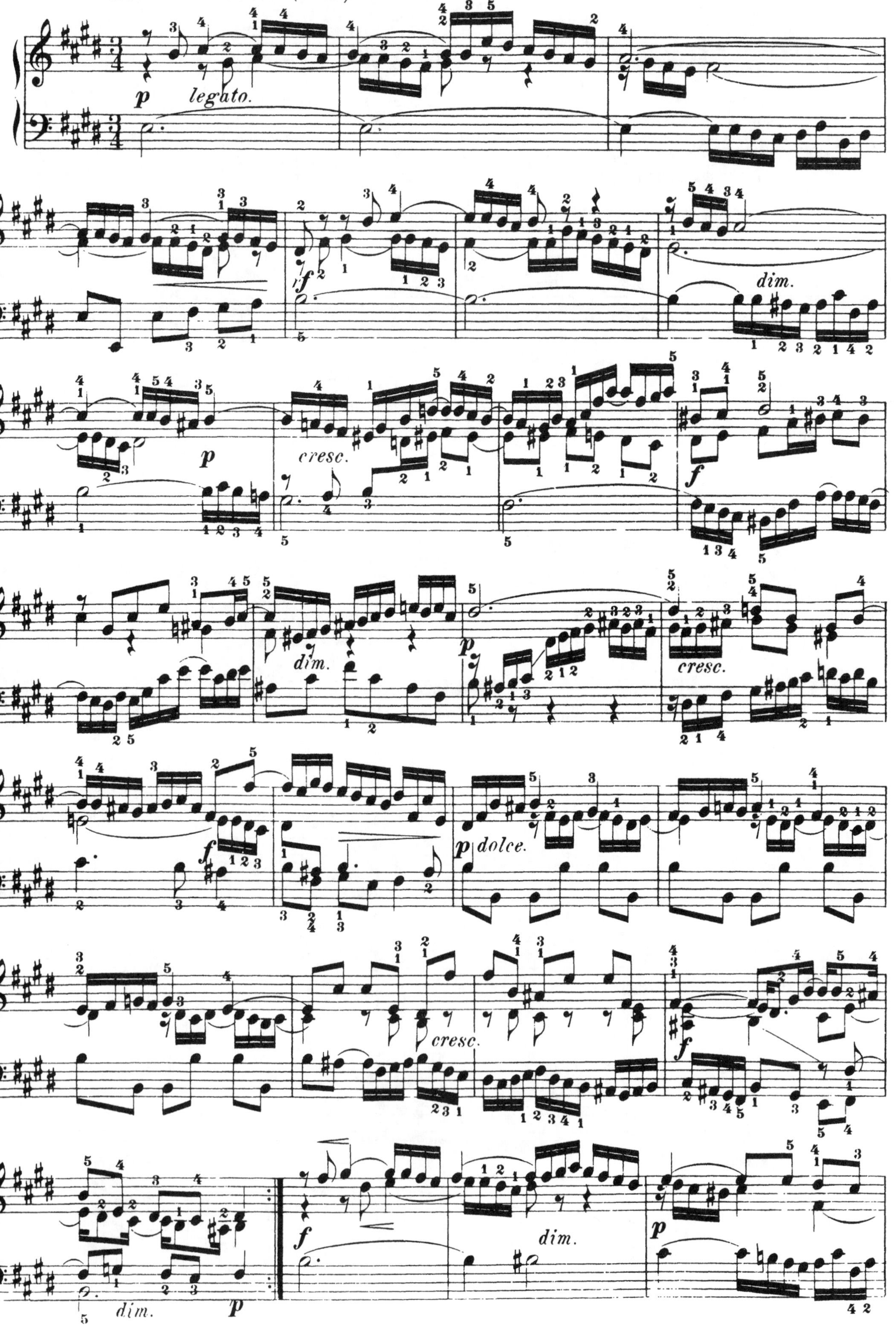

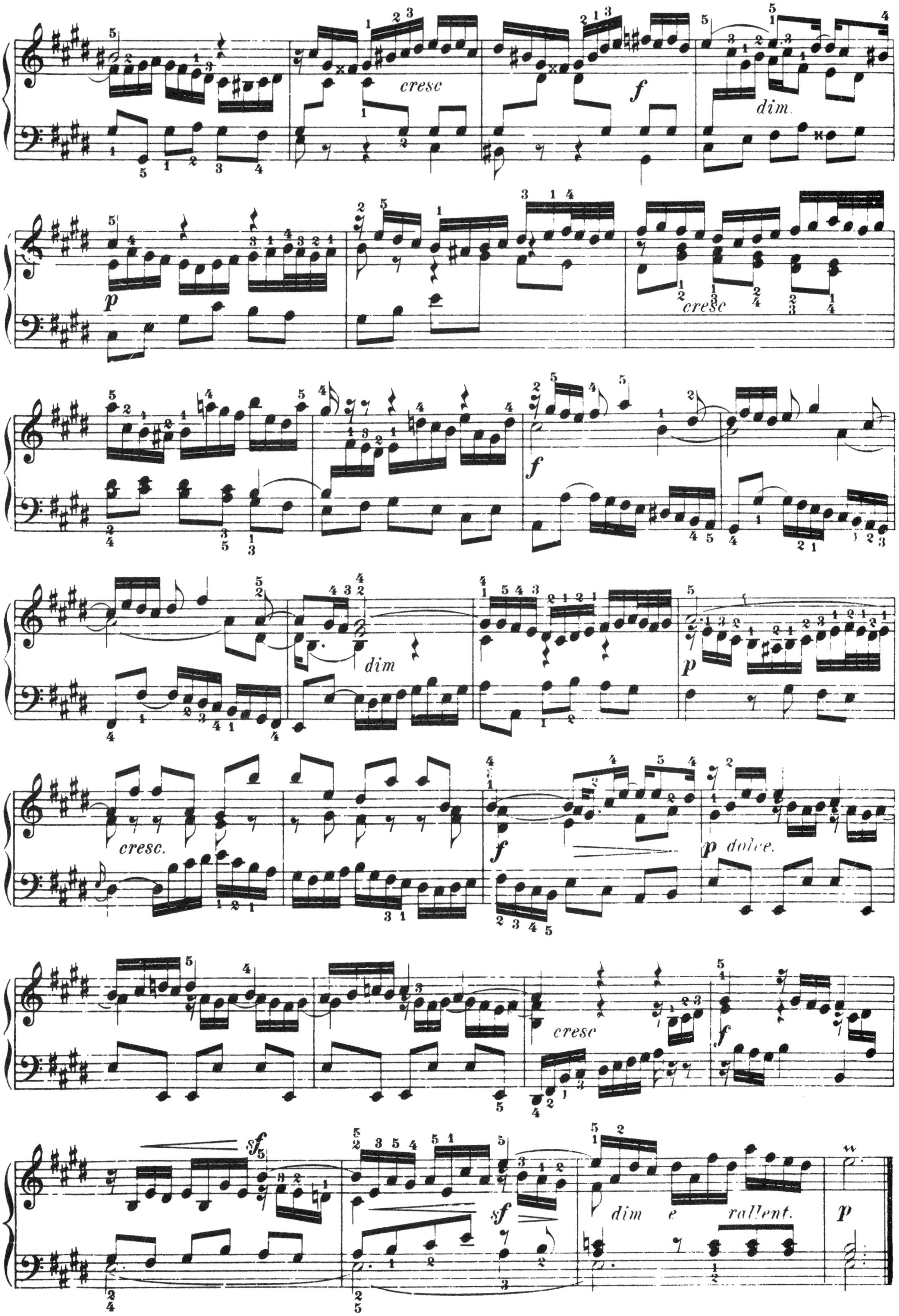
cresc
f
dim.
p
cresc
f
dim
p
cresc.
f
p dolce.
f
cresc
sf
dim e rallent.
p

Fuga IX.

a 4 Voci.

Adagio alla Breve. (𝅗𝅥 = 60.)

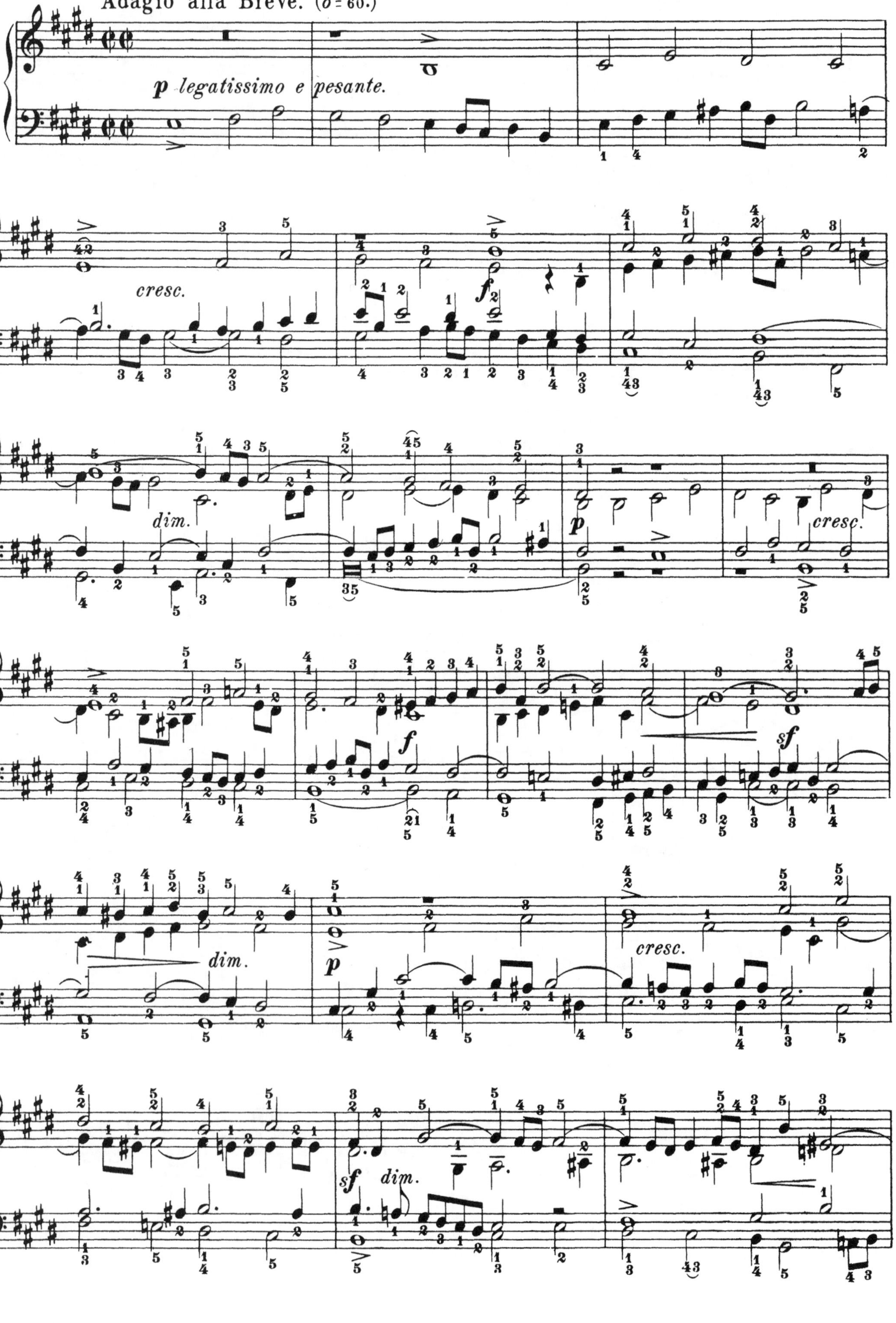

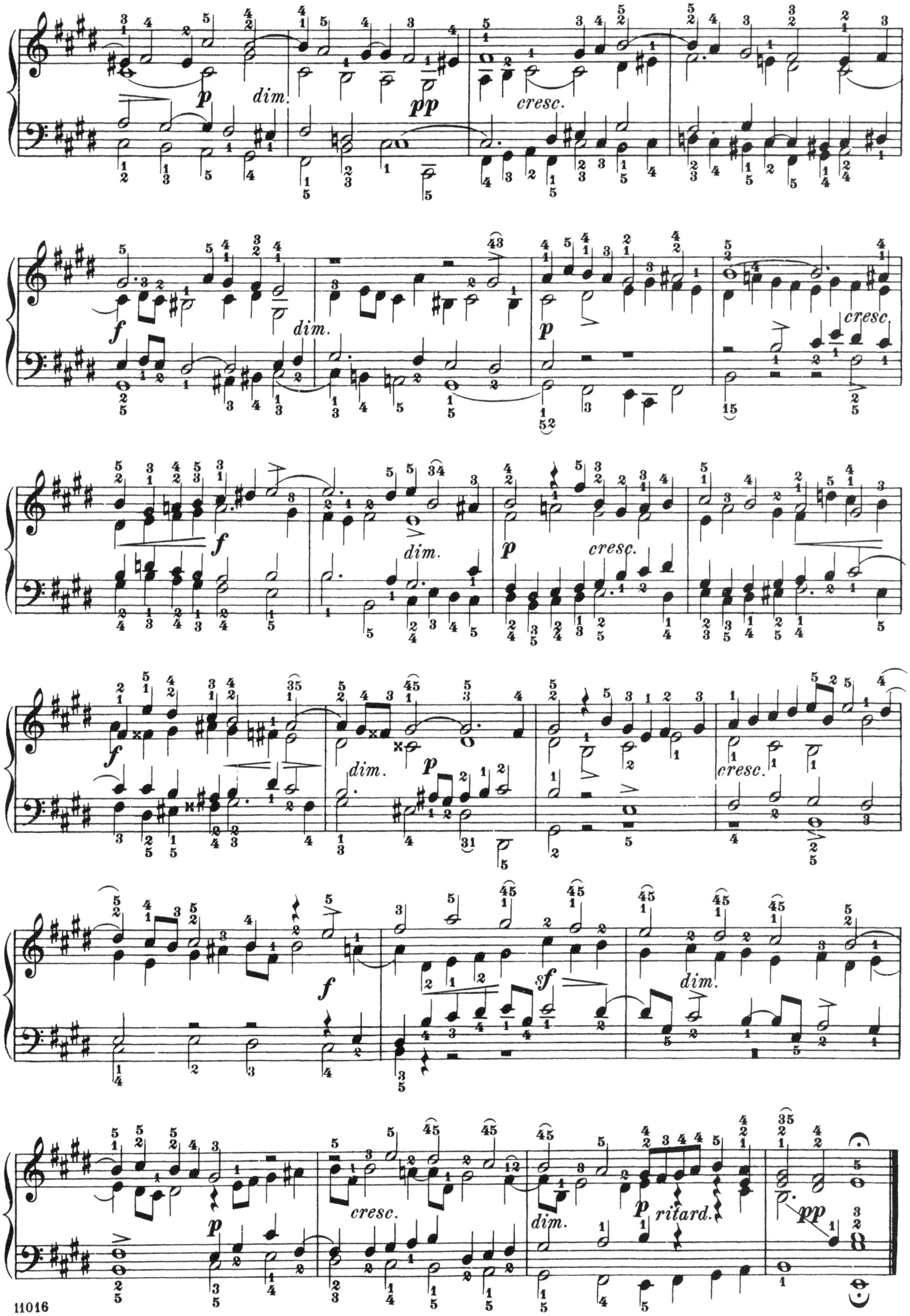
p
dim.
pp
cresc.
f
dim.
p
cresc.
f
dim.
p
cresc.
f
dim.
p
cresc.
f
sf
dim.
p
cresc.
dim.
p ritard.
pp

Preludio X.

Allegretto vivace. (♩. = 66.)

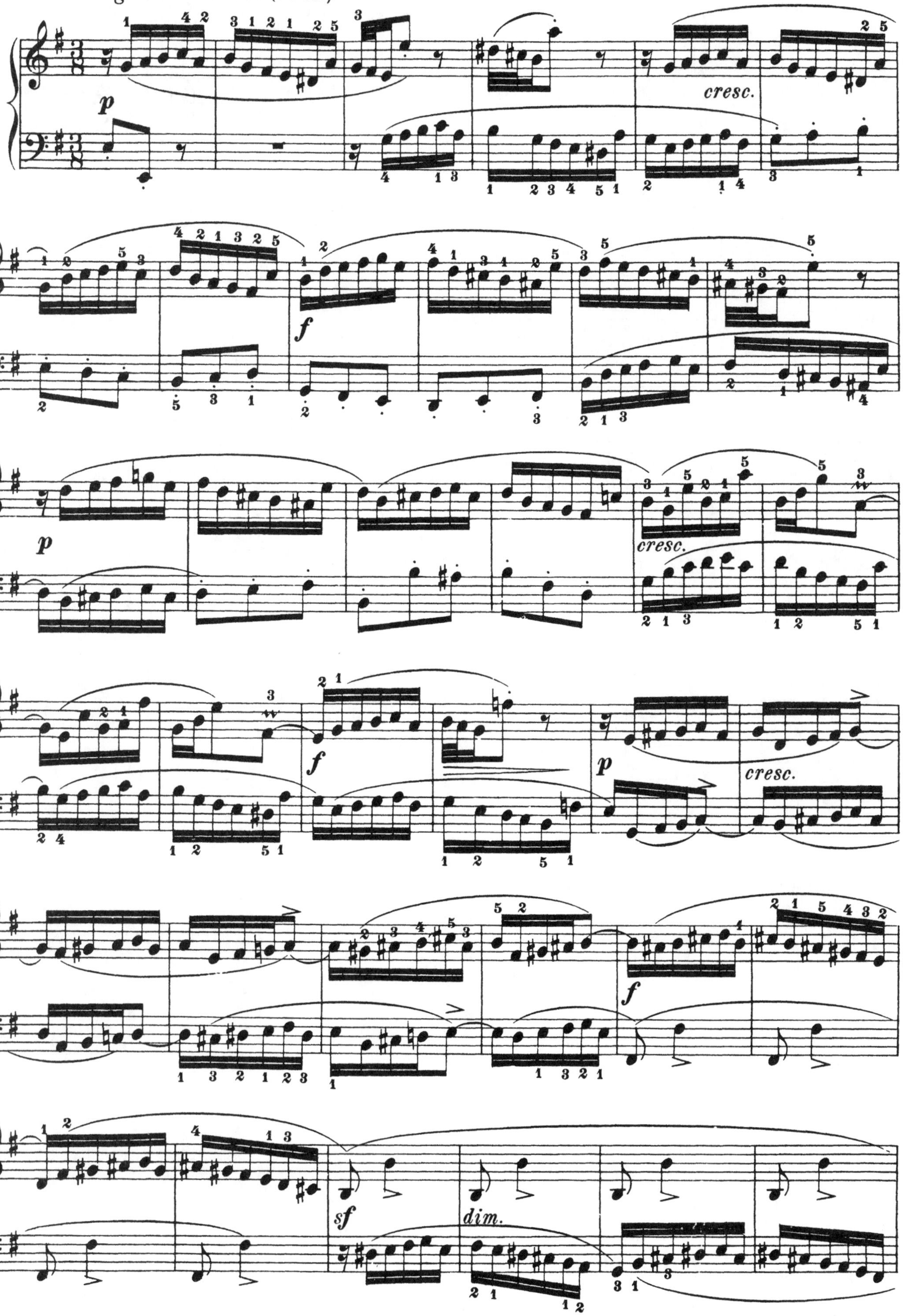

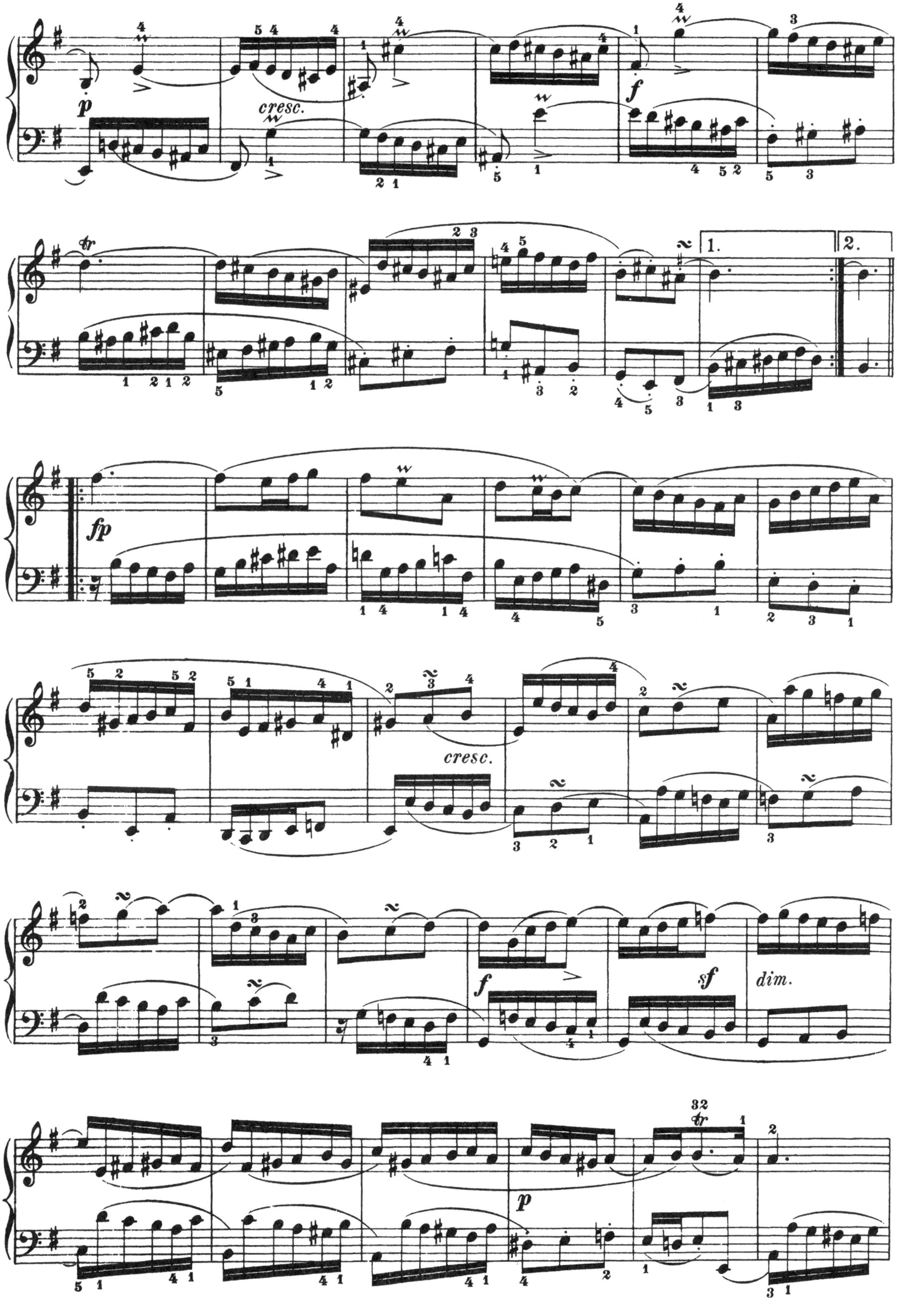
p
cresc.
f
tr
1.
2.
fp
cresc.
f
sf
dim.
p
tr

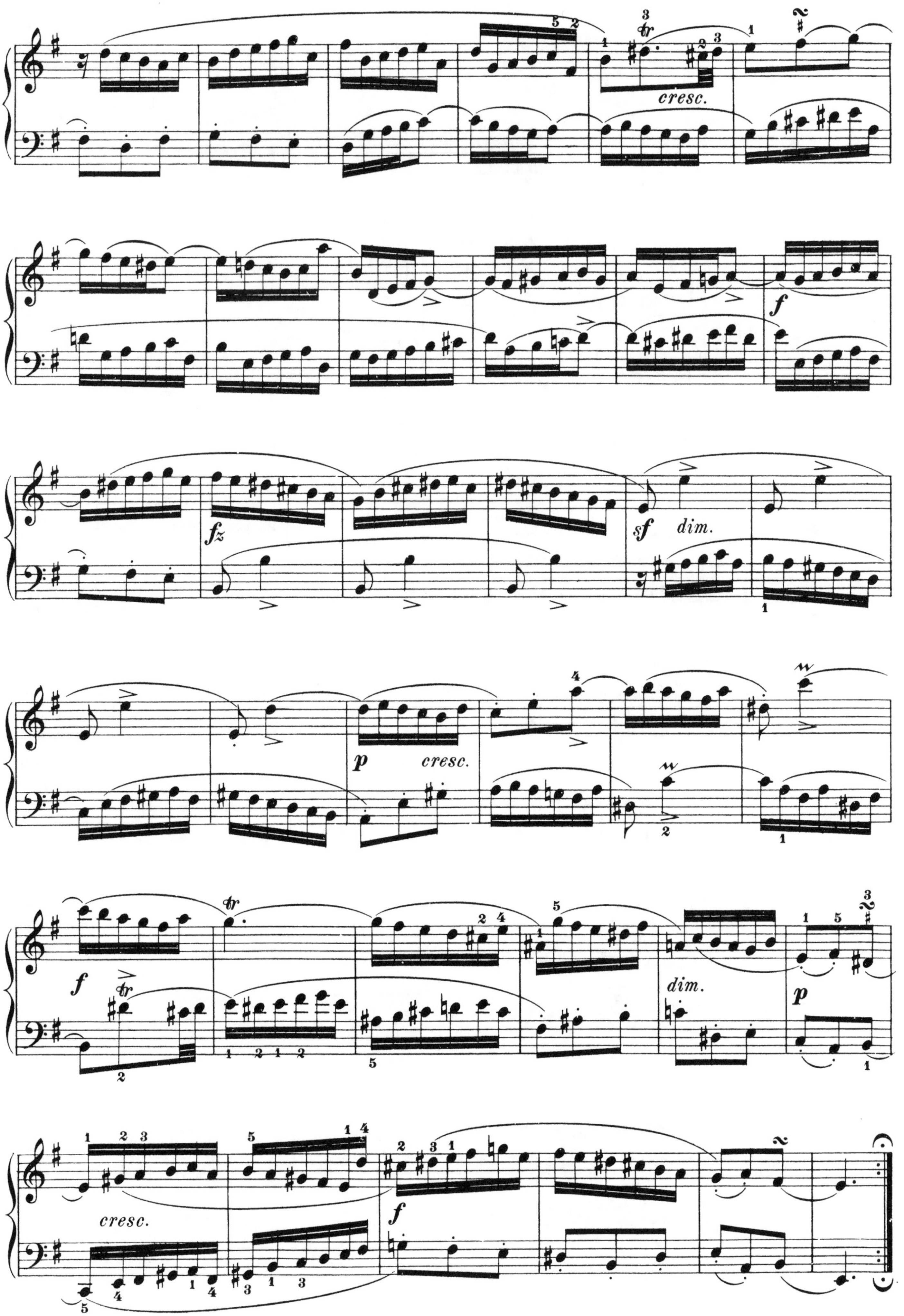
cresc.
f
fz
sf
dim.
p
cresc.
f
dim.
p
cresc.
f

Fuga X.

a 3 Voci.

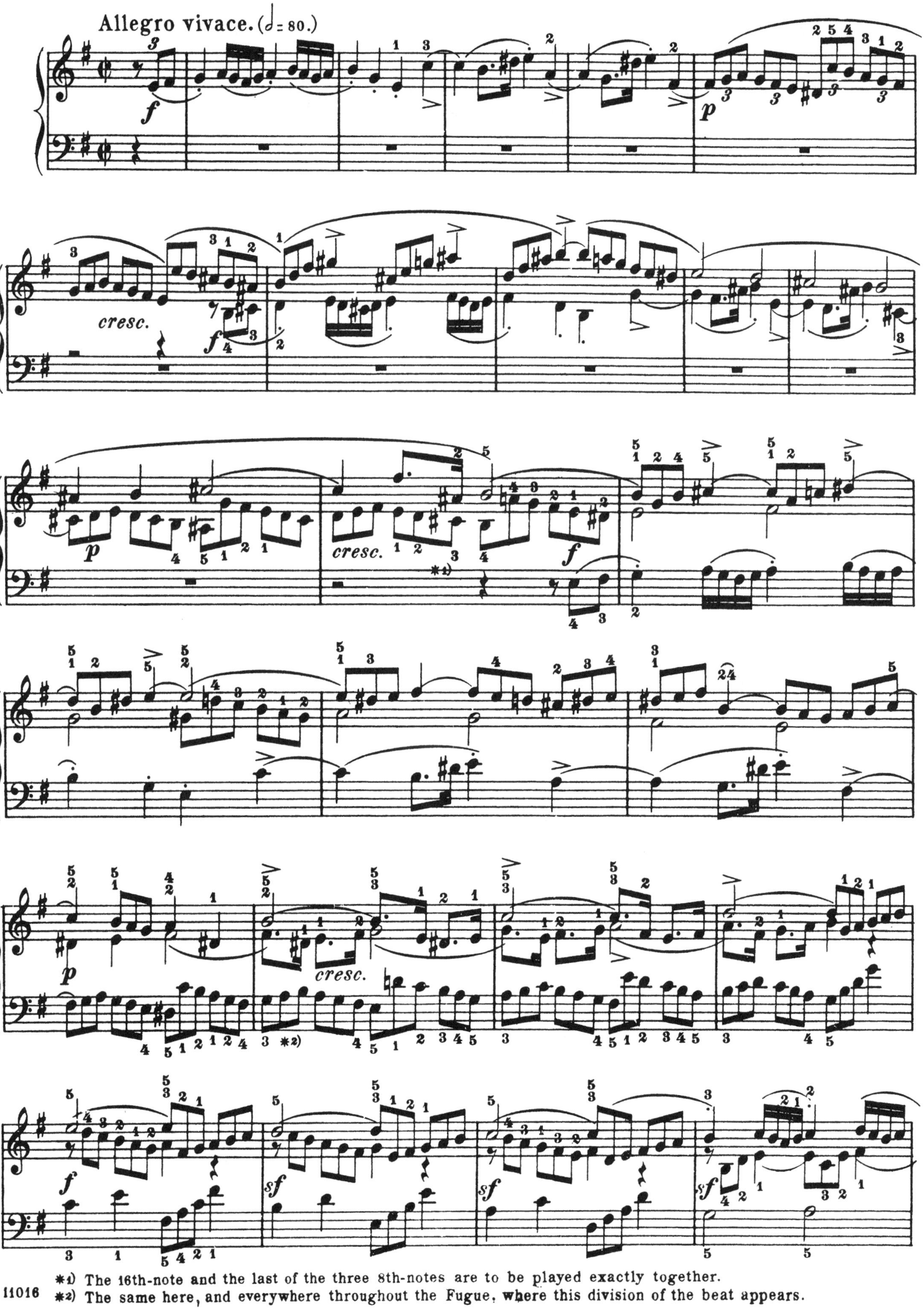

*1) The 16th-note and the last of the three 8th-notes are to be played exactly together.

*2) The same here, and everywhere throughout the Fugue, where this division of the beat appears.

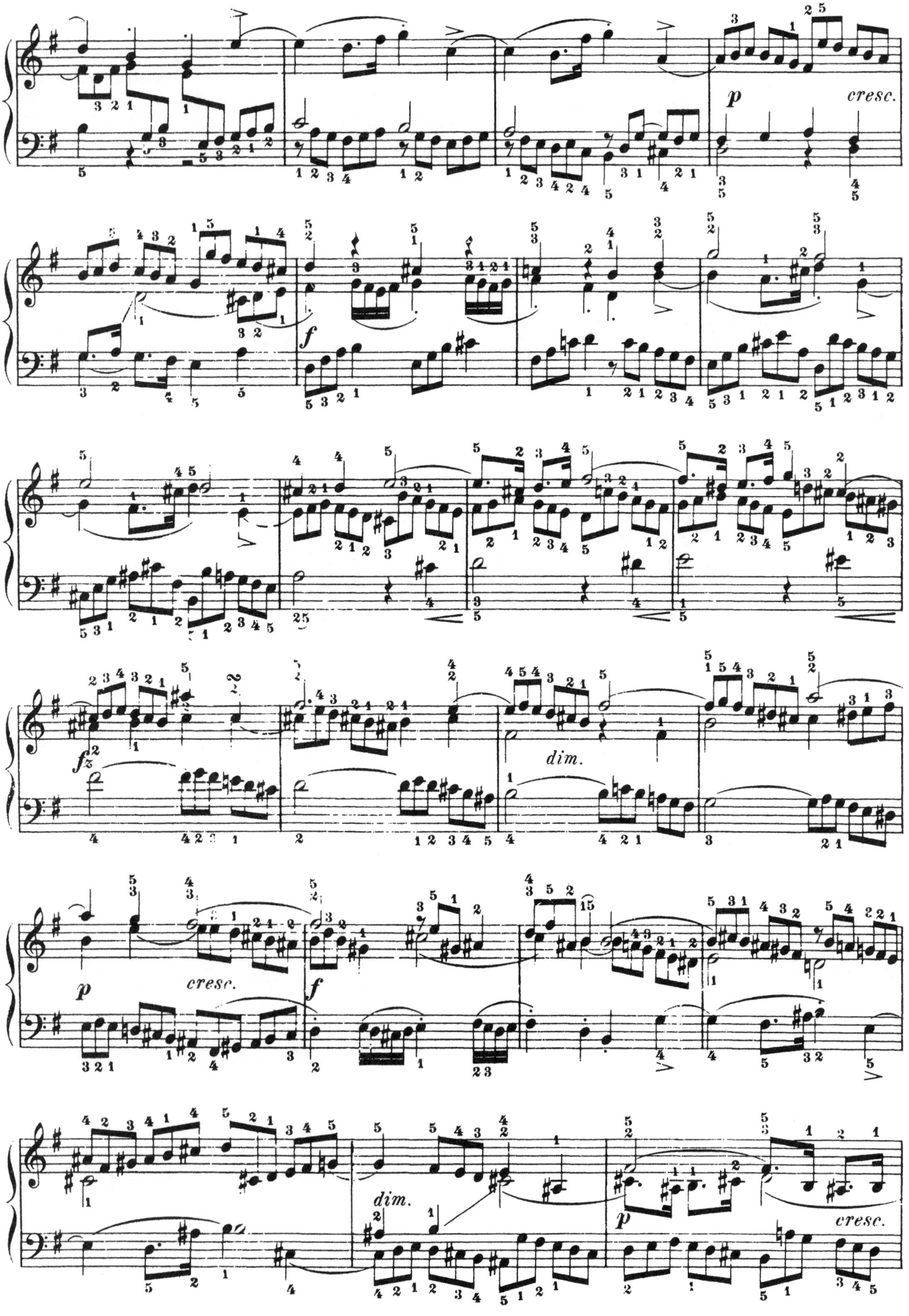
p
cresc.
f
fz
dim.
p
cresc.
f
dim.
p
cresc.

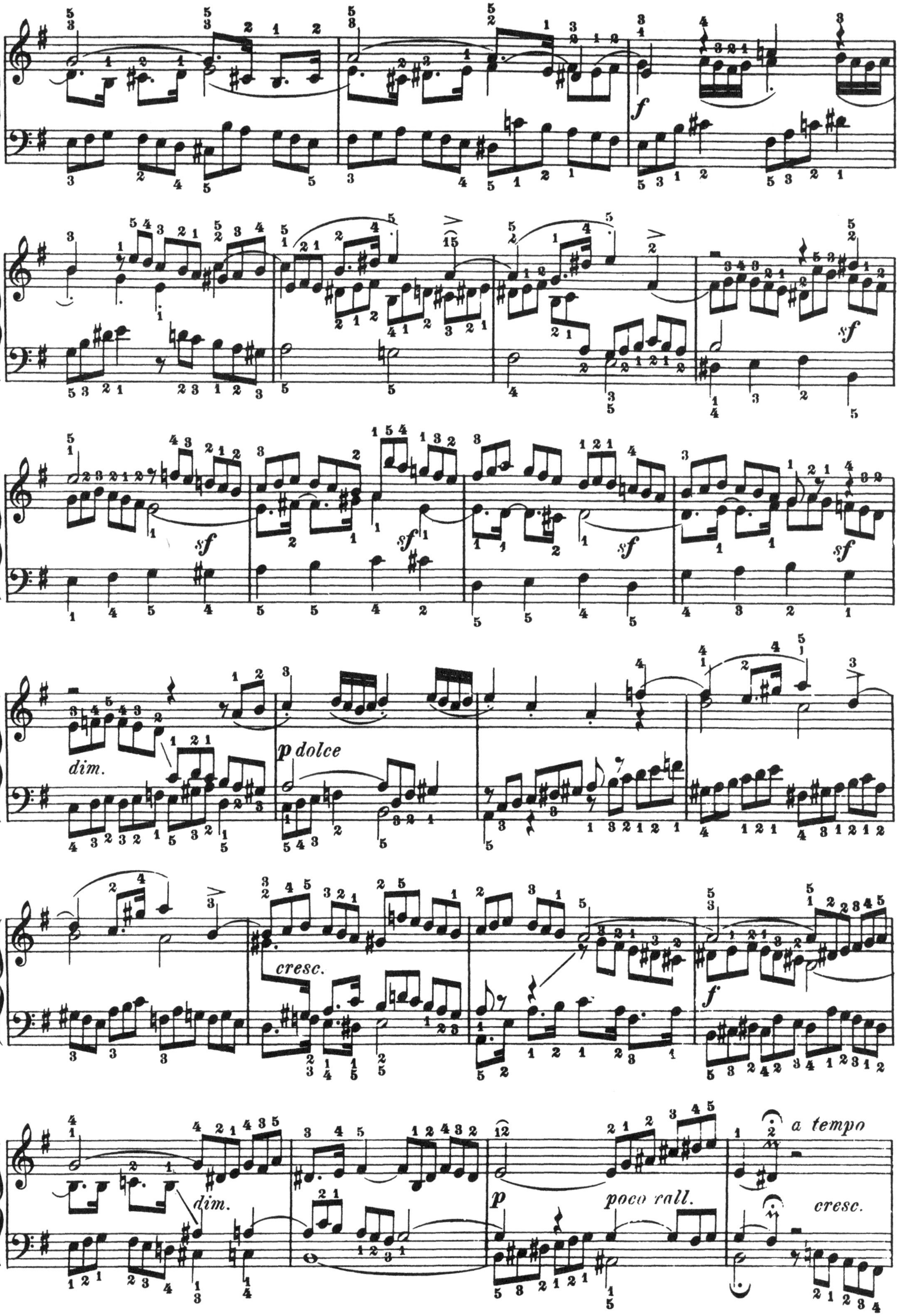

f
sf
sf
sf
sf
sf
dim.
p dolce
cresc.
f
dim.
p
poco rall.
a tempo
cresc.

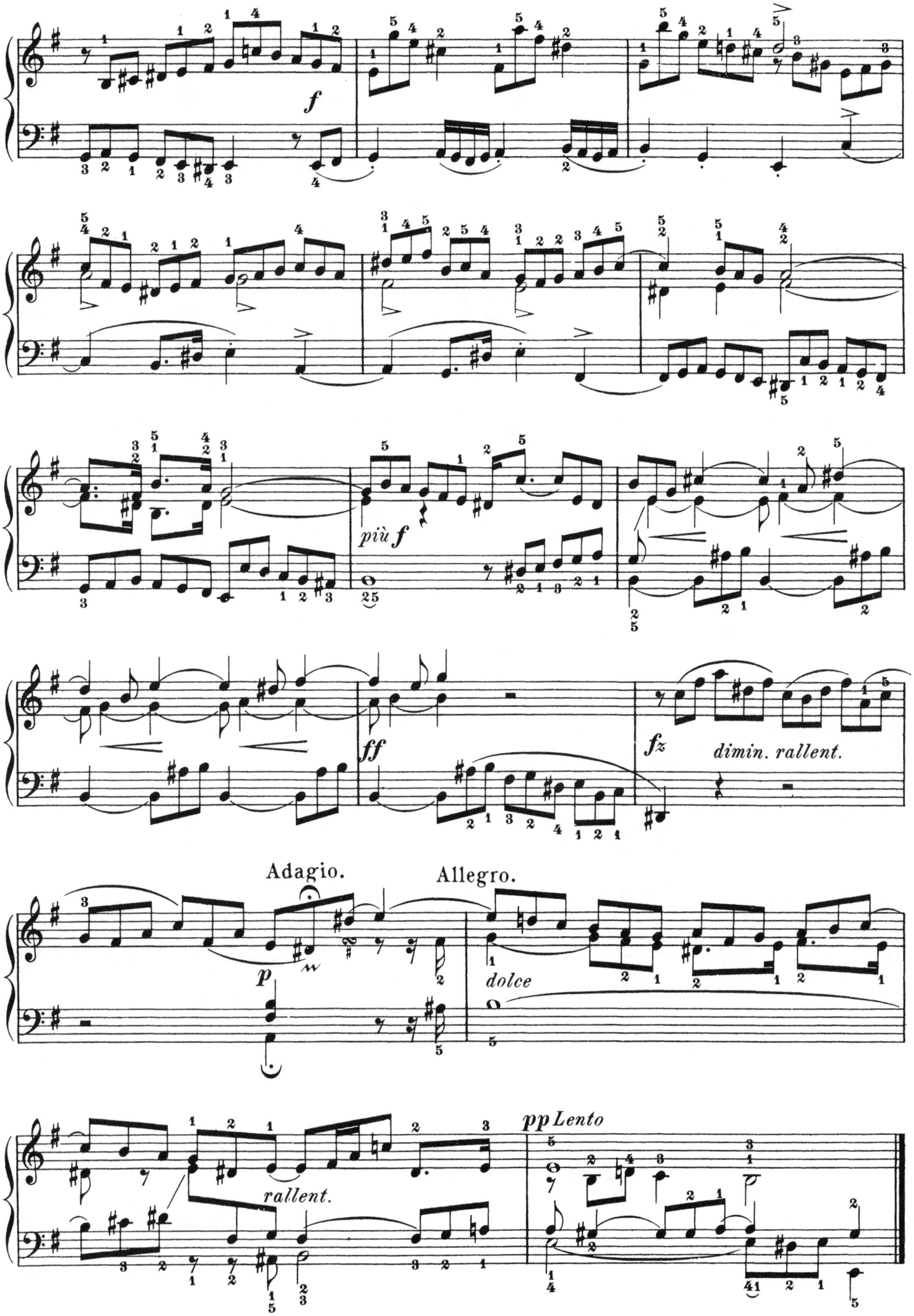
f
più f
ff
fz
dimin. rallent.
Adagio.
Allegro.
p
dolce
rallent.
pp Lento

Preludio XI.

Andante espressivo. (𝅗𝅥 = 104.)

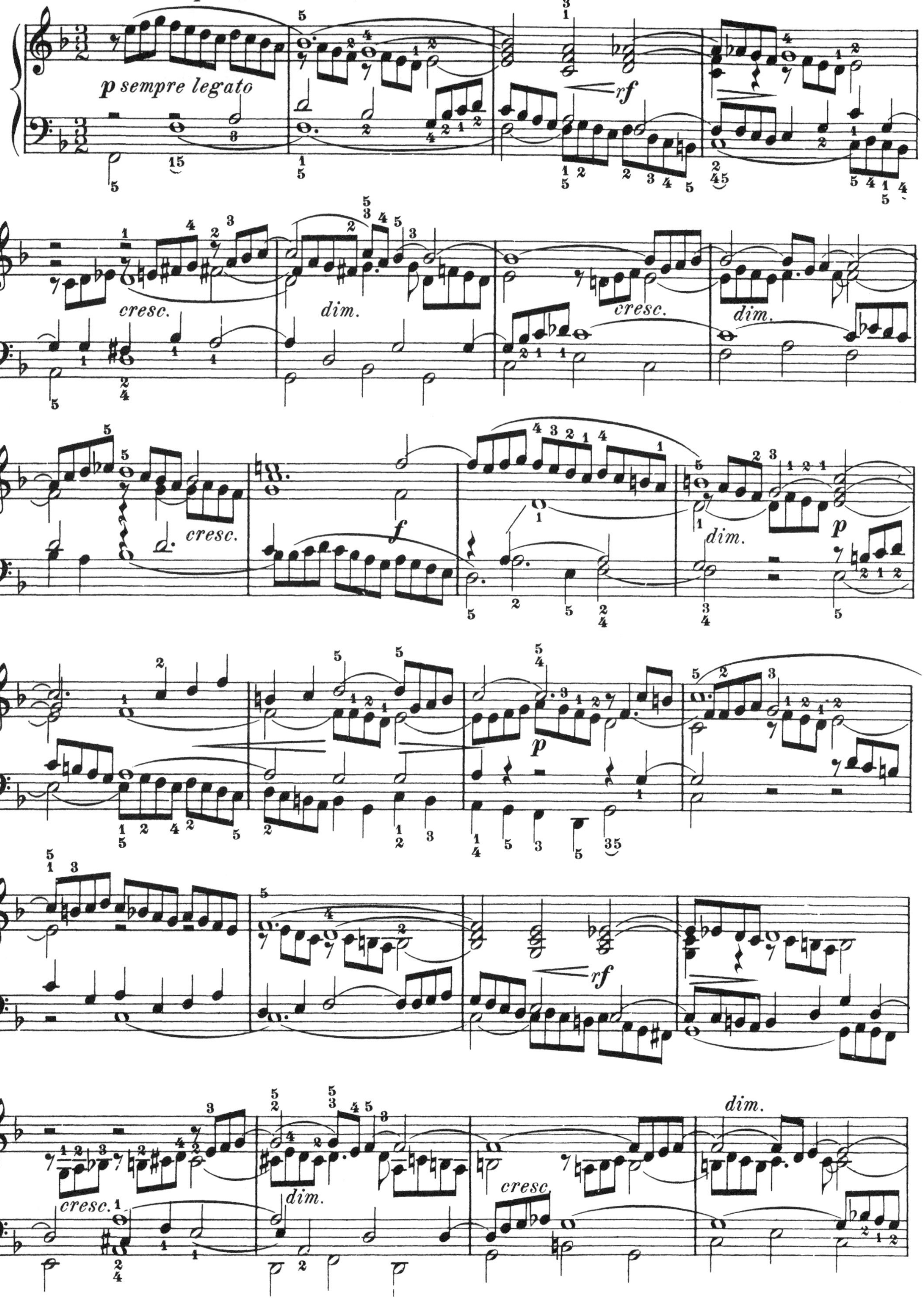

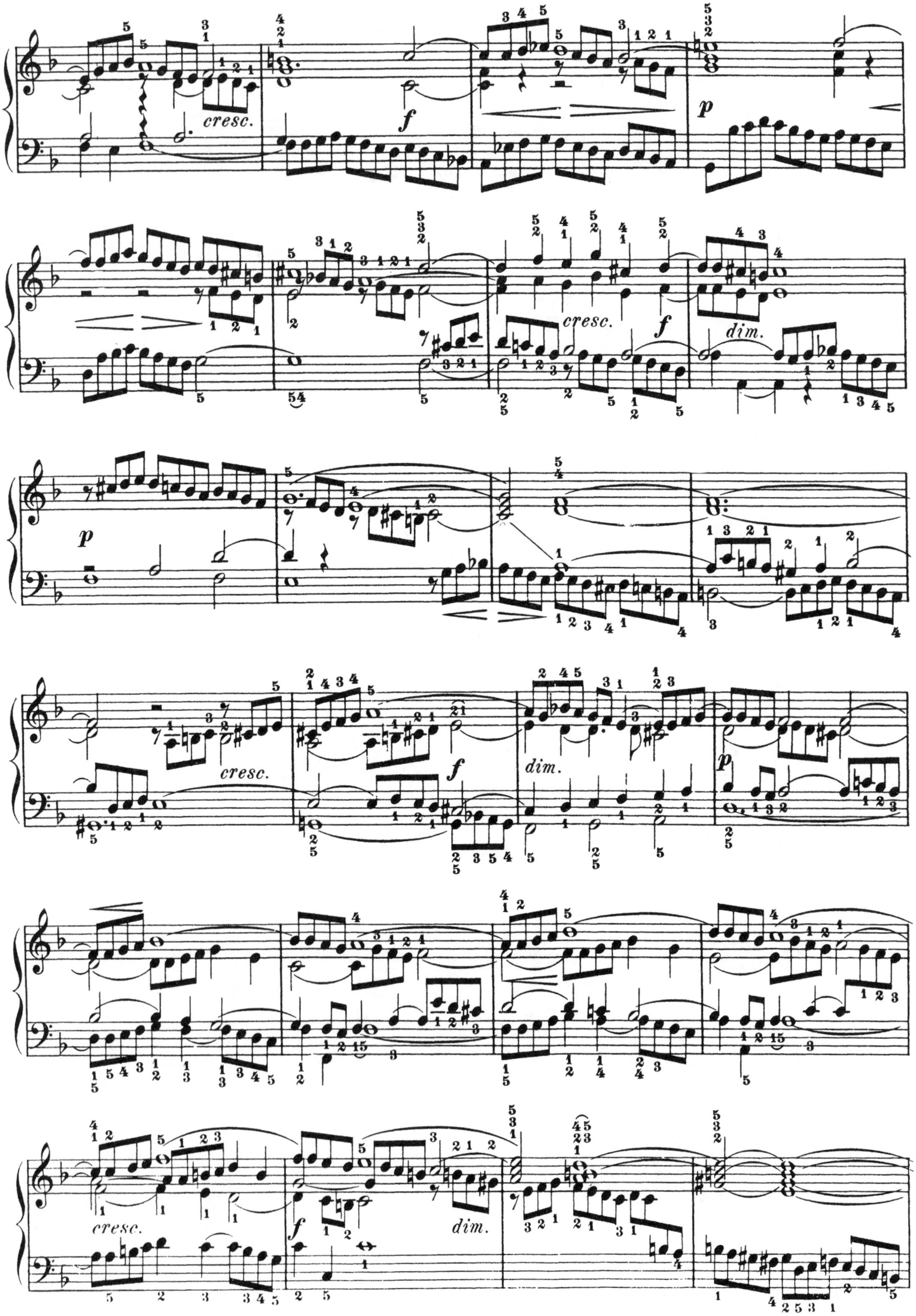
cresc.
f
p
cresc.
f
dim.
p
cresc.
f
dim.
p
cresc.
f
dim.

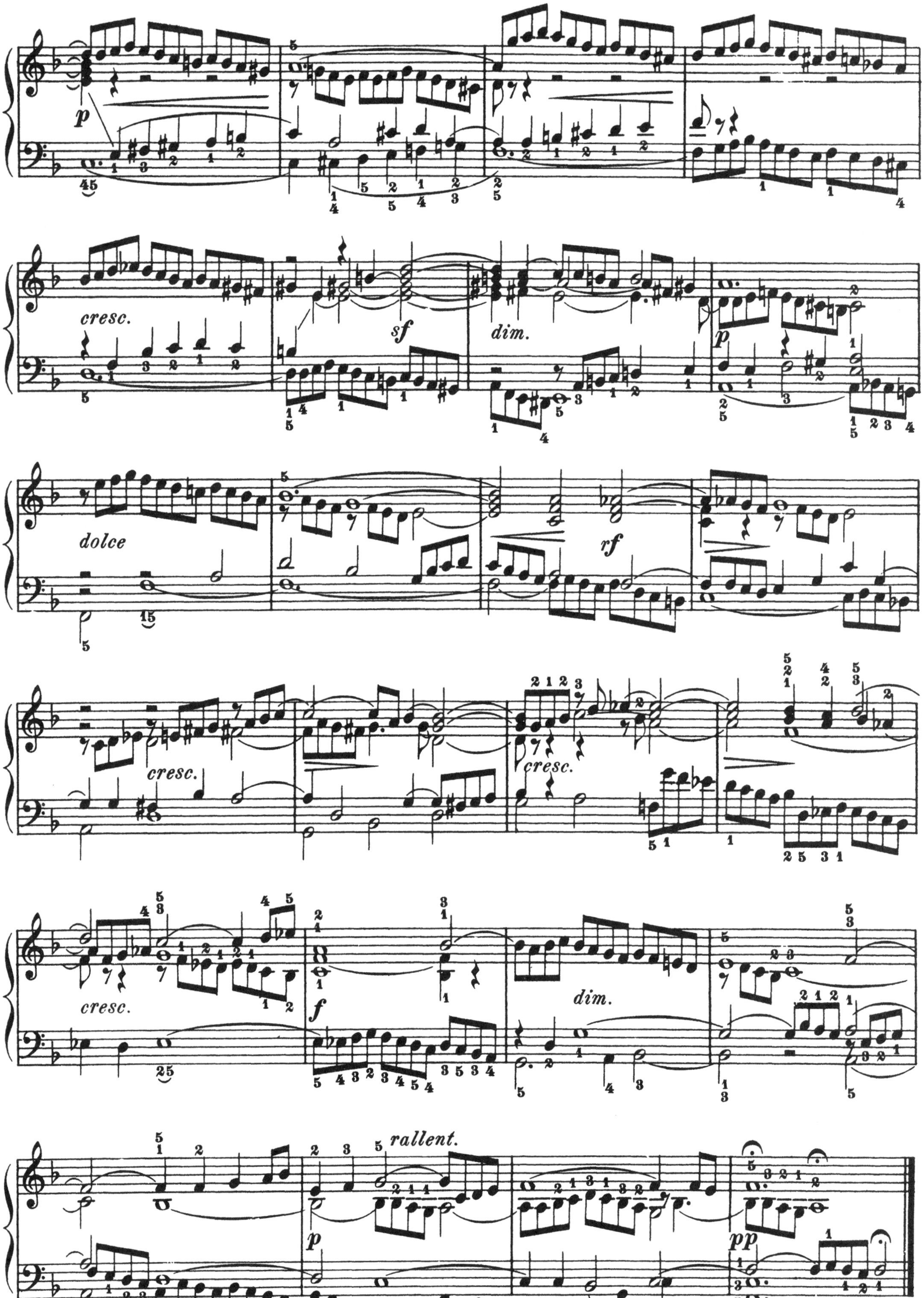
p
cresc.
sf
dim.
p
dolce
rf
cresc.
cresc.
cresc.
f
dim.
rallent.
p
pp

Fuga XI.

a 3 Voci.

Allegretto. (♪. = 112.)

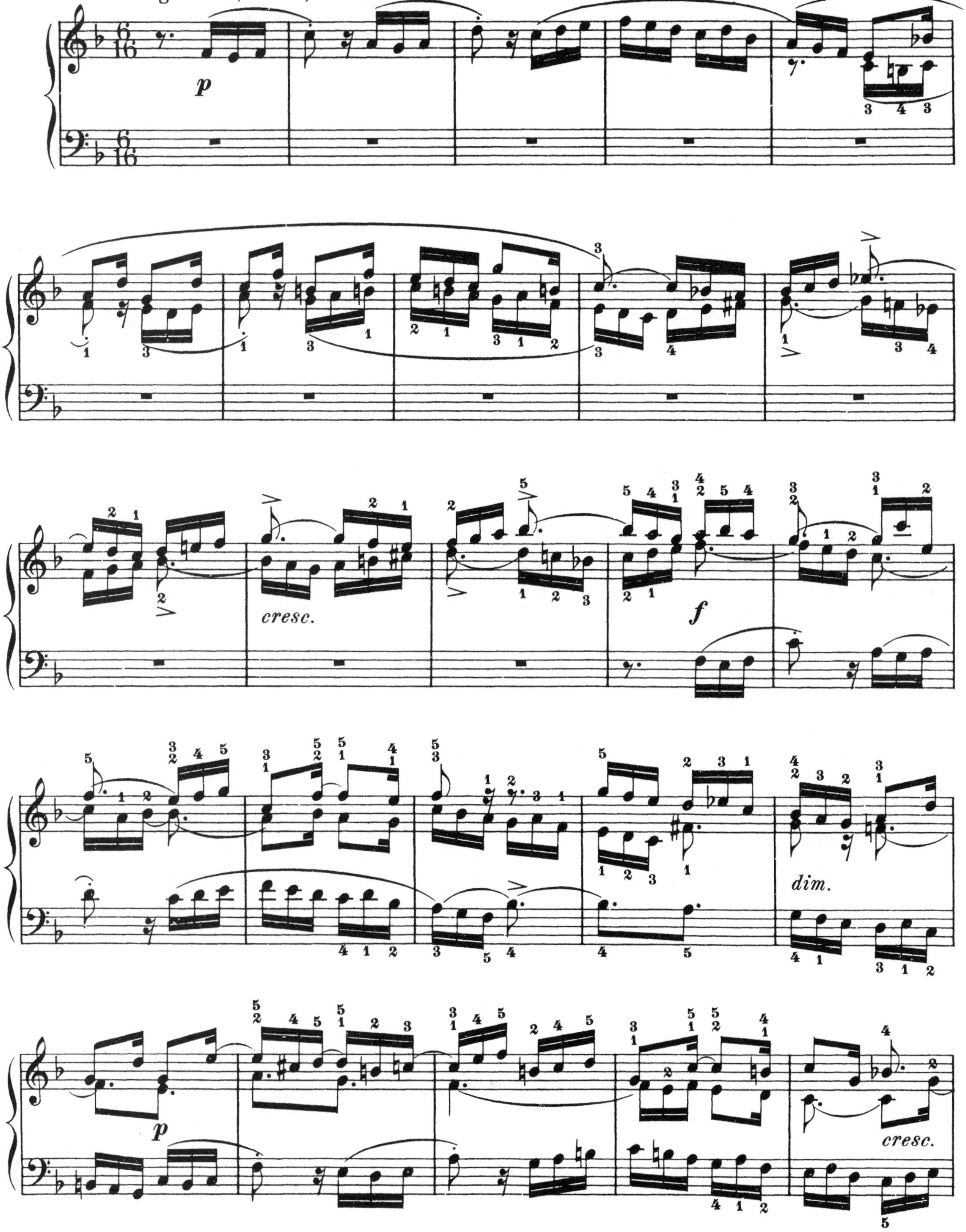

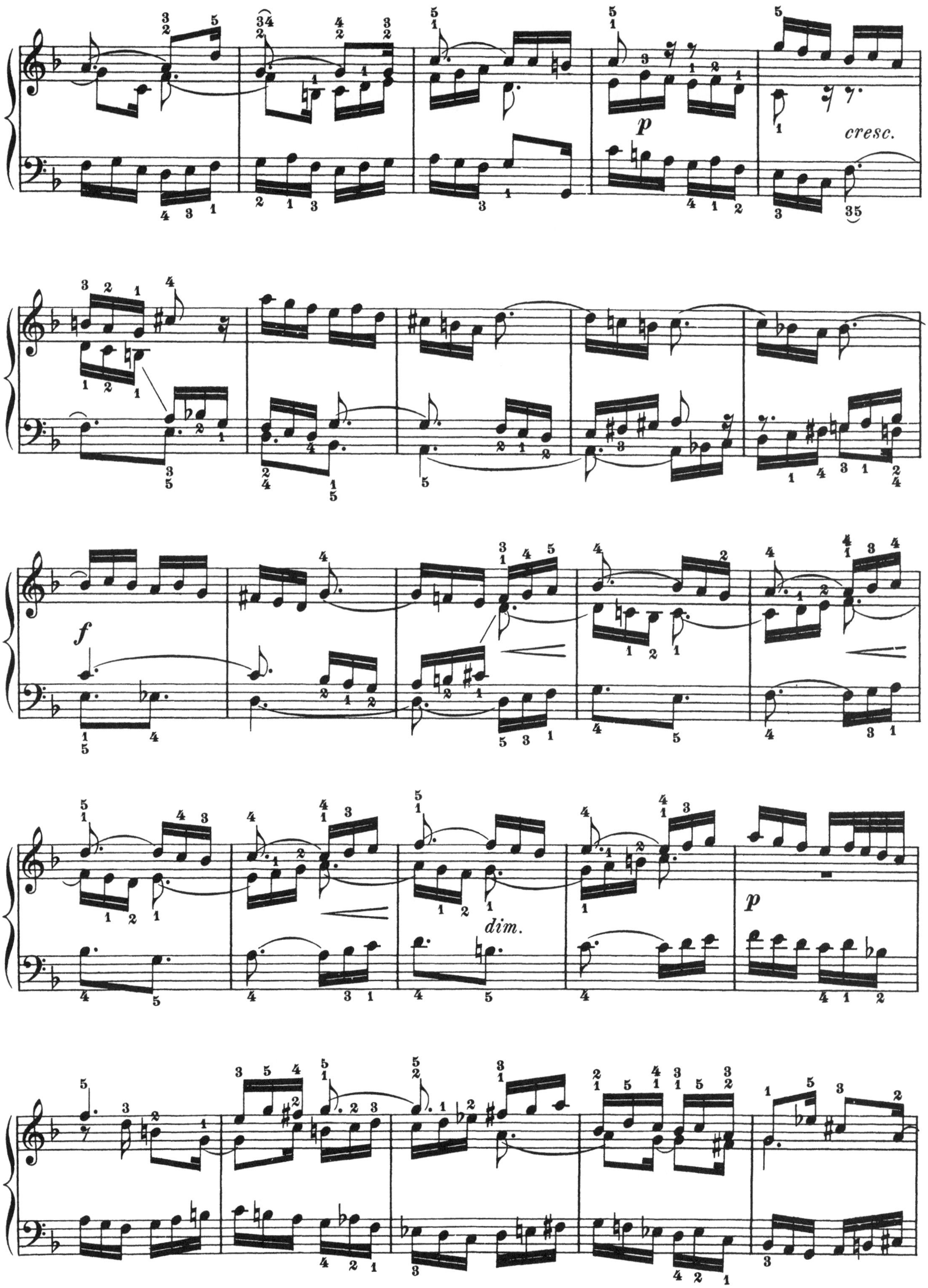
p
cresc.
f
dim.
p

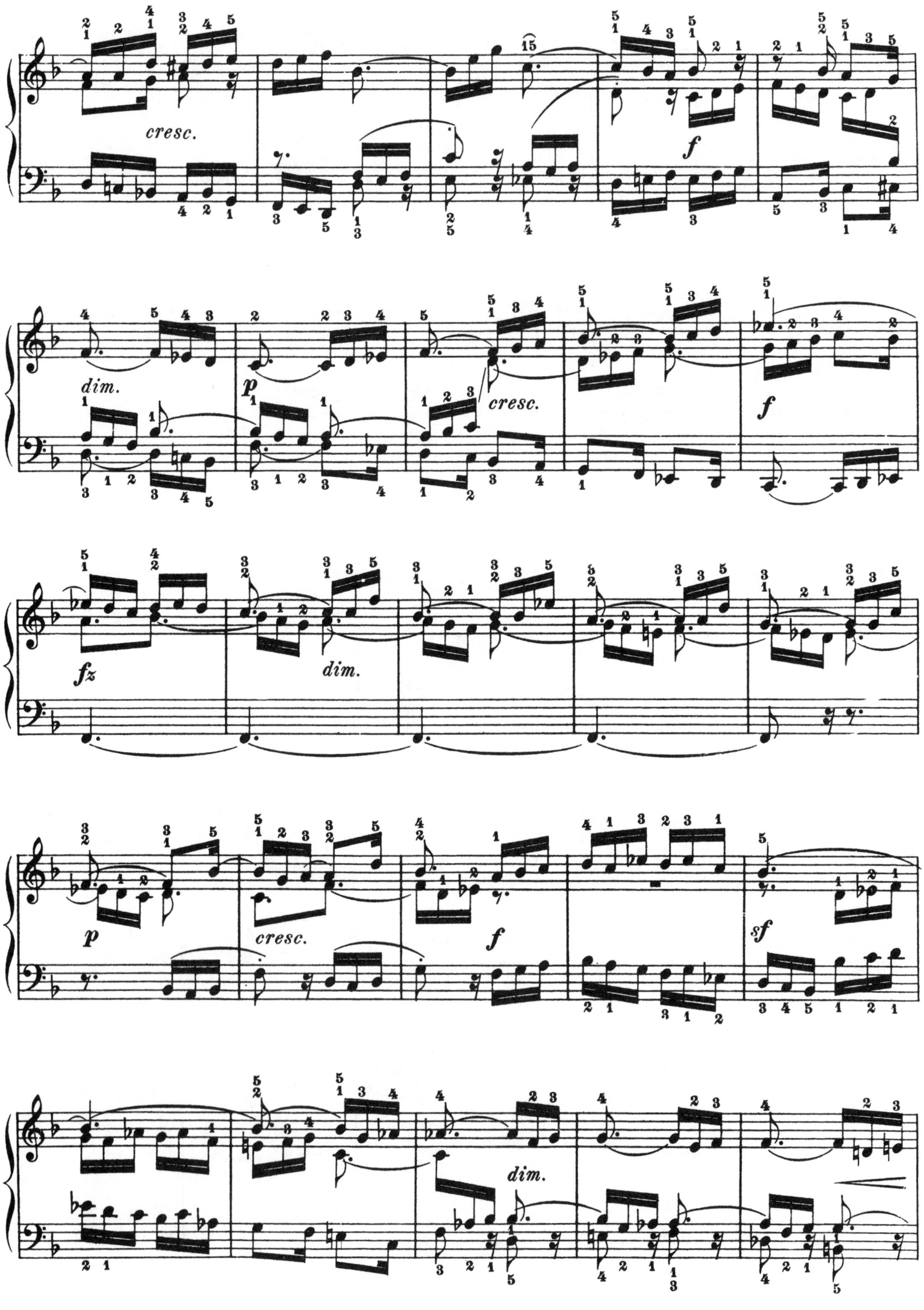
cresc.
f
dim.
p
cresc.
f
fz
dim.
p
cresc.
f
sf
dim.

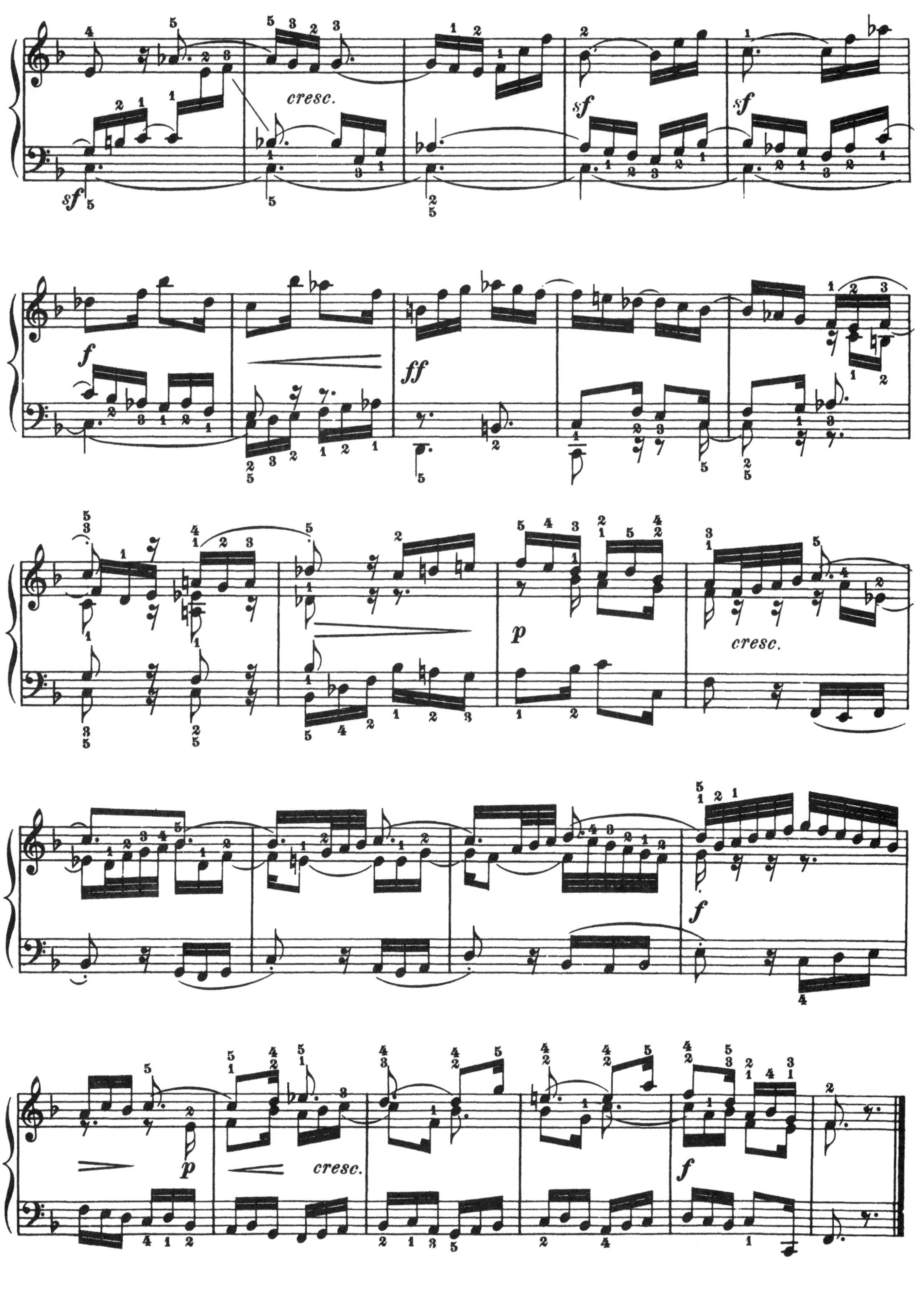

sf
cresc.
sf
sf
f
ff
p
cresc.
f
p
cresc.
f

Preludio XII.

Andante espressivo. (♩= 80.)

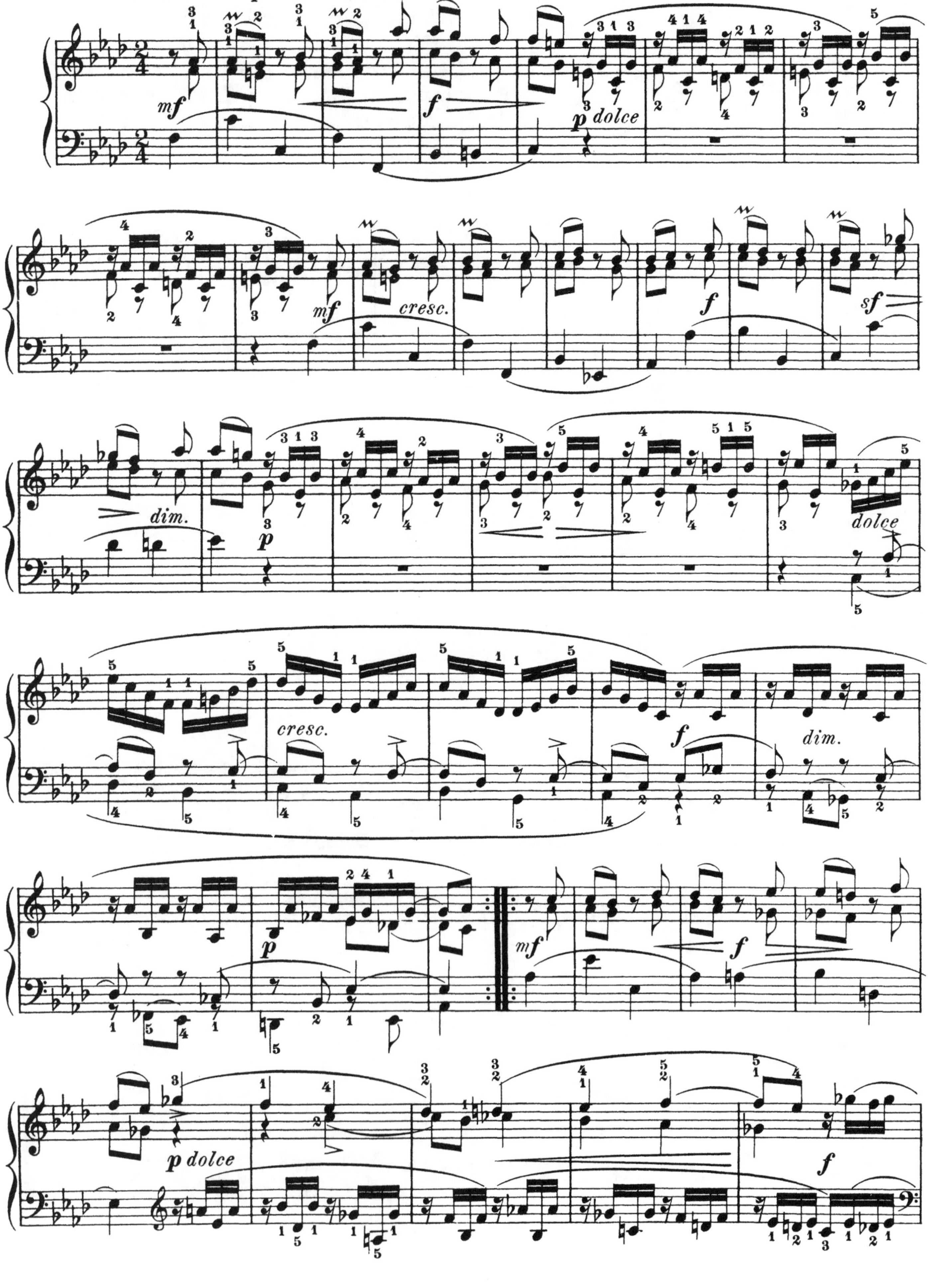

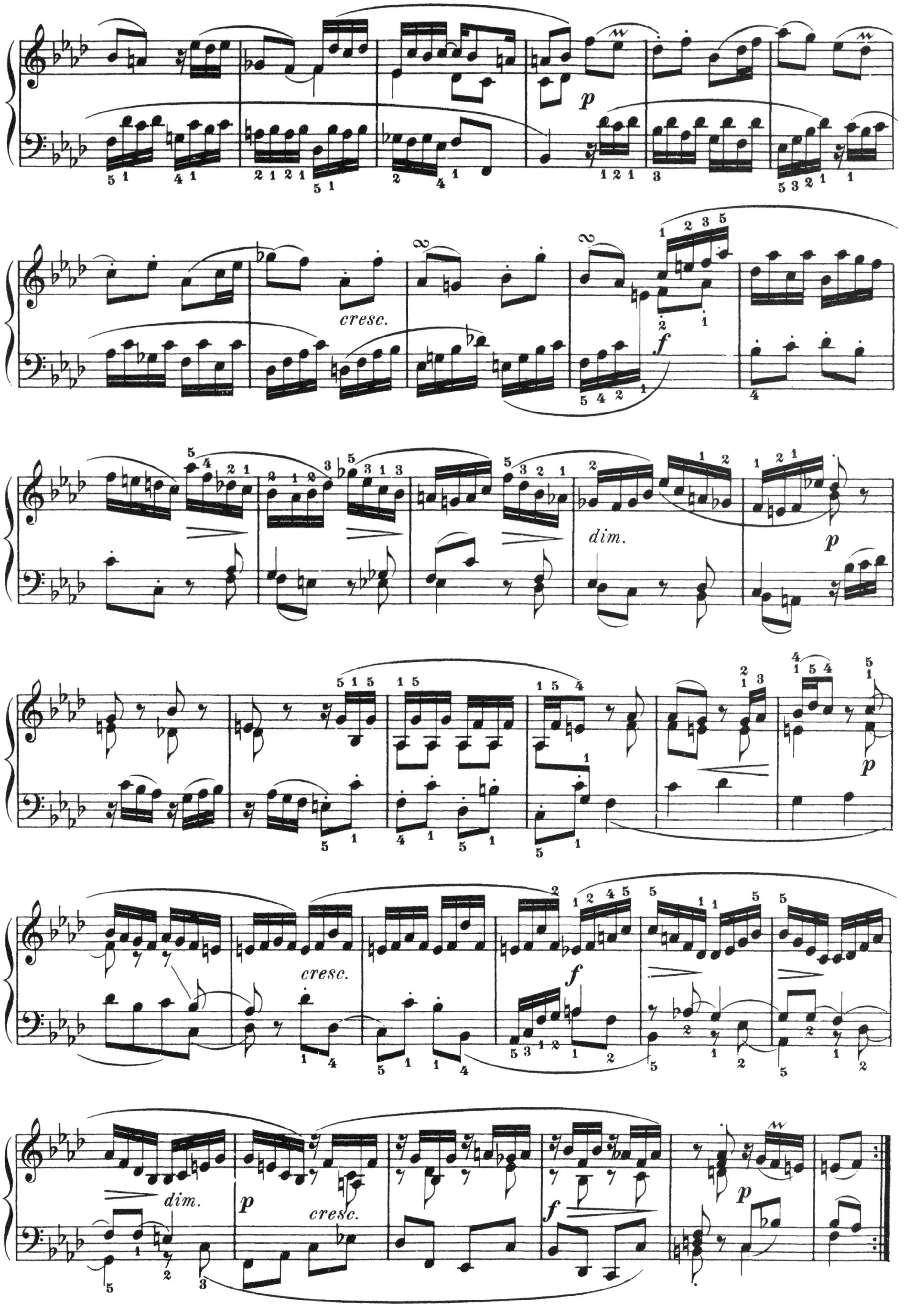
p
cresc.
f
dim.
p
cresc.
f
dim.
p
cresc.
f
p

Fuga XII.

a 3 Voci.

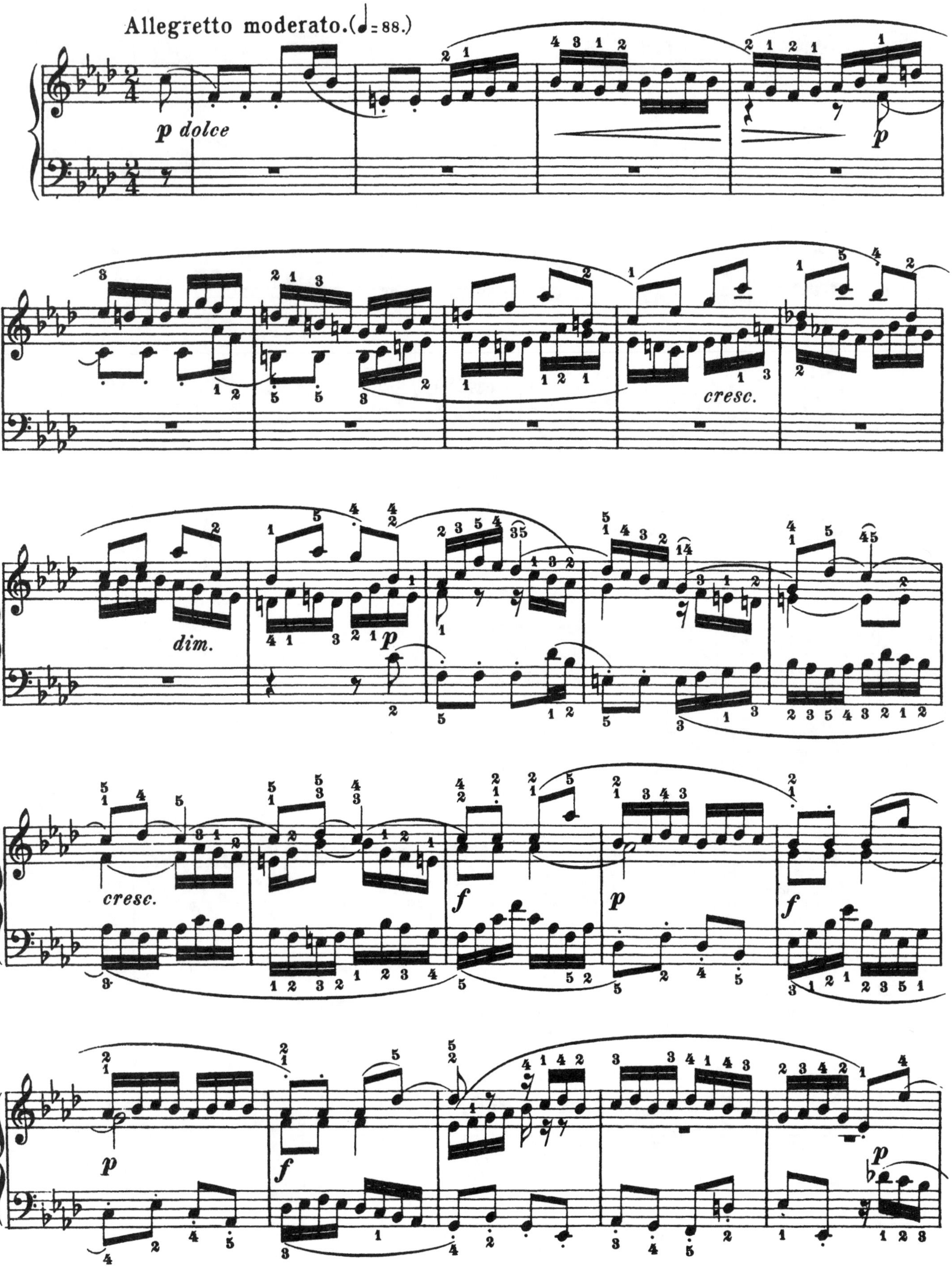

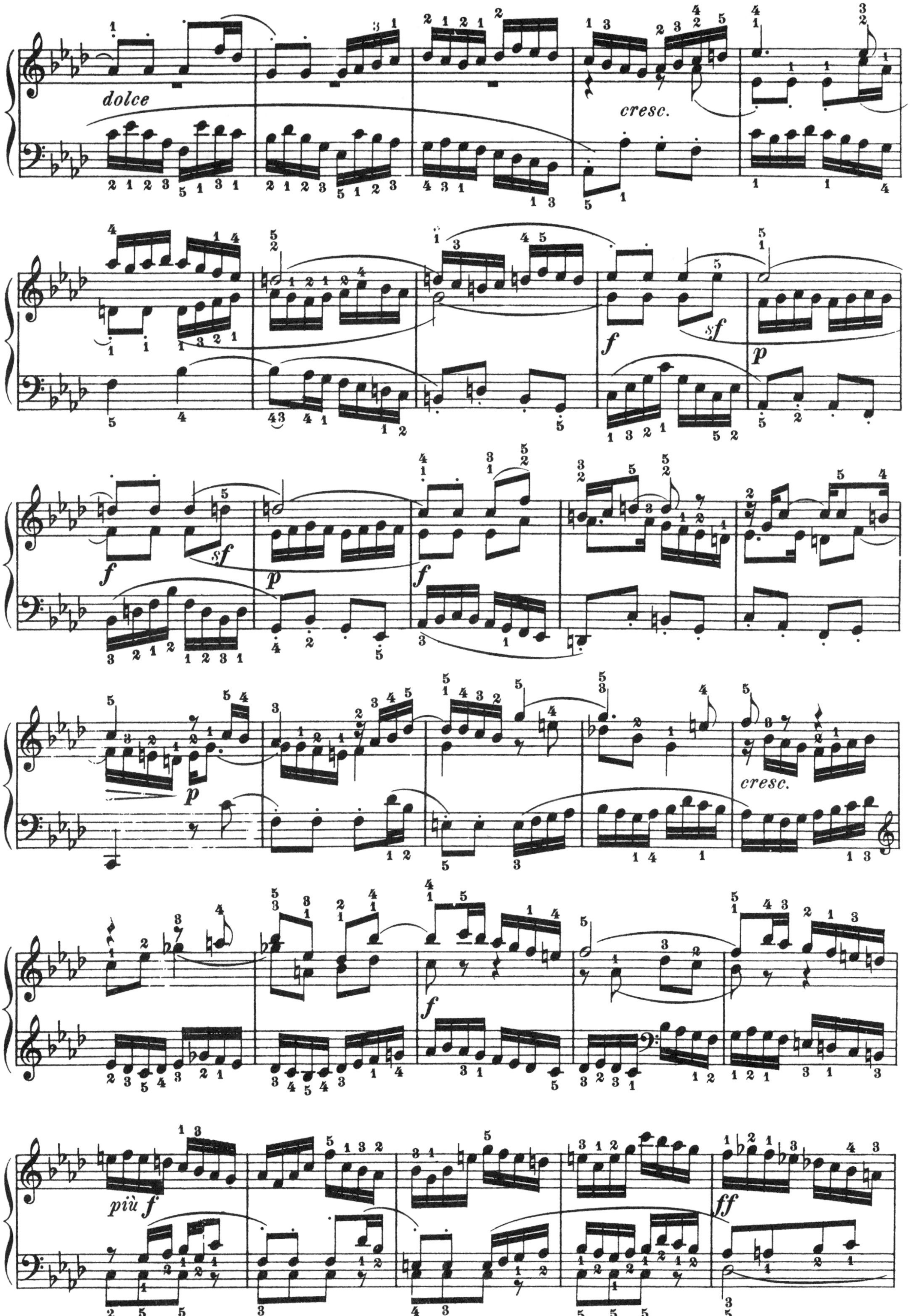
dolce
cresc.
f
sf
p
f
sf
p
f
p
cresc.
f
più f
ff

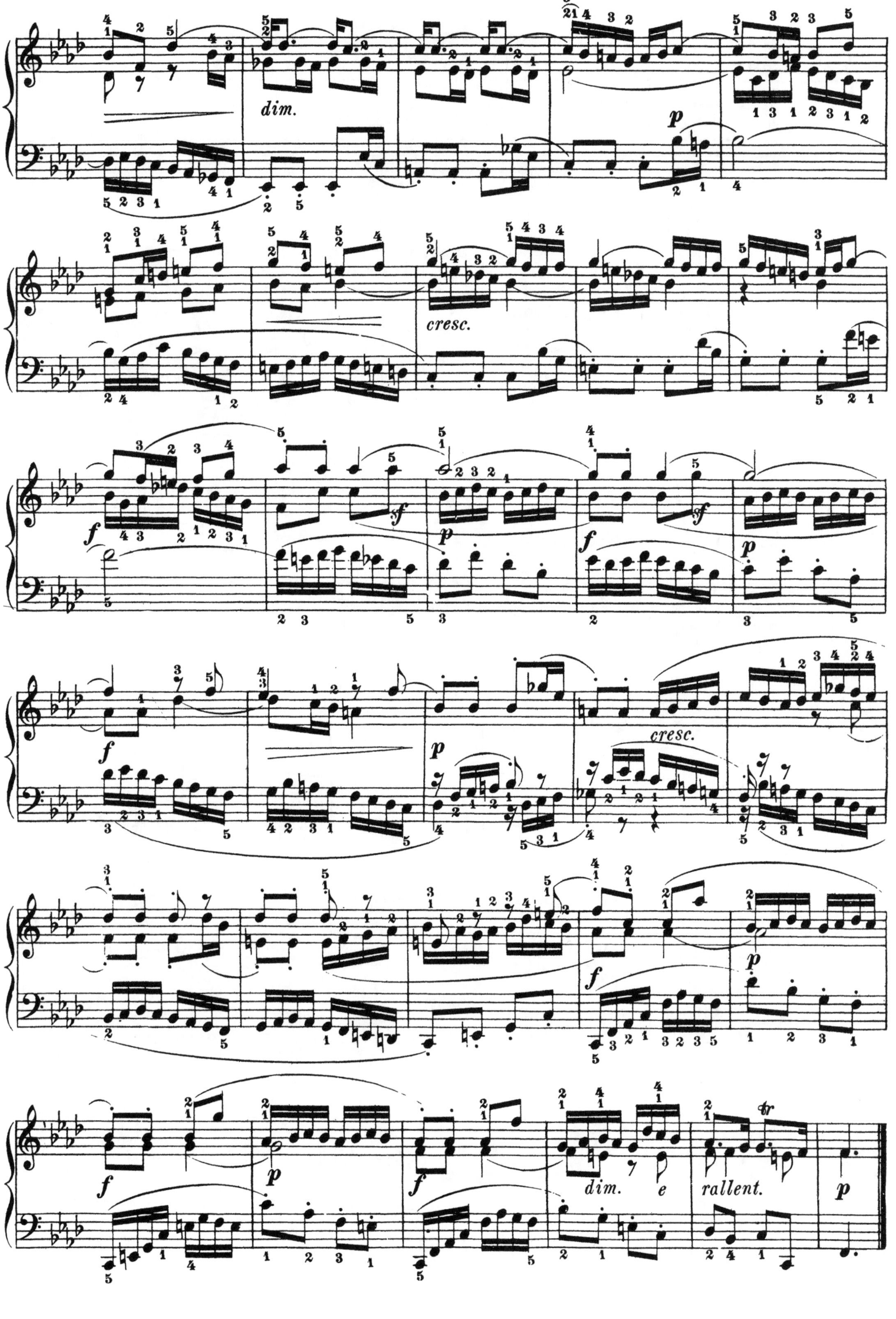
dim.
p
cresc.
f
sf
p
f
sf
p
f
p
cresc.
f
p
f
p
f
dim.
e
rallent.
tr
p

Preludio XIII.

Allegretto con moto. (♩ = 92)

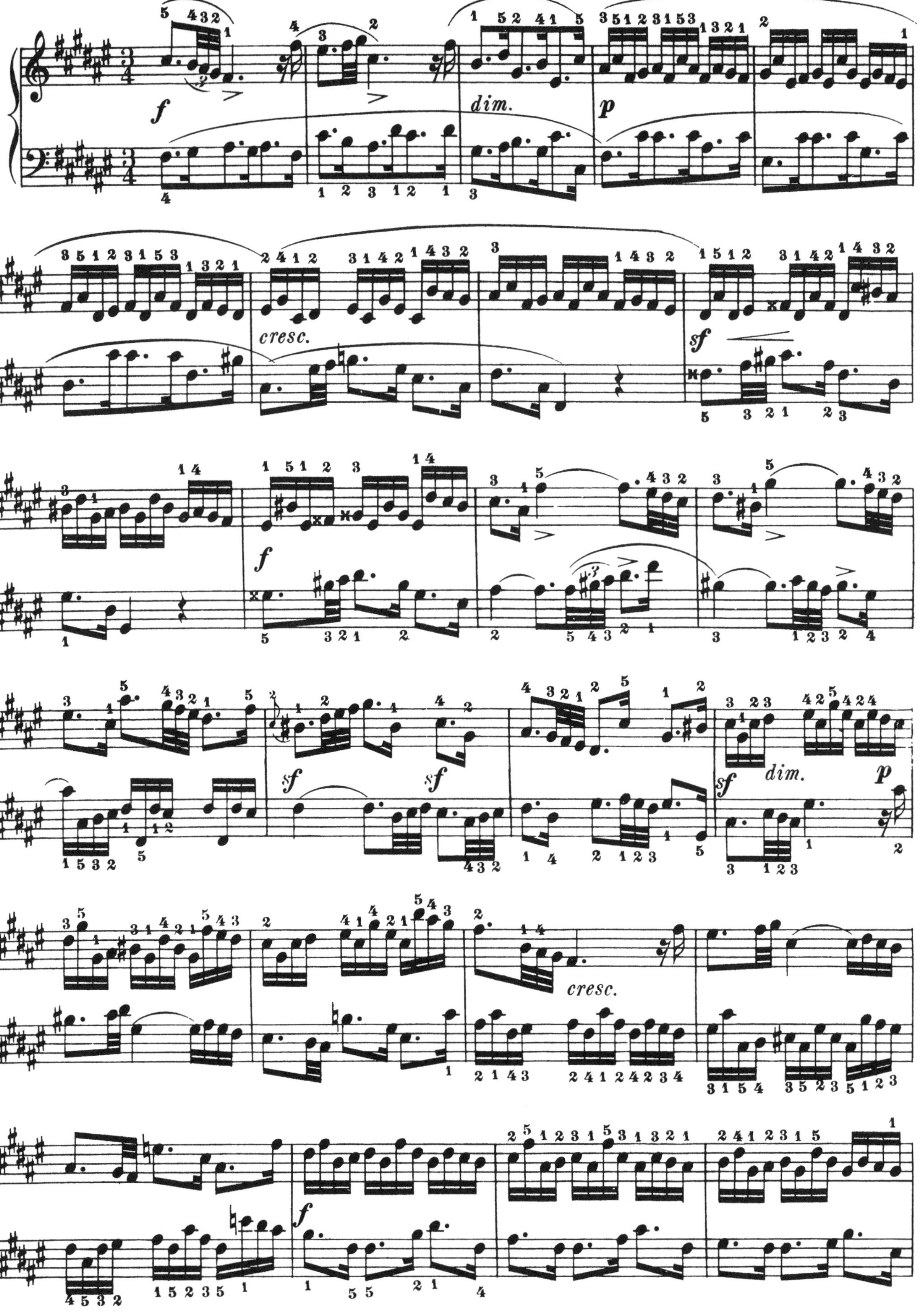

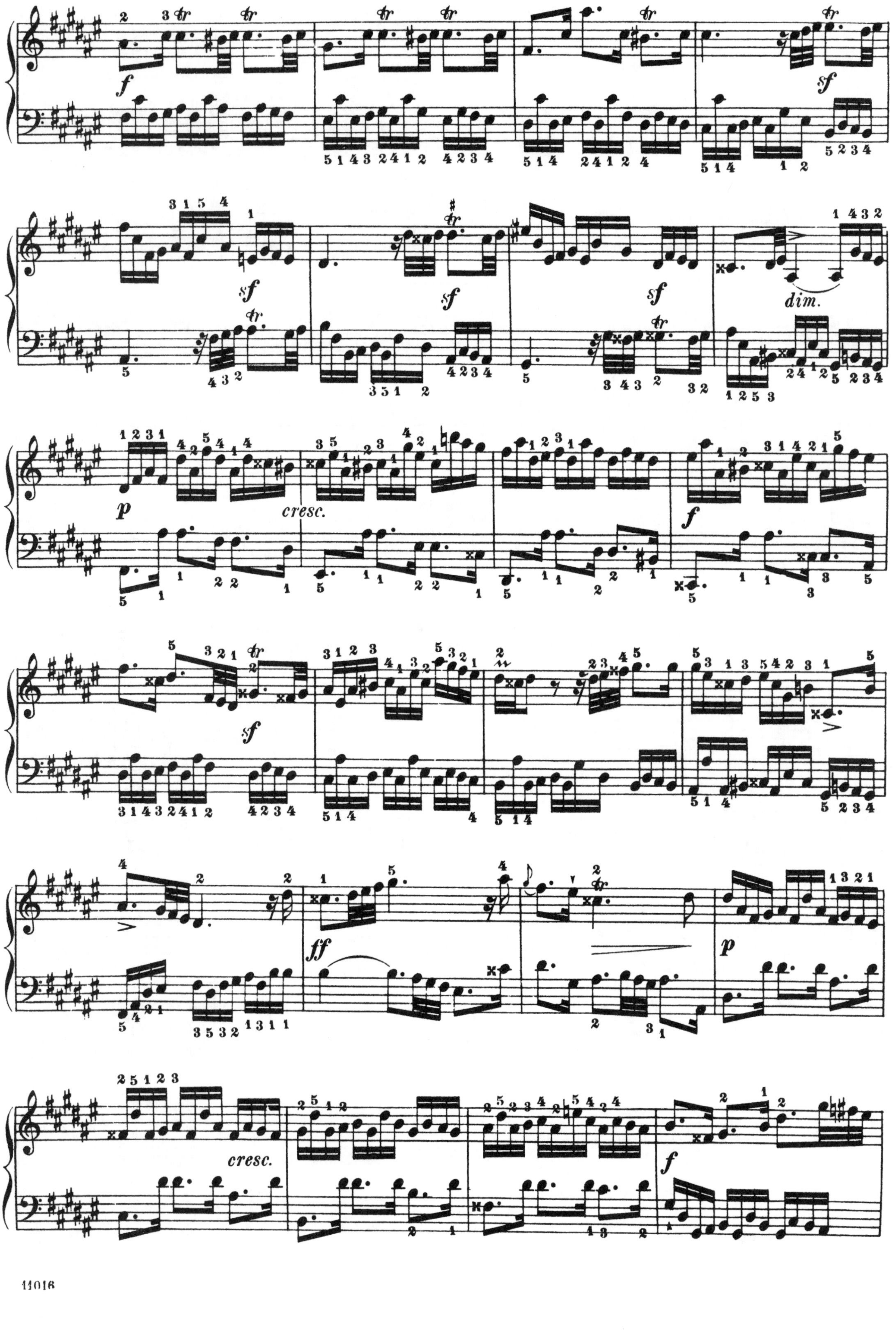
f
sf
sf
sf
sf
dim.
p
cresc.
f
sf
ff
p
cresc.
f

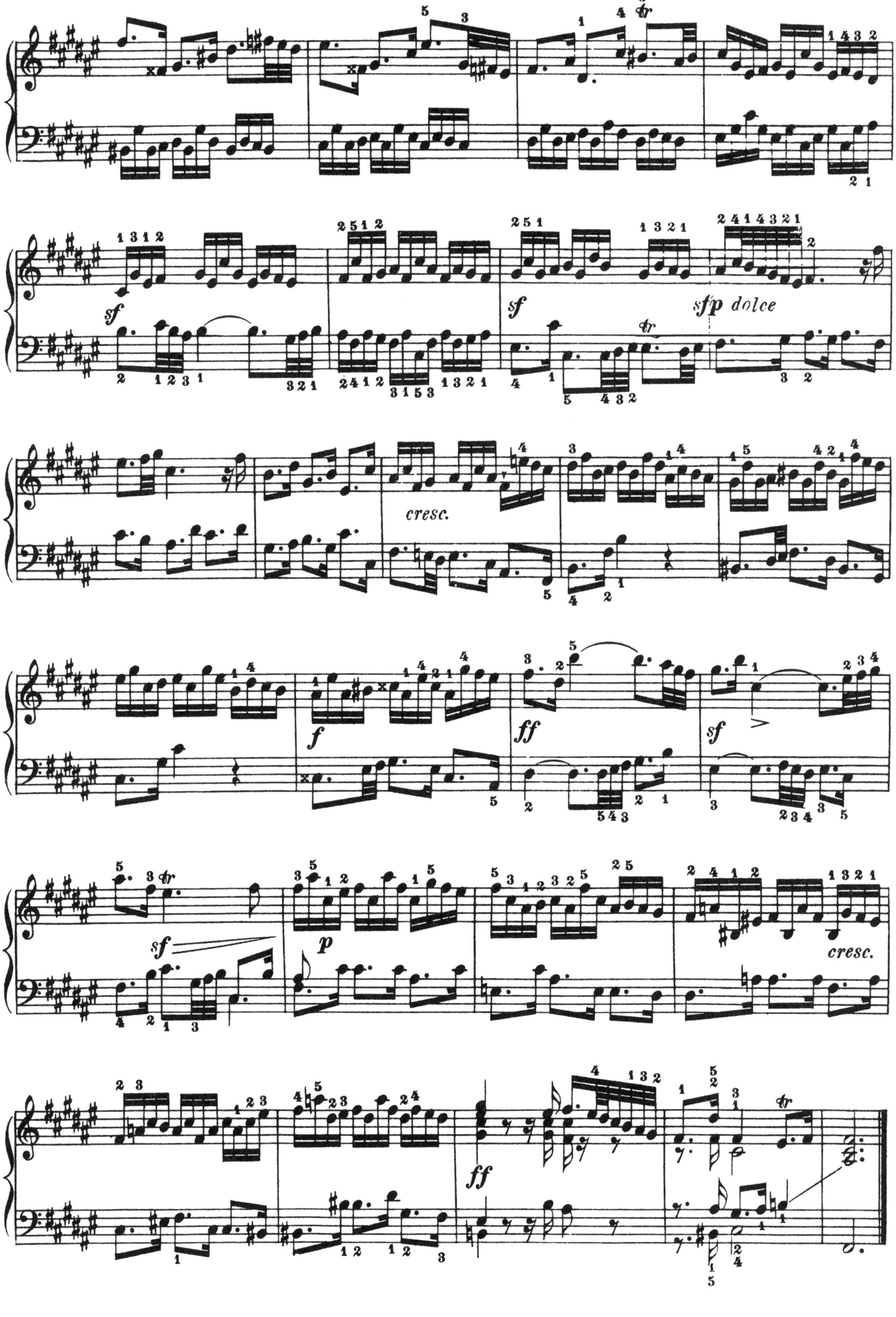
sf
sf
sfp dolce
cresc.
f
ff
sf
sf
p
cresc.
ff

Fuga XIII.

a 3 Voci.

Allegro moderato. (𝅗𝅥 = 58)

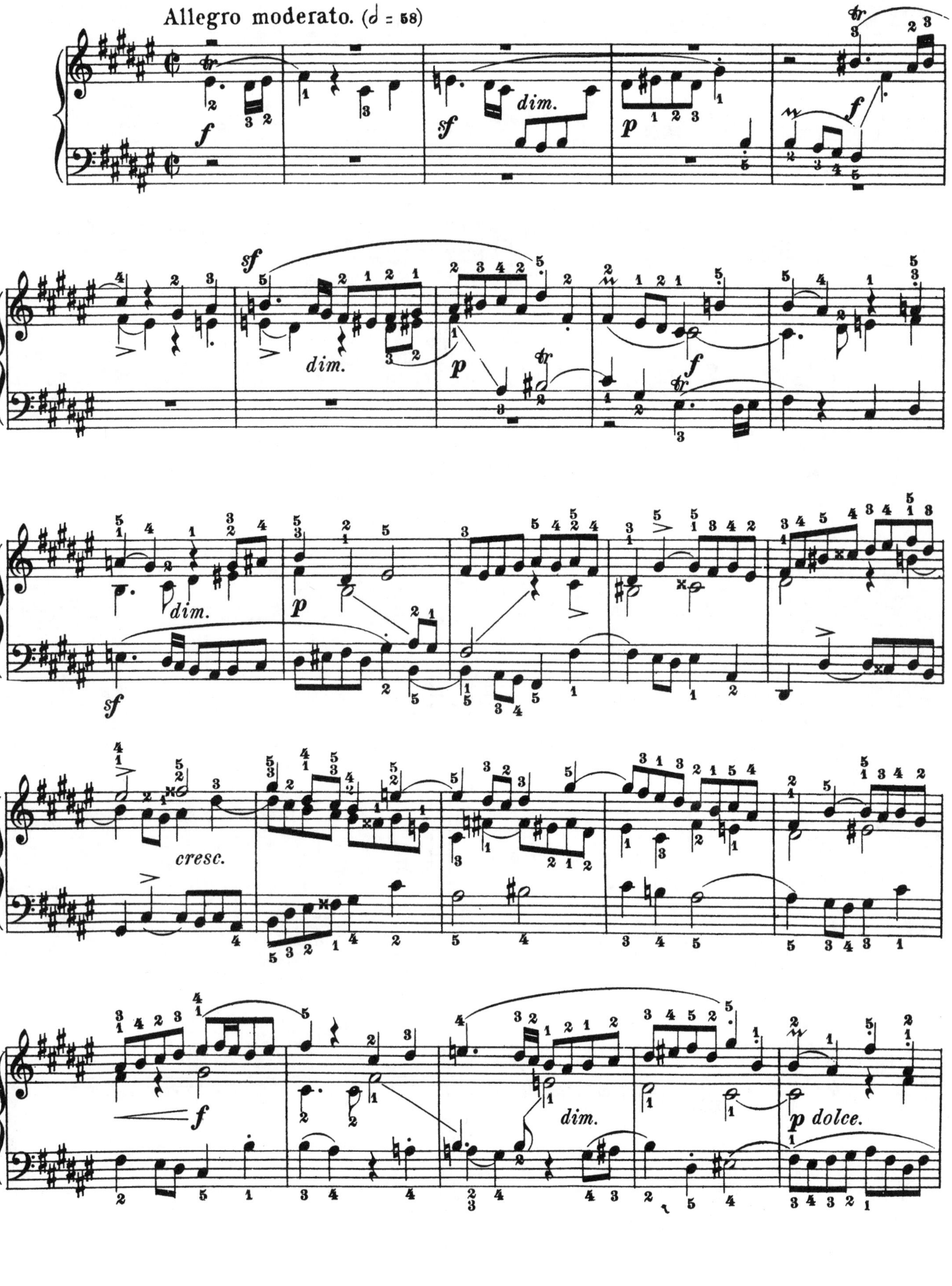

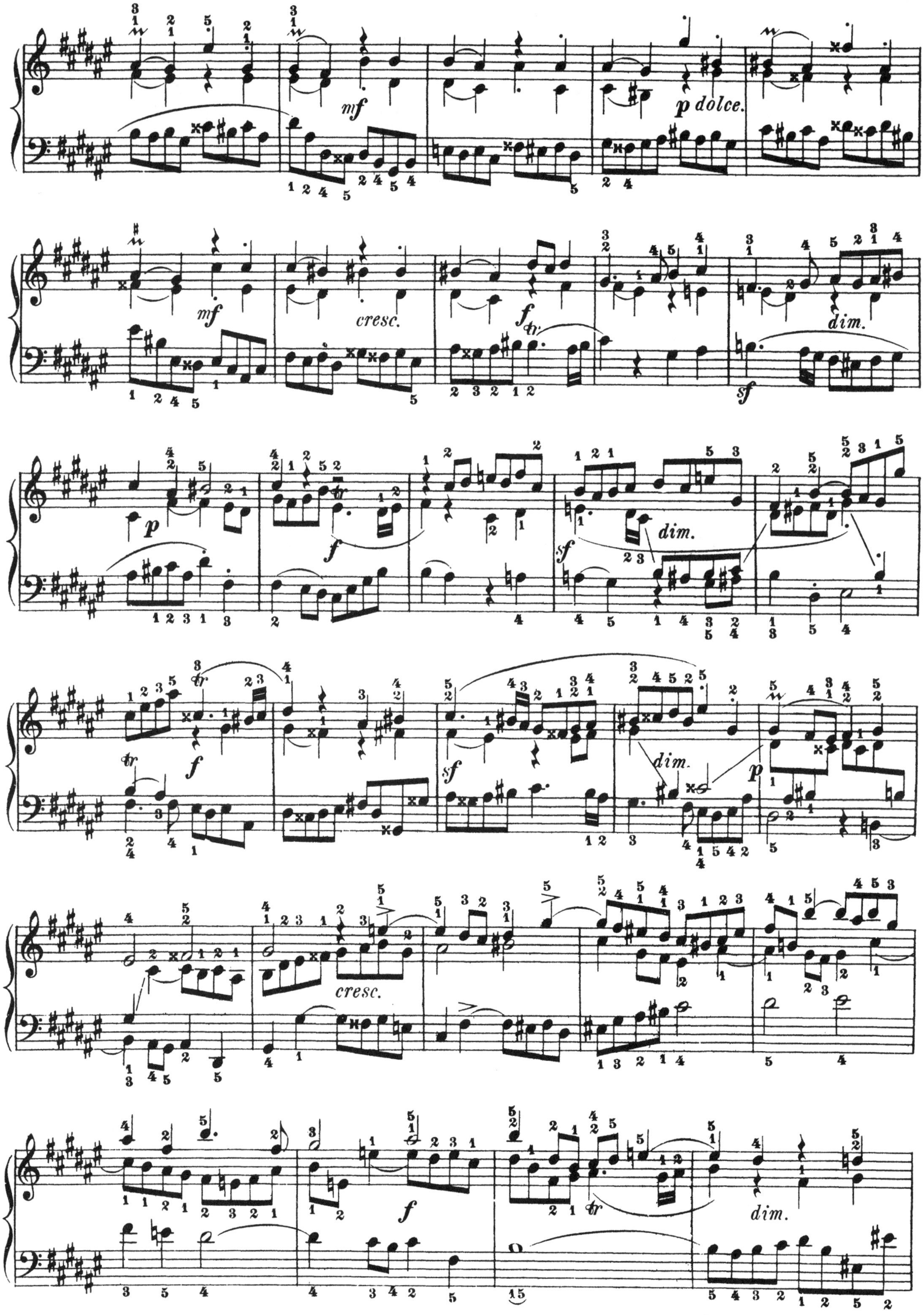
mf
p dolce.
mf
cresc.
f
dim.
sf
p
f
sf
dim.
p
f
sf
dim.
p
cresc.
f
dim.

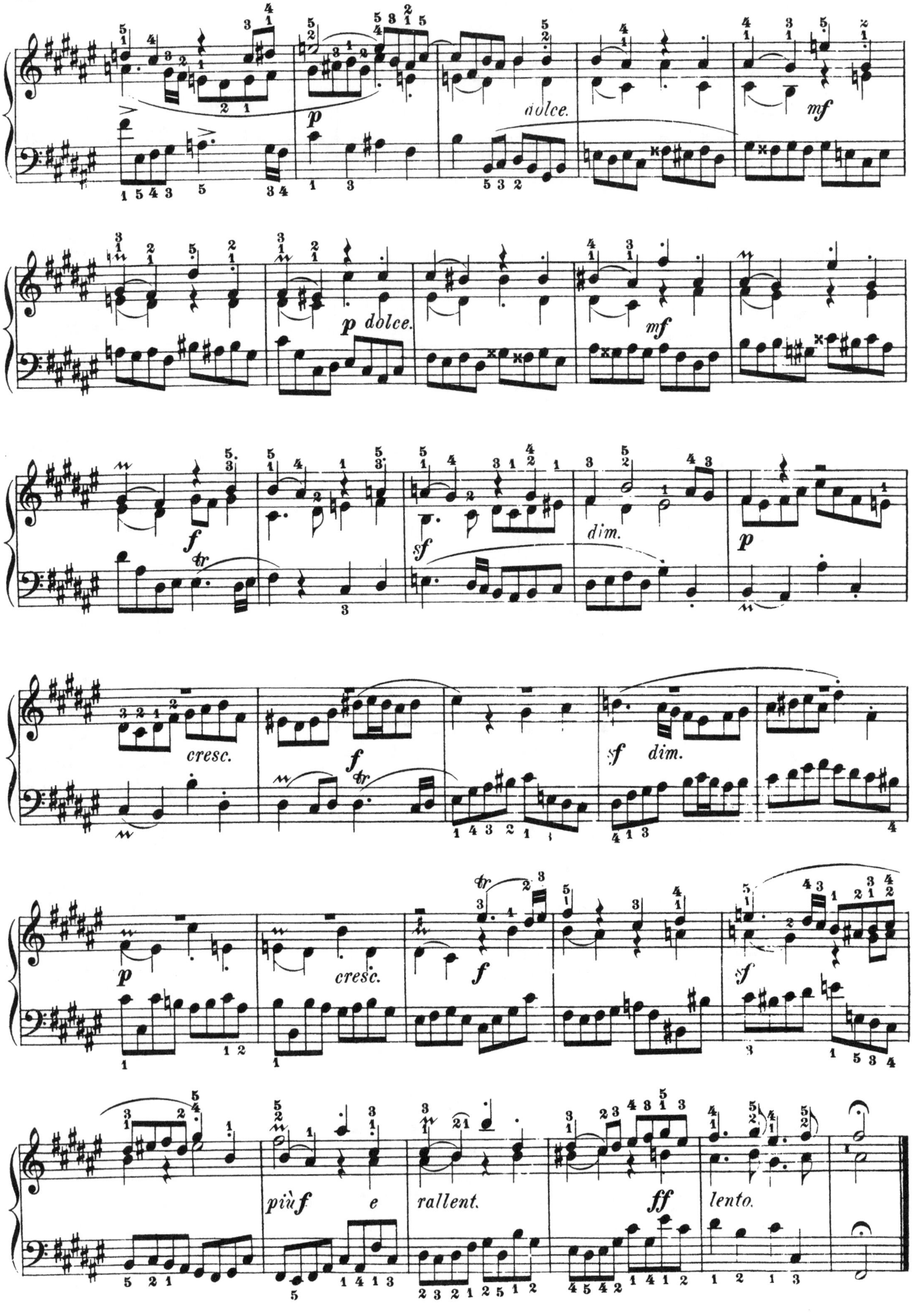
p
dolce.
mf
p dolce.
mf
f
sf
dim.
p
cresc.
f
sf
dim.
p
cresc.
f
sf
più f
e
rallent.
ff
lento.

Preludio XIV.

Andante con moto. (♪ = 116)

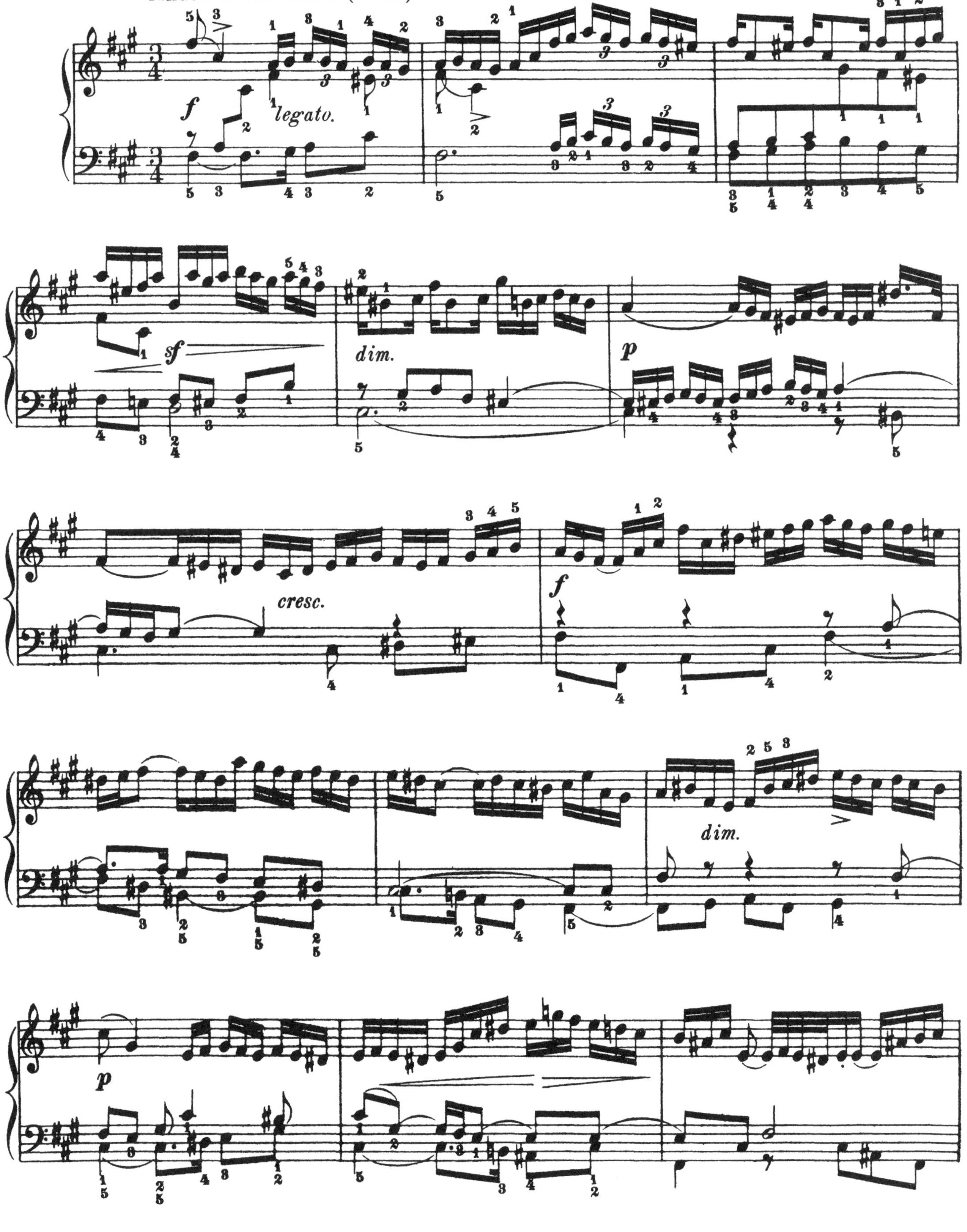

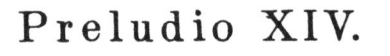

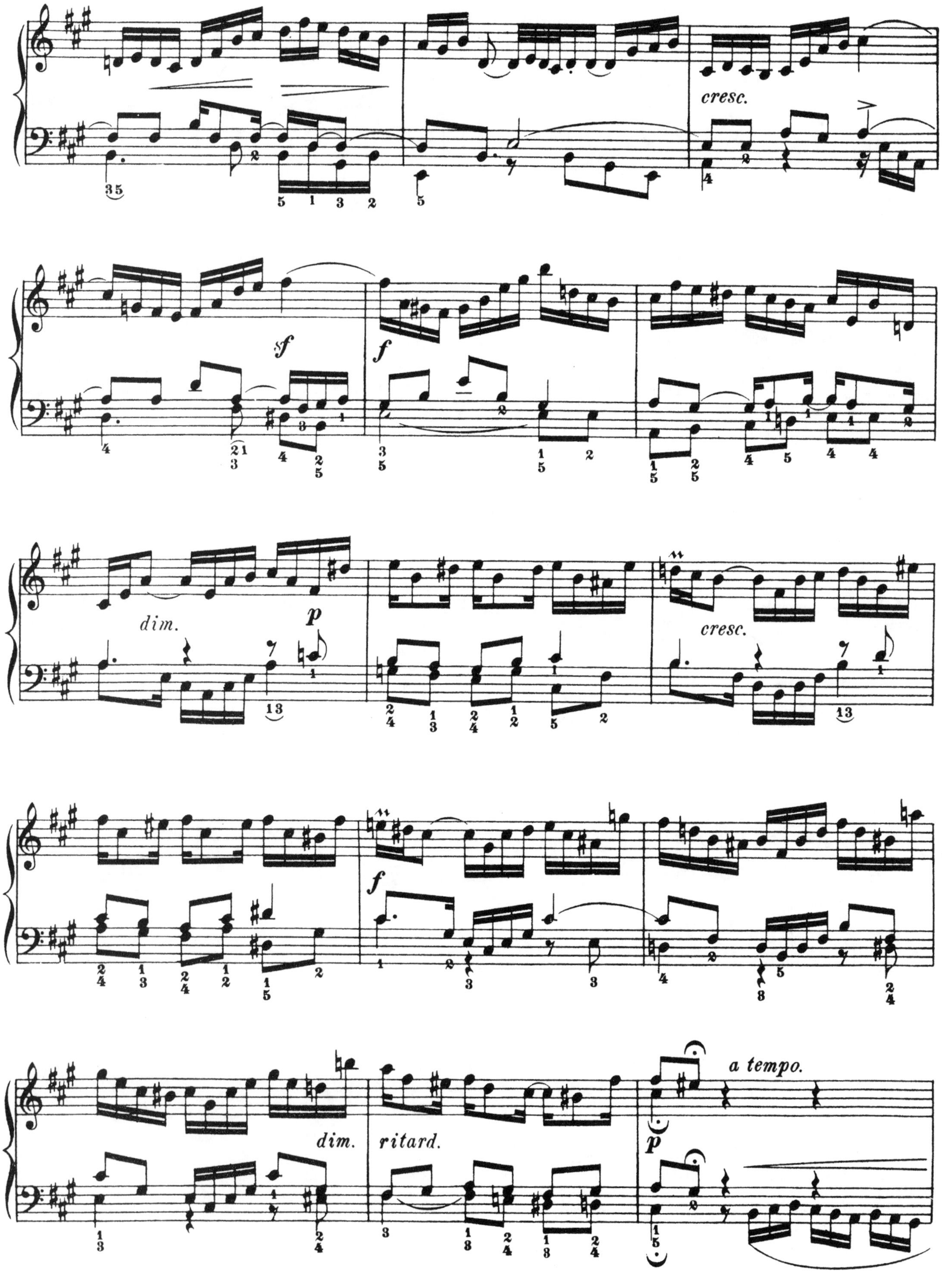
cresc.
sf
f
dim.
p
cresc.
f
dim.
ritard.
a tempo.
p

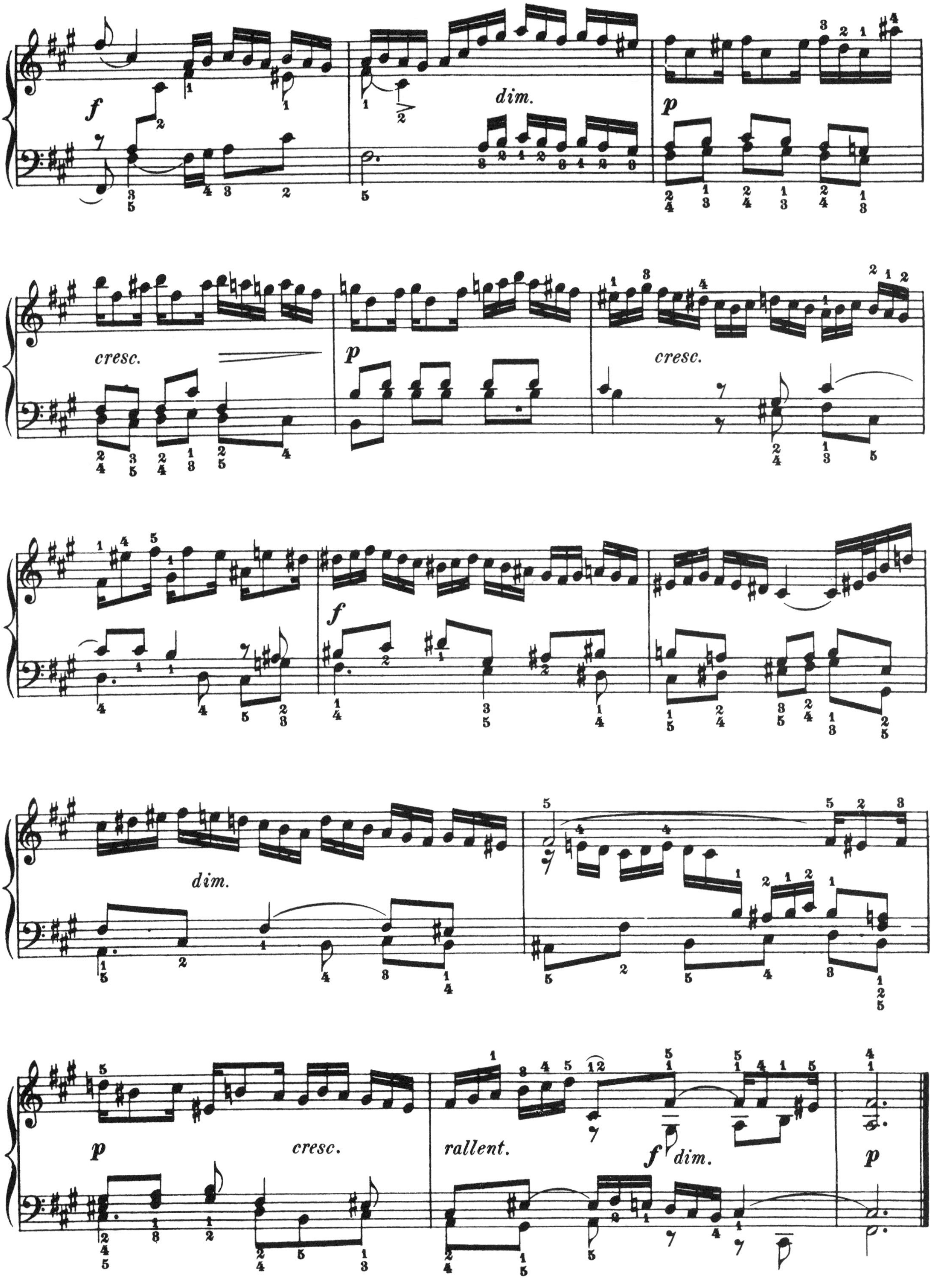
f
dim.
p
cresc.
p
cresc.
f
dim.
p
cresc.
rallent.
f dim.
p

Fuga XIV.

a 3 Voci.

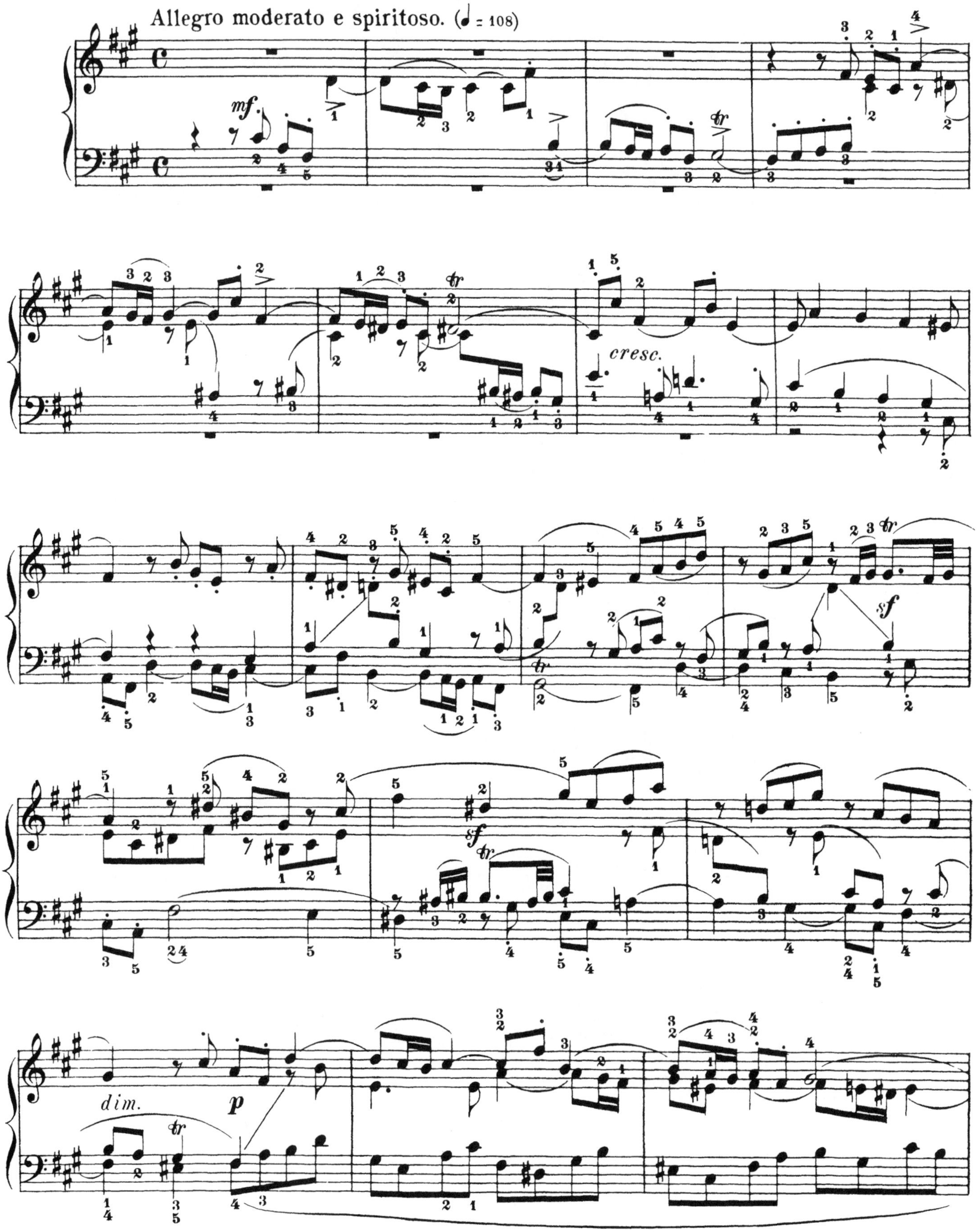

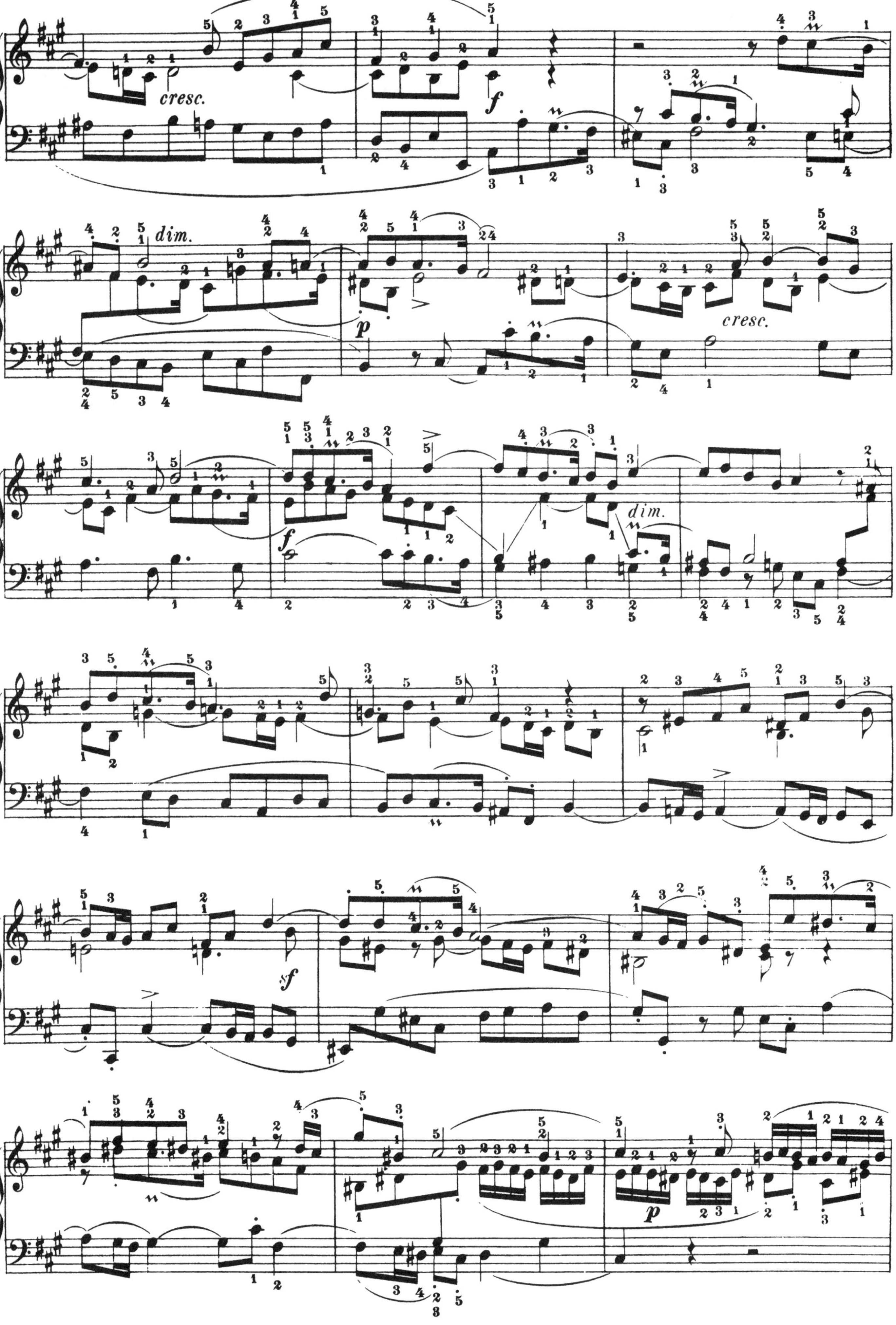
cresc.
f
dim.
p
cresc.
f
dim.
sf
p

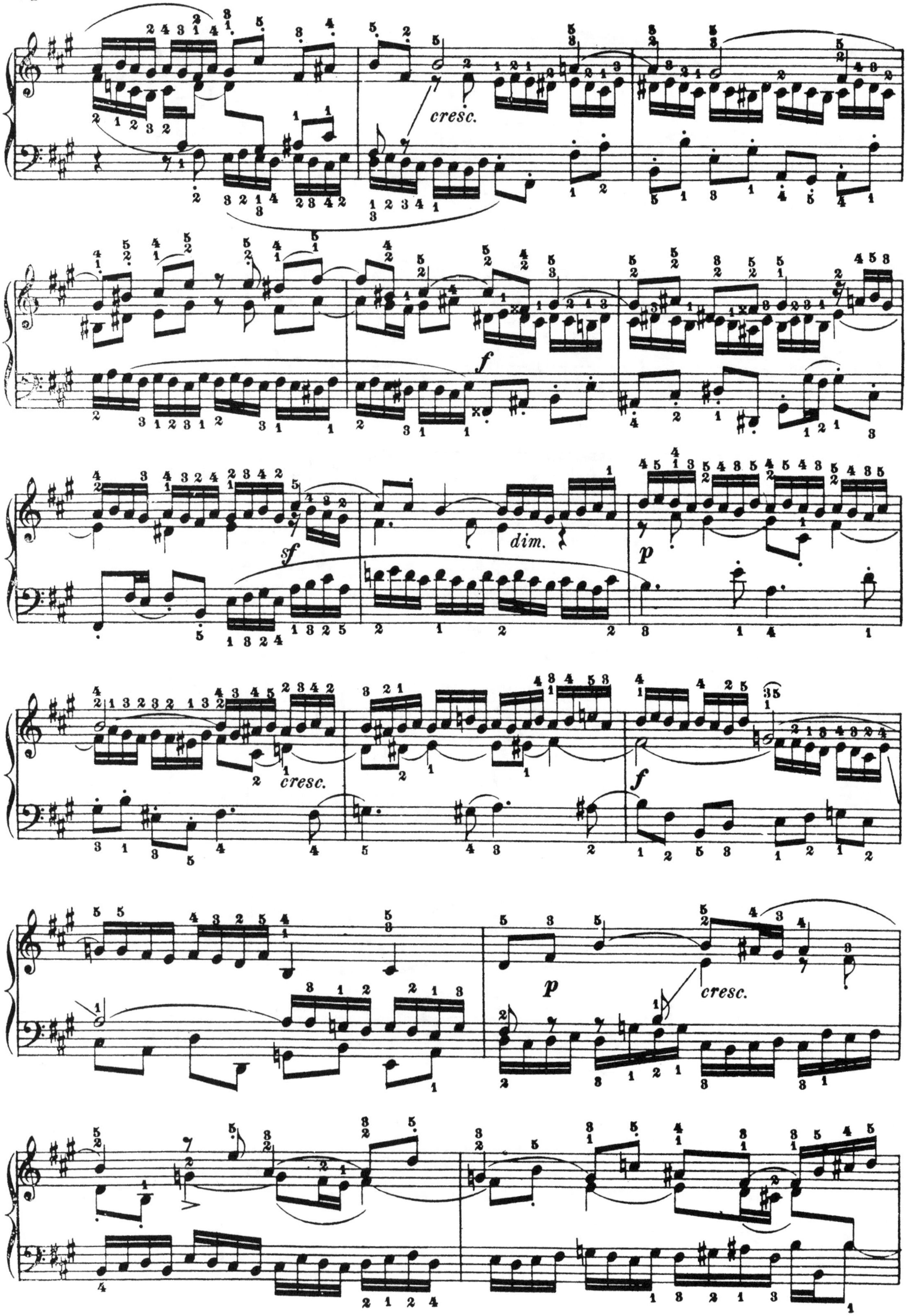
cresc.
f
sf
dim.
p
cresc.
f
p
cresc.

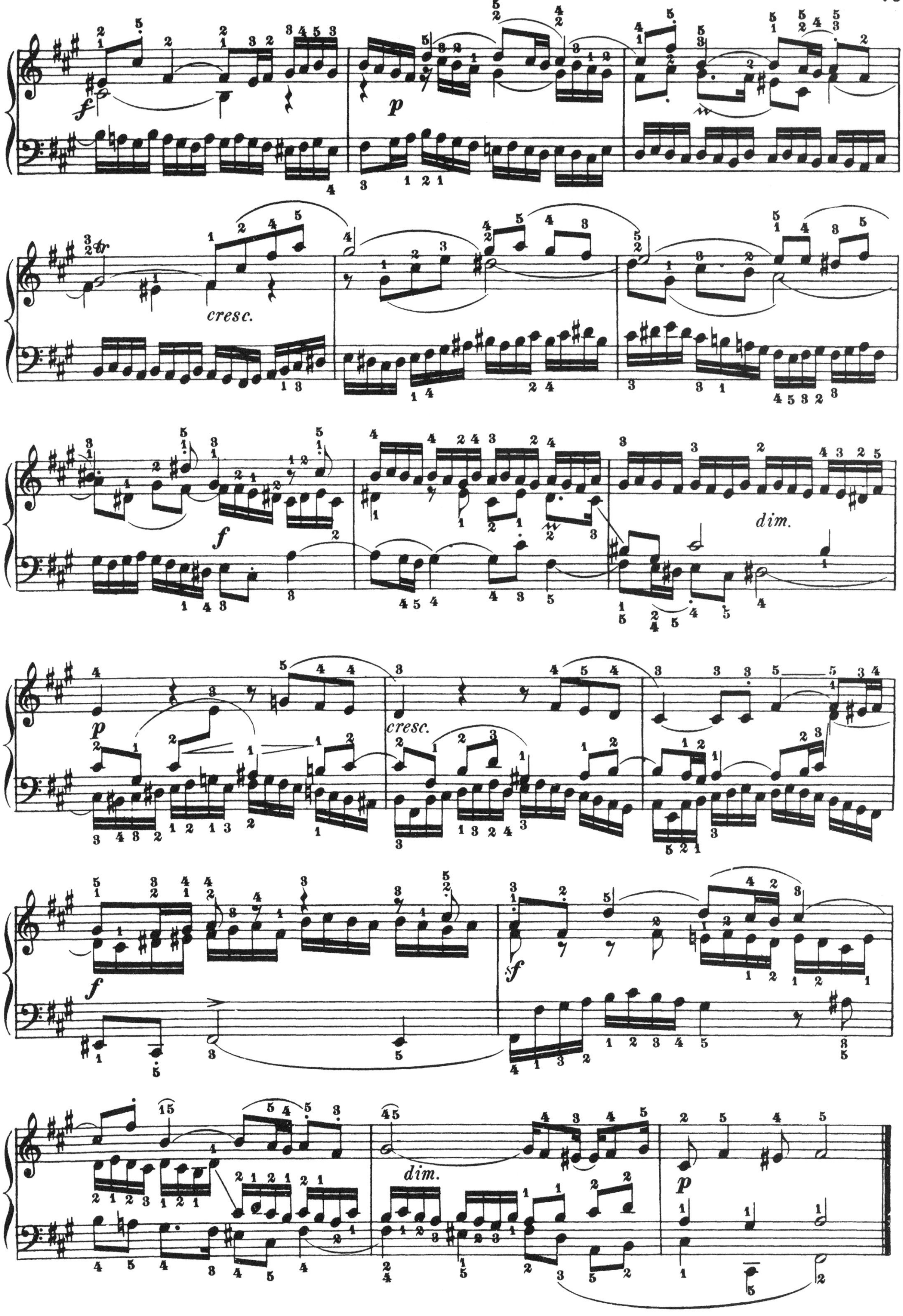
cresc.
dim.
cresc.
dim.

Preludio XV.

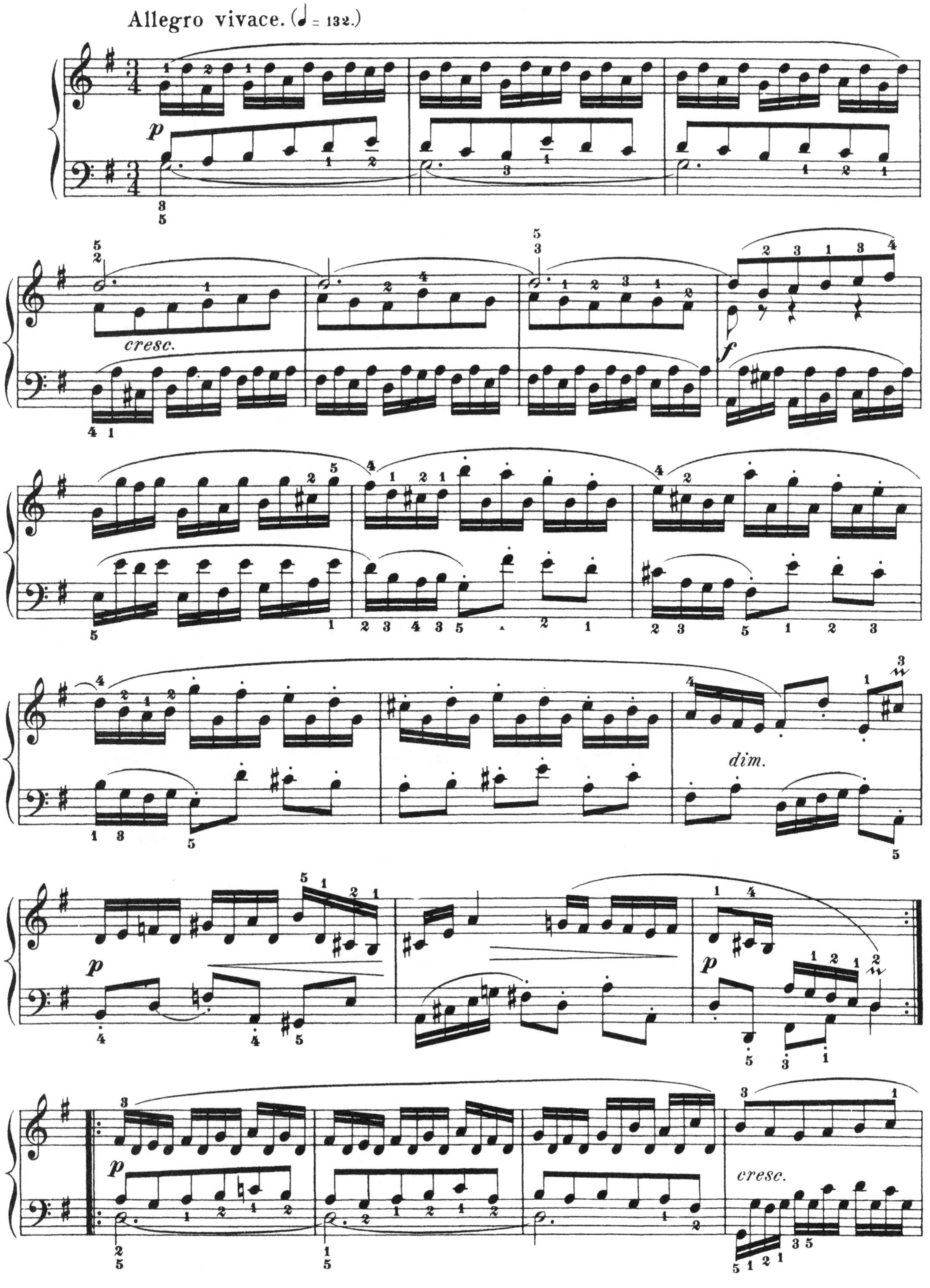

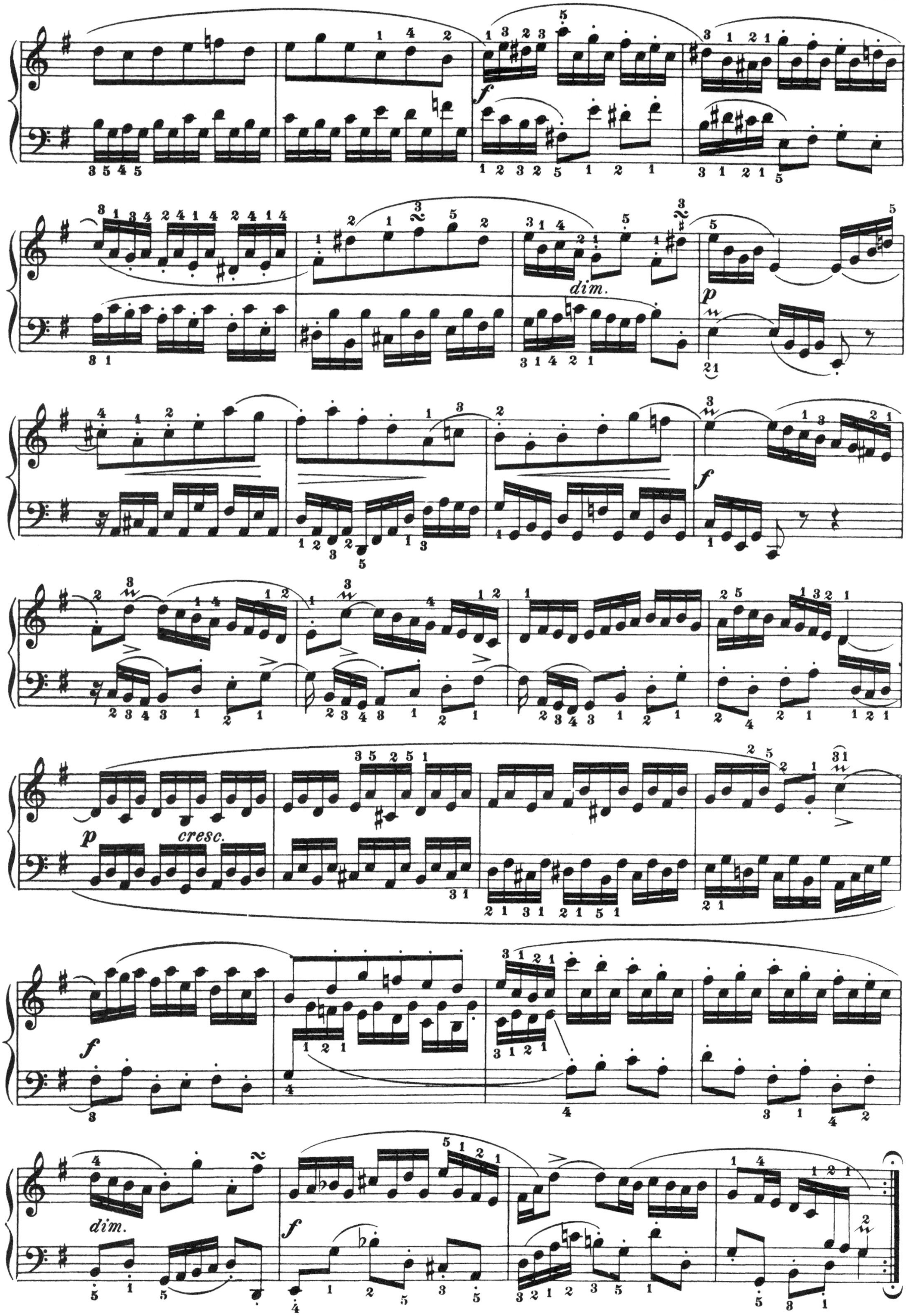
dim.
p
f
p
cresc.
f
dim.
f

Fuga XV.

a 3 Voci.

Allegretto vivace. (♩. = 76.)

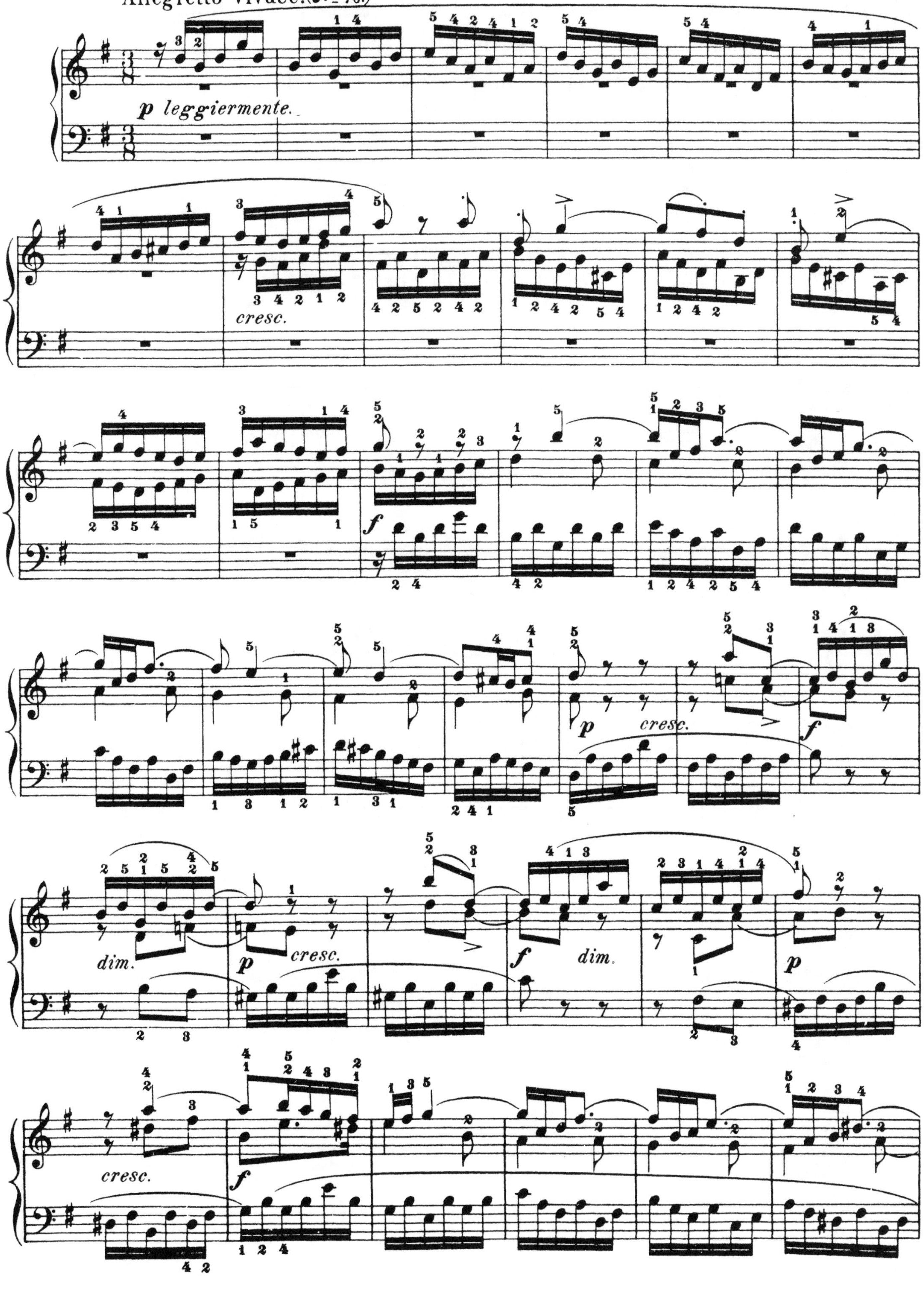

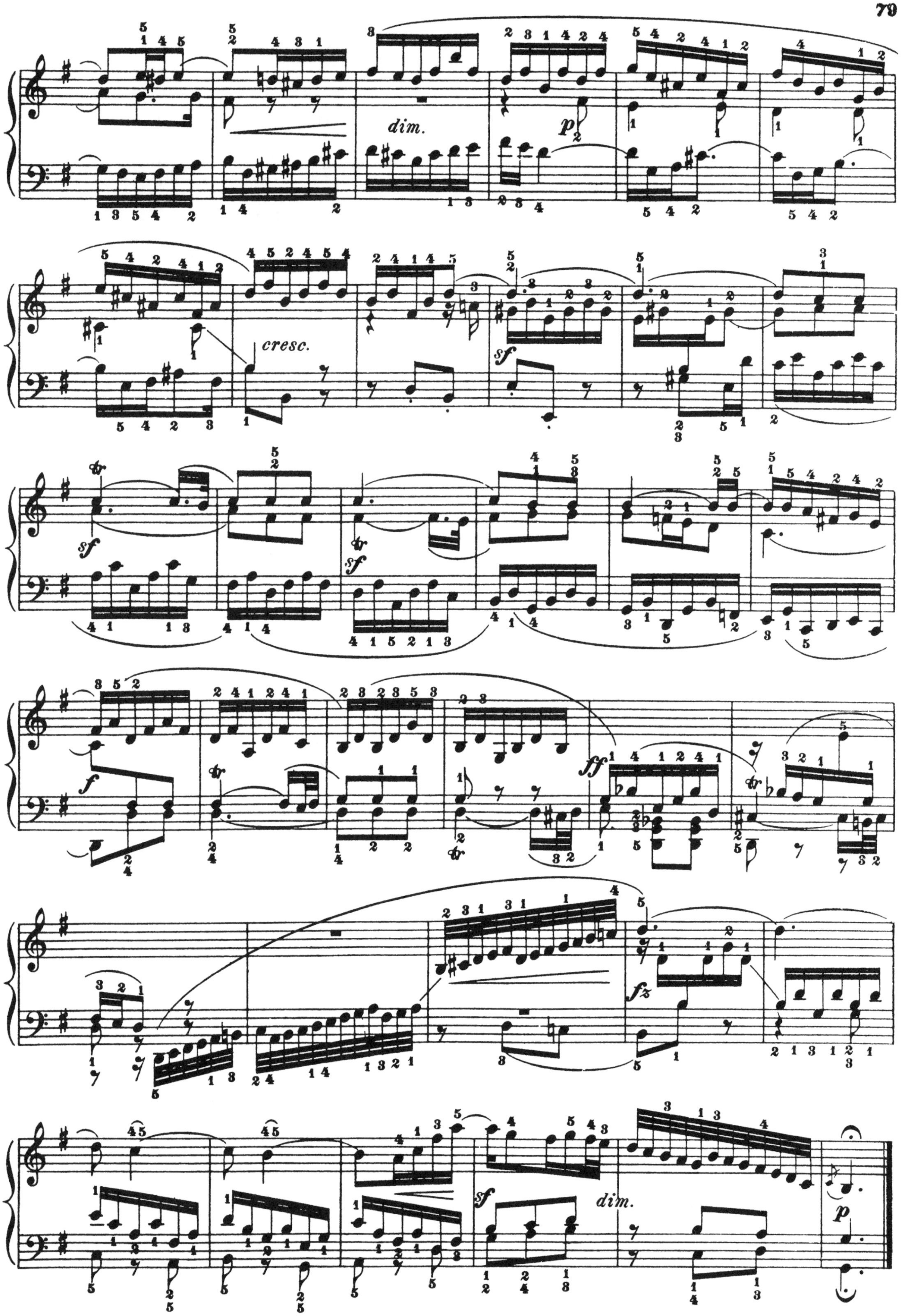
dim.
p
cresc.
sf
sf
sf
f
ff
fz
sf
dim.
p

Preludio XVI.

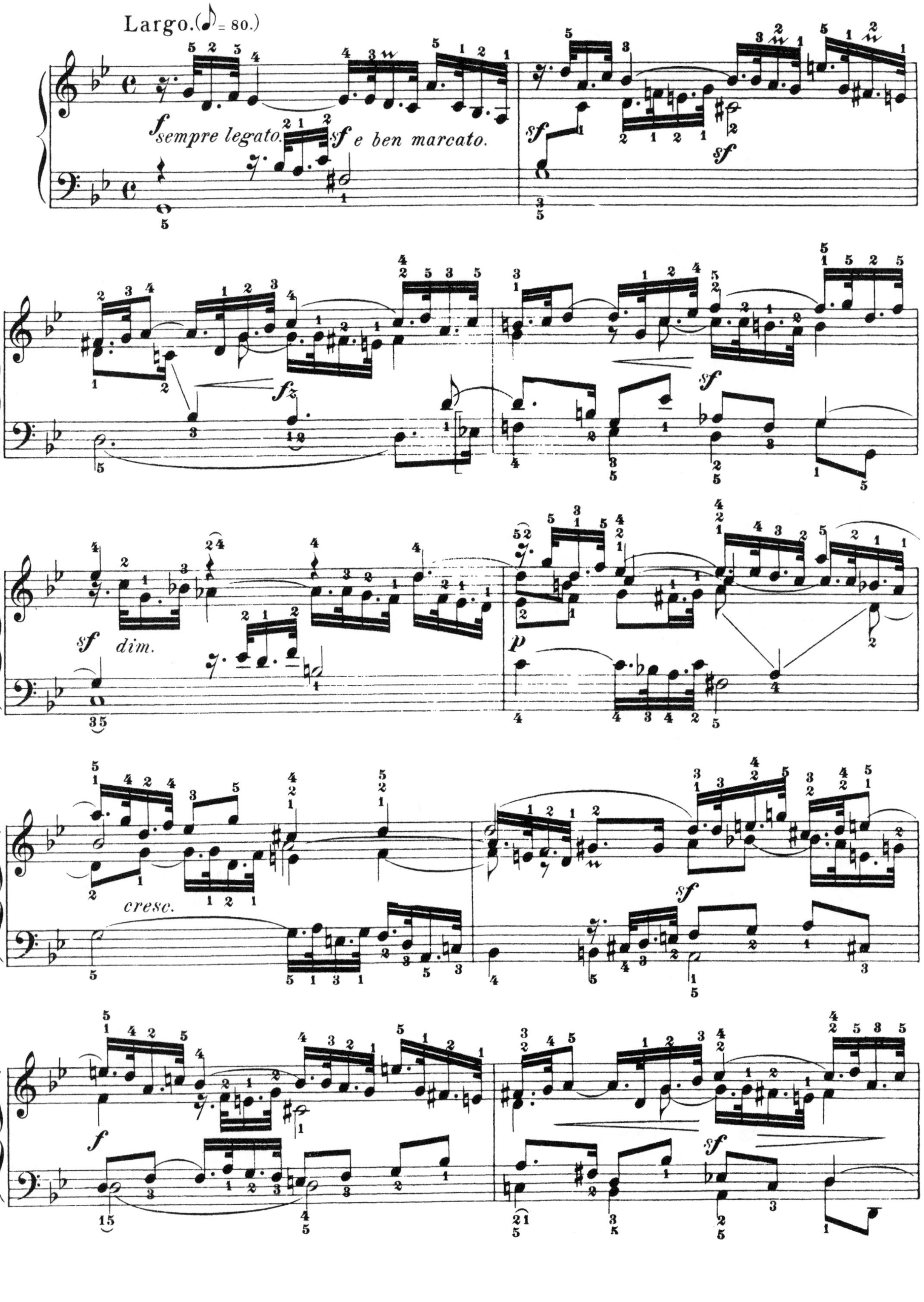

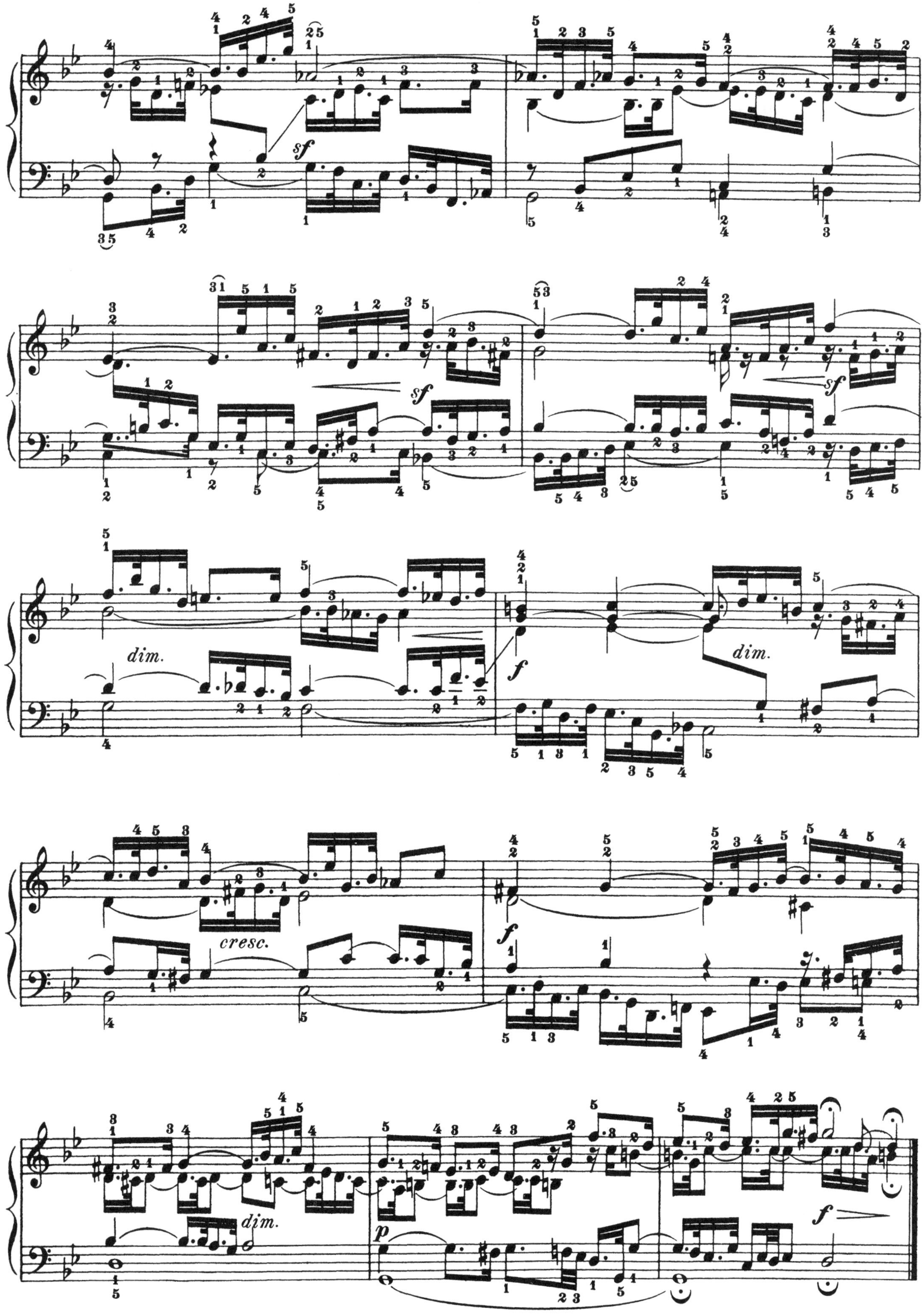
sf
sf
sf
dim.
f
dim.
cresc.
f
dim.
p
f

Fuga XVI.

a 4 Voci.

Andante con moto. (♩ = 84.)

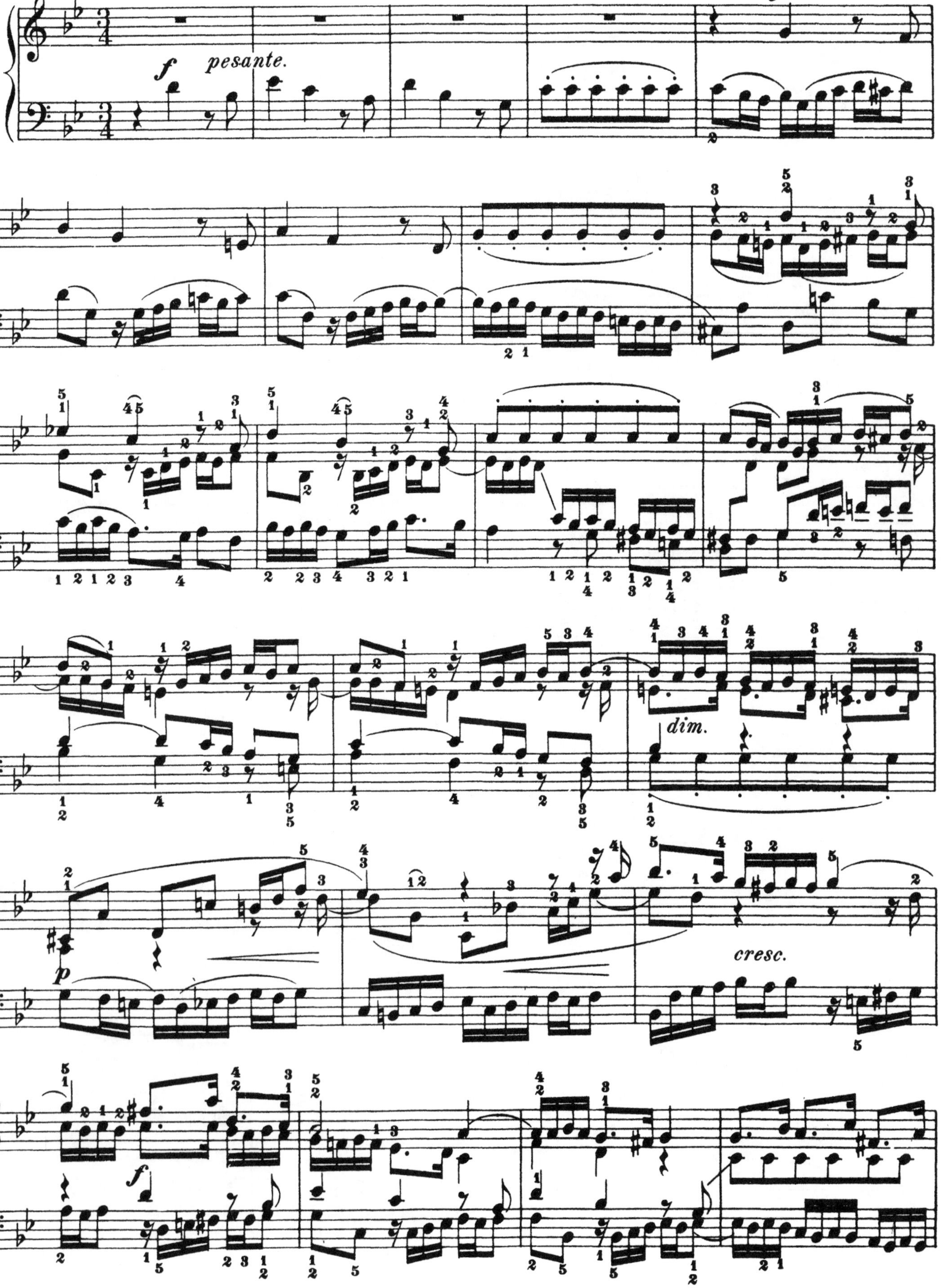

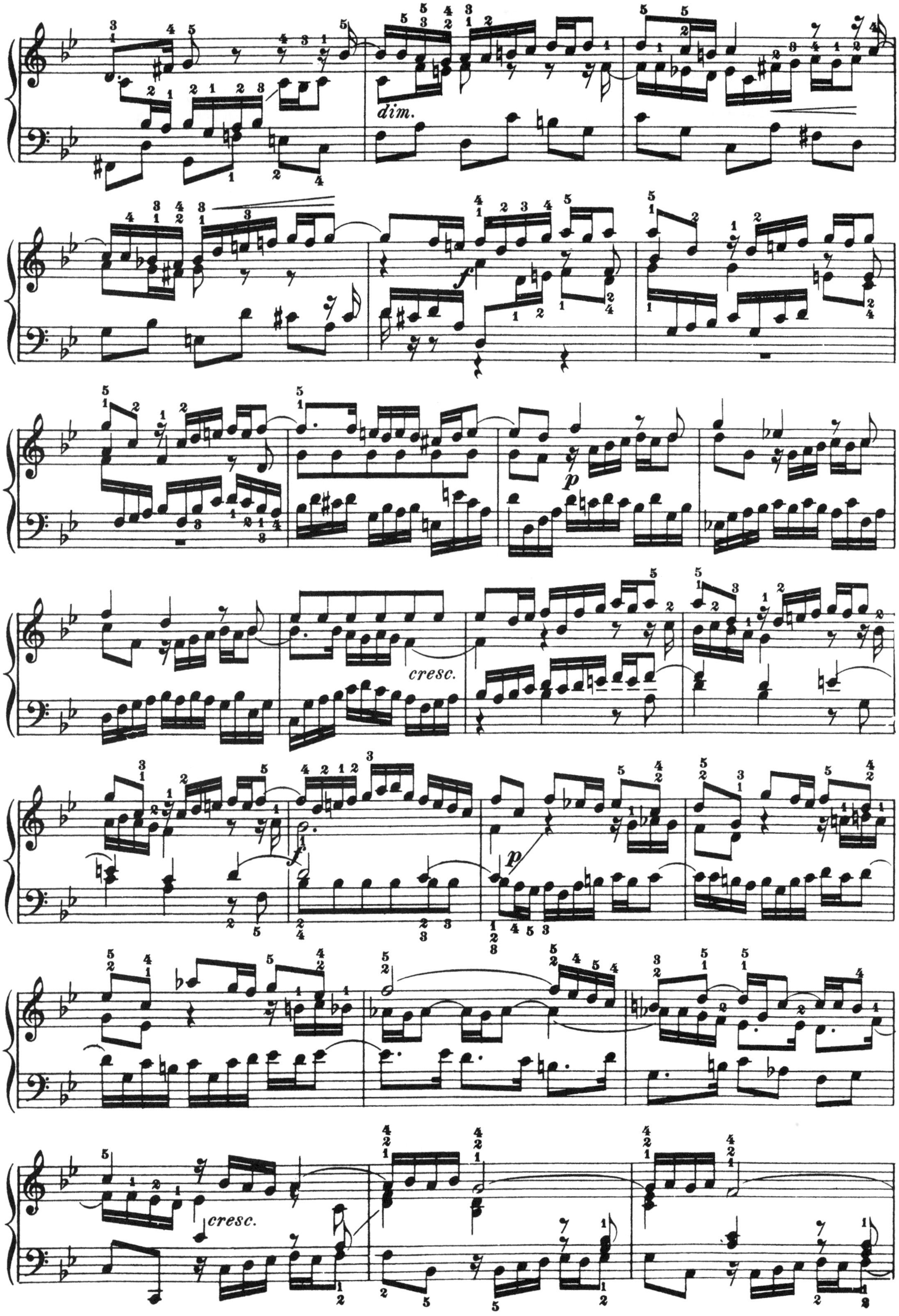
dim.
f
p
cresc.
f
p
cresc.

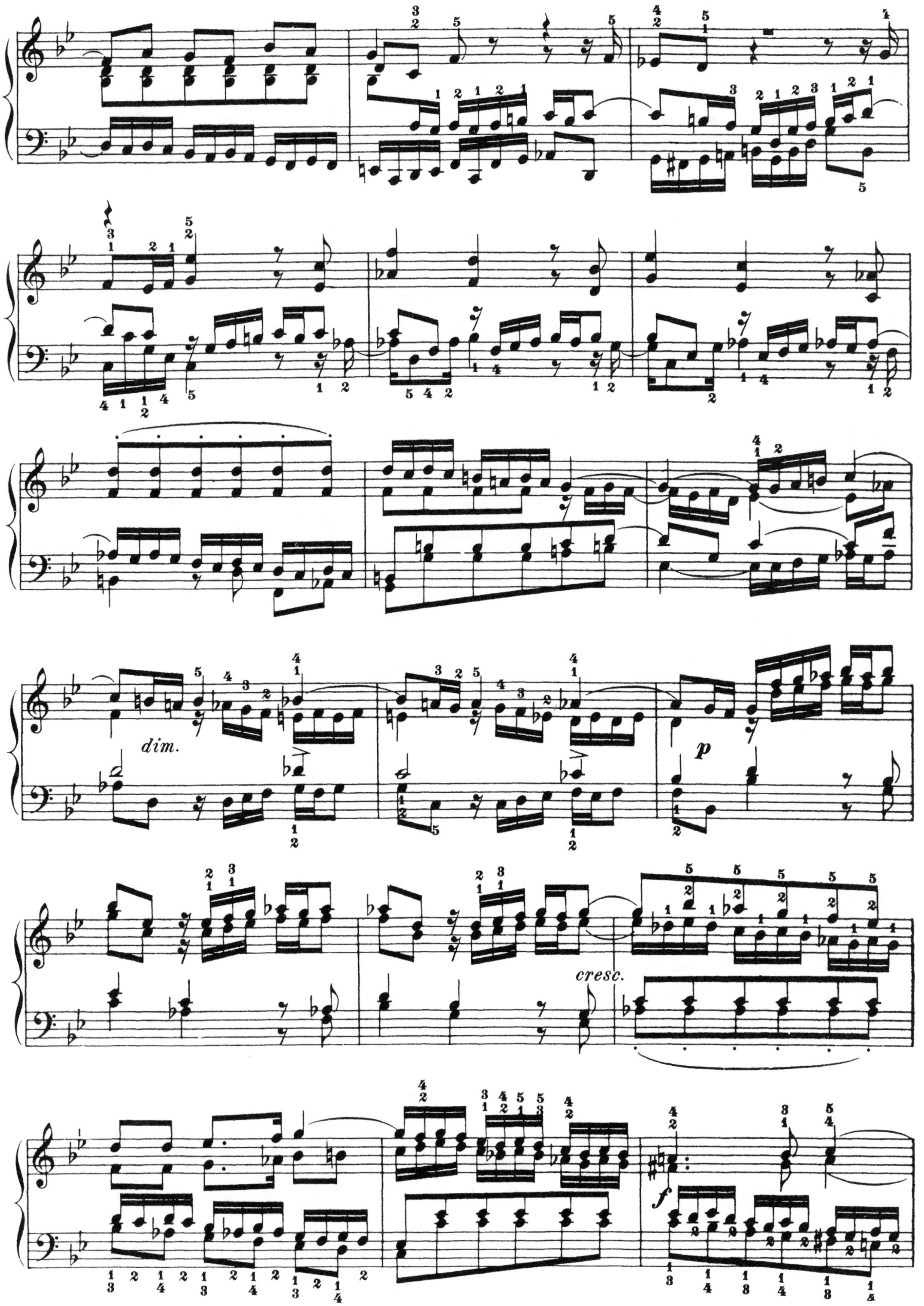
dim.
p
cresc.
f

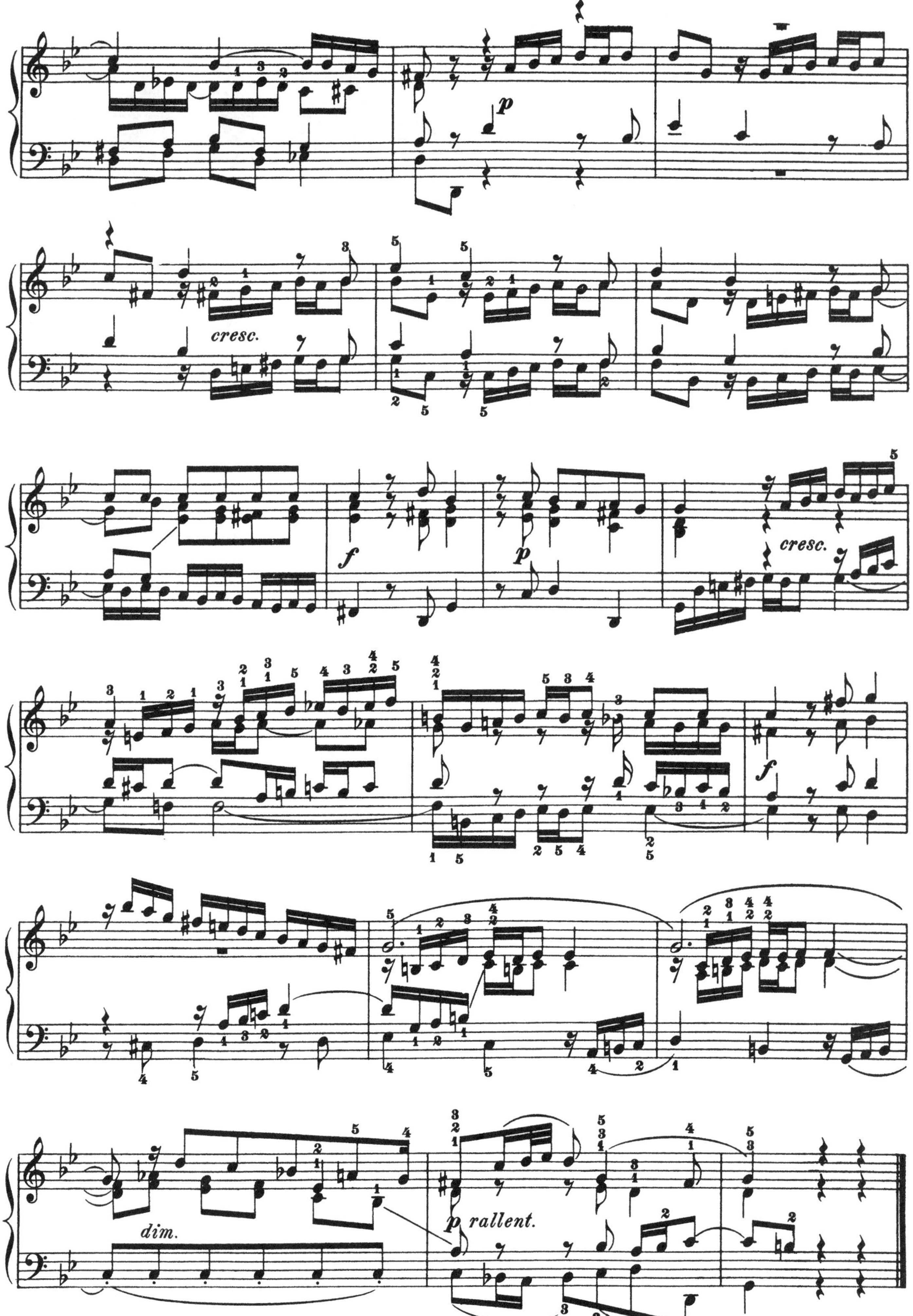
p
cresc.
f
p
cresc.
f
dim.
p rallent.

Preludio XVII.

Andante con moto. (♩ = 72.)

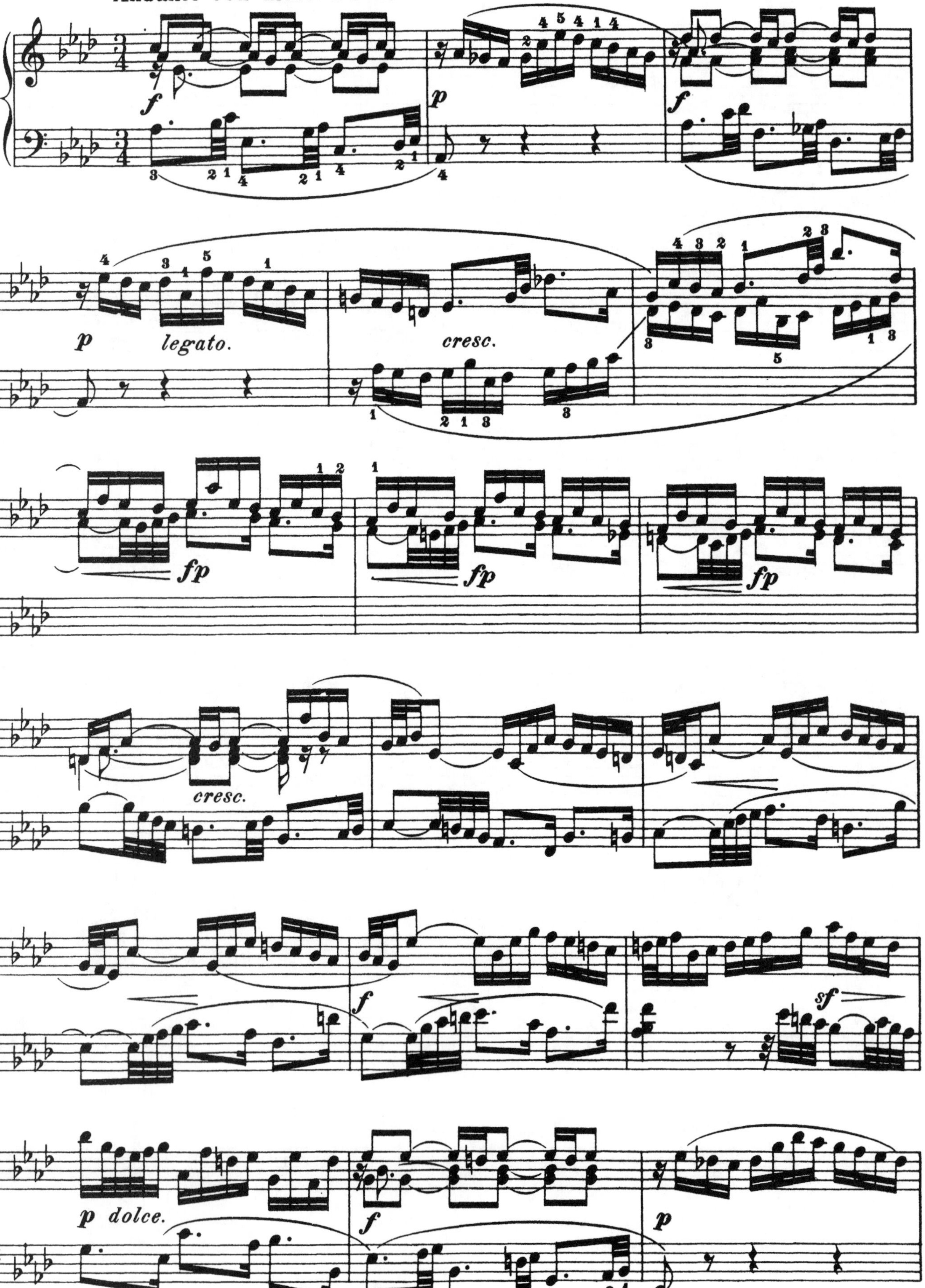

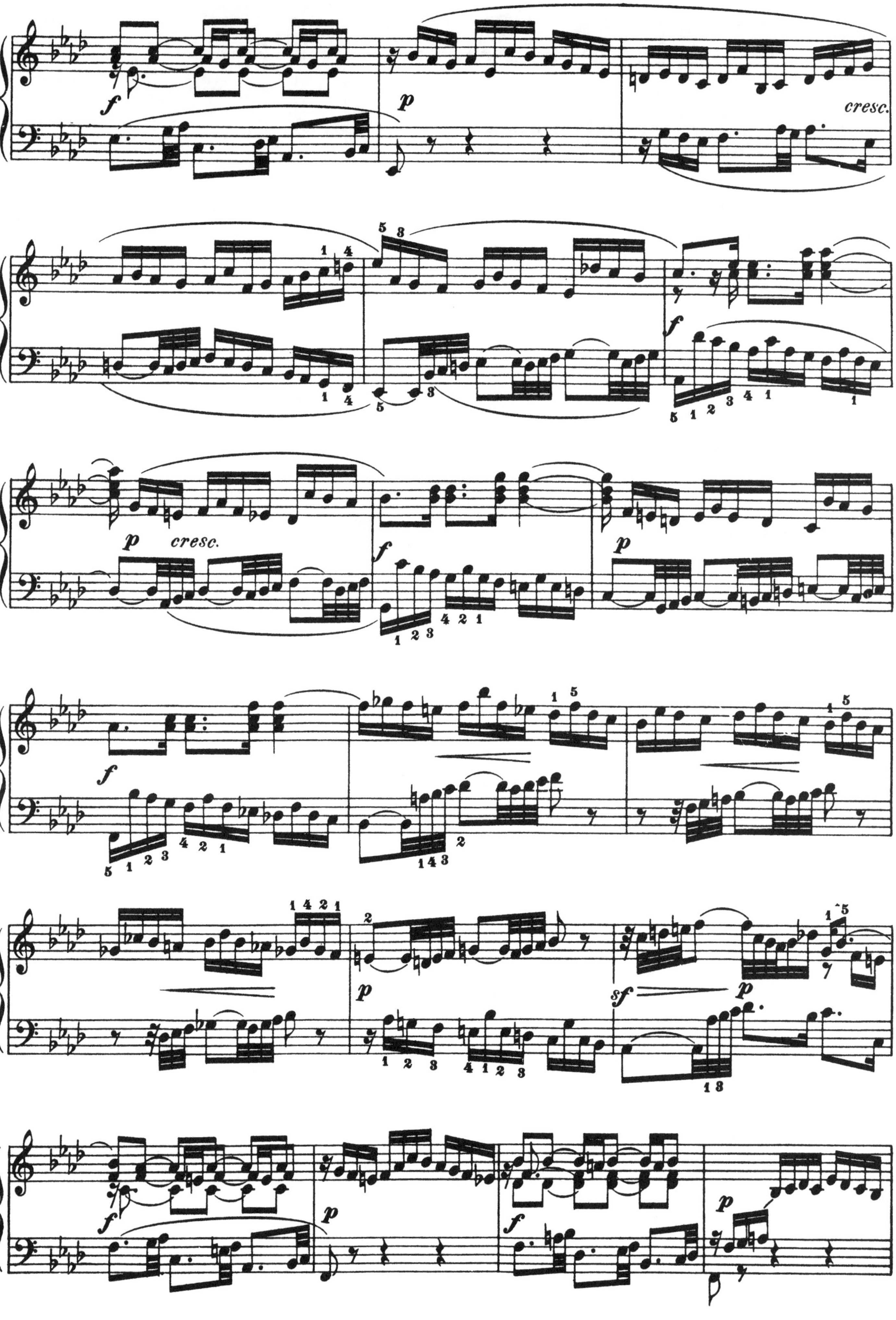
cresc.
cresc.

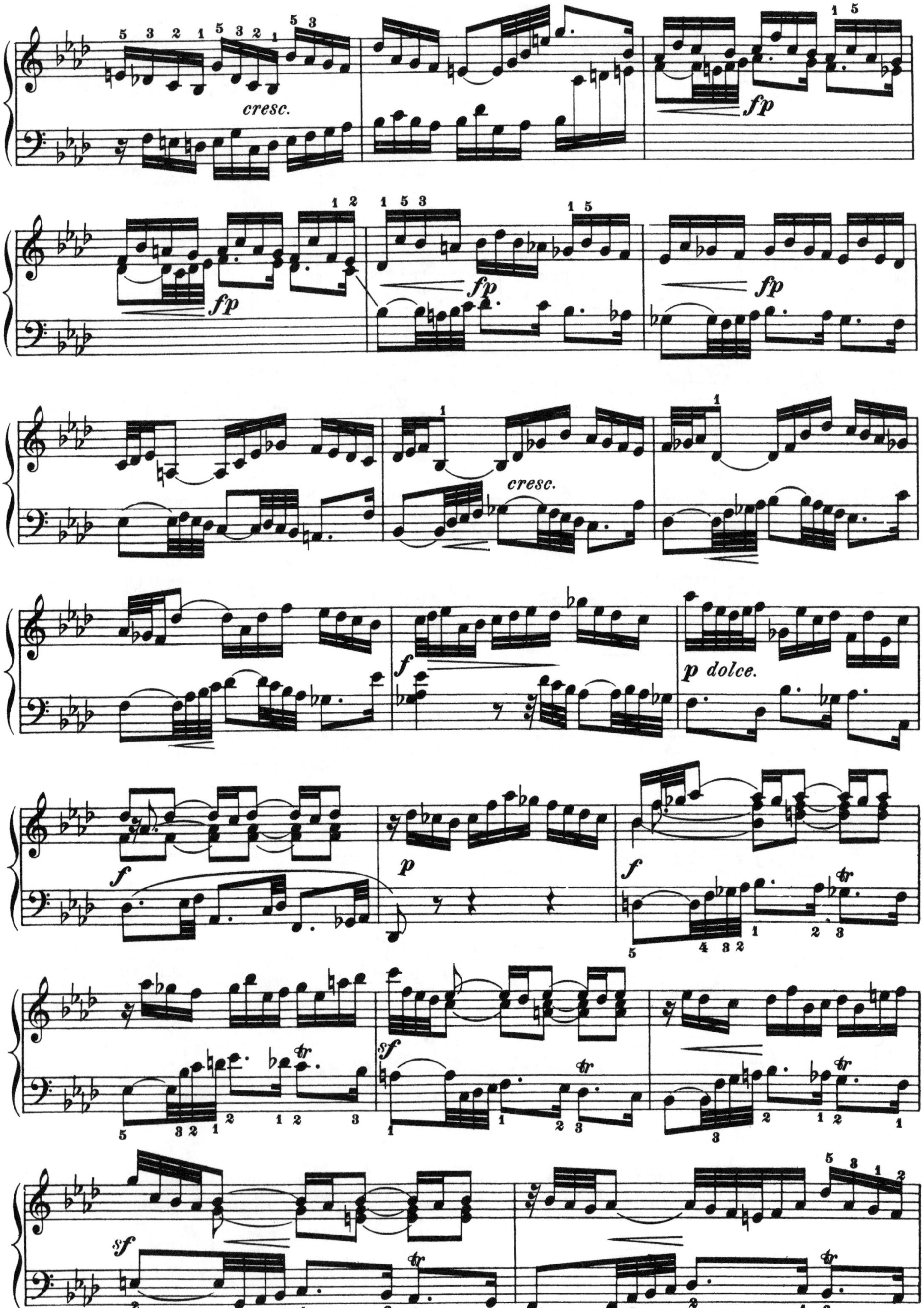
cresc.
fp
fp
fp
fp
cresc.
f
p dolce.
f
p
f
sf
sf

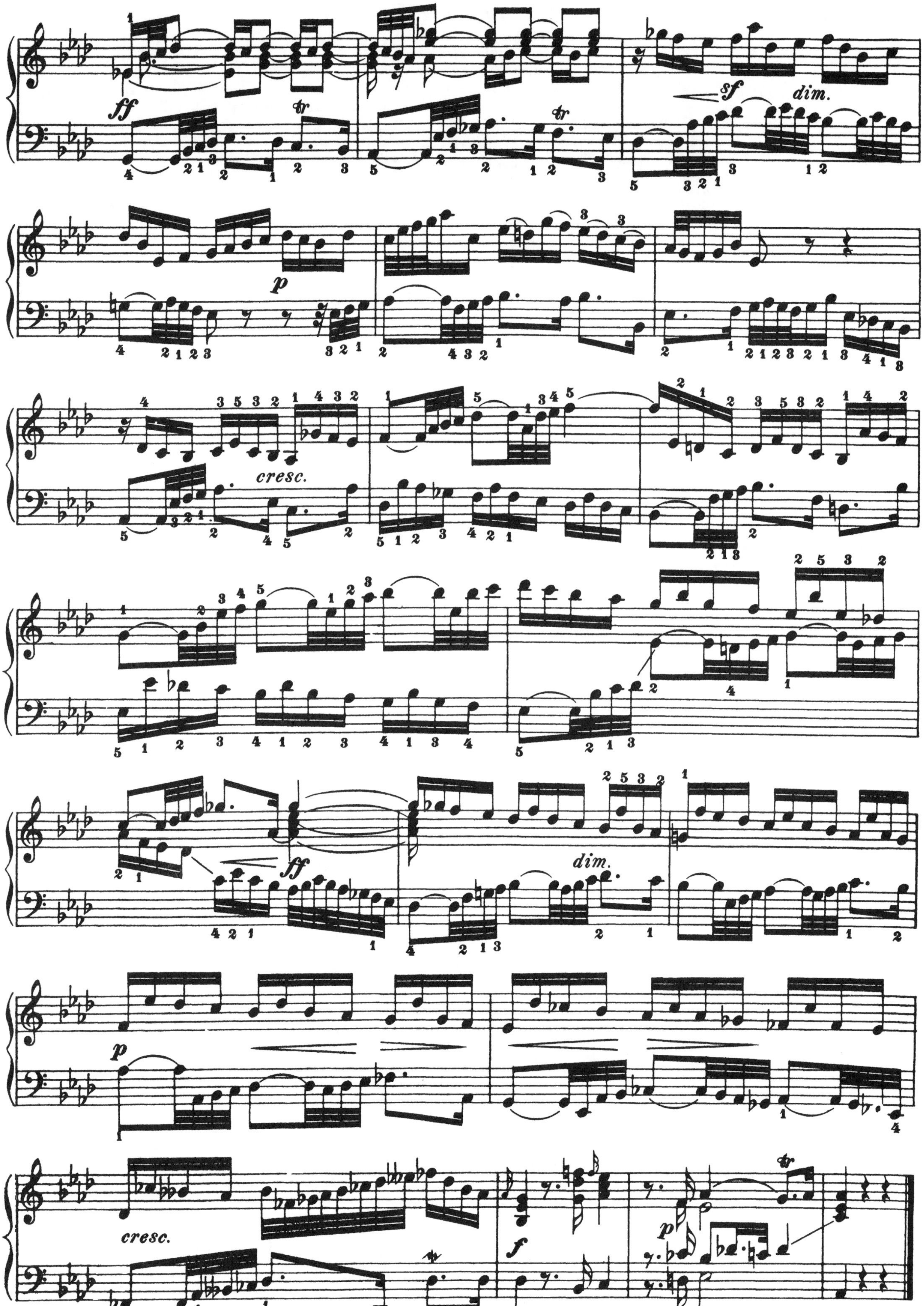
ff
tr
sf
dim.
p
cresc.
ff
dim.
p
cresc.
f
p
tr

Fuga XVII.

a 4 Voci.

Lento. (𝅗𝅥 = 69.)

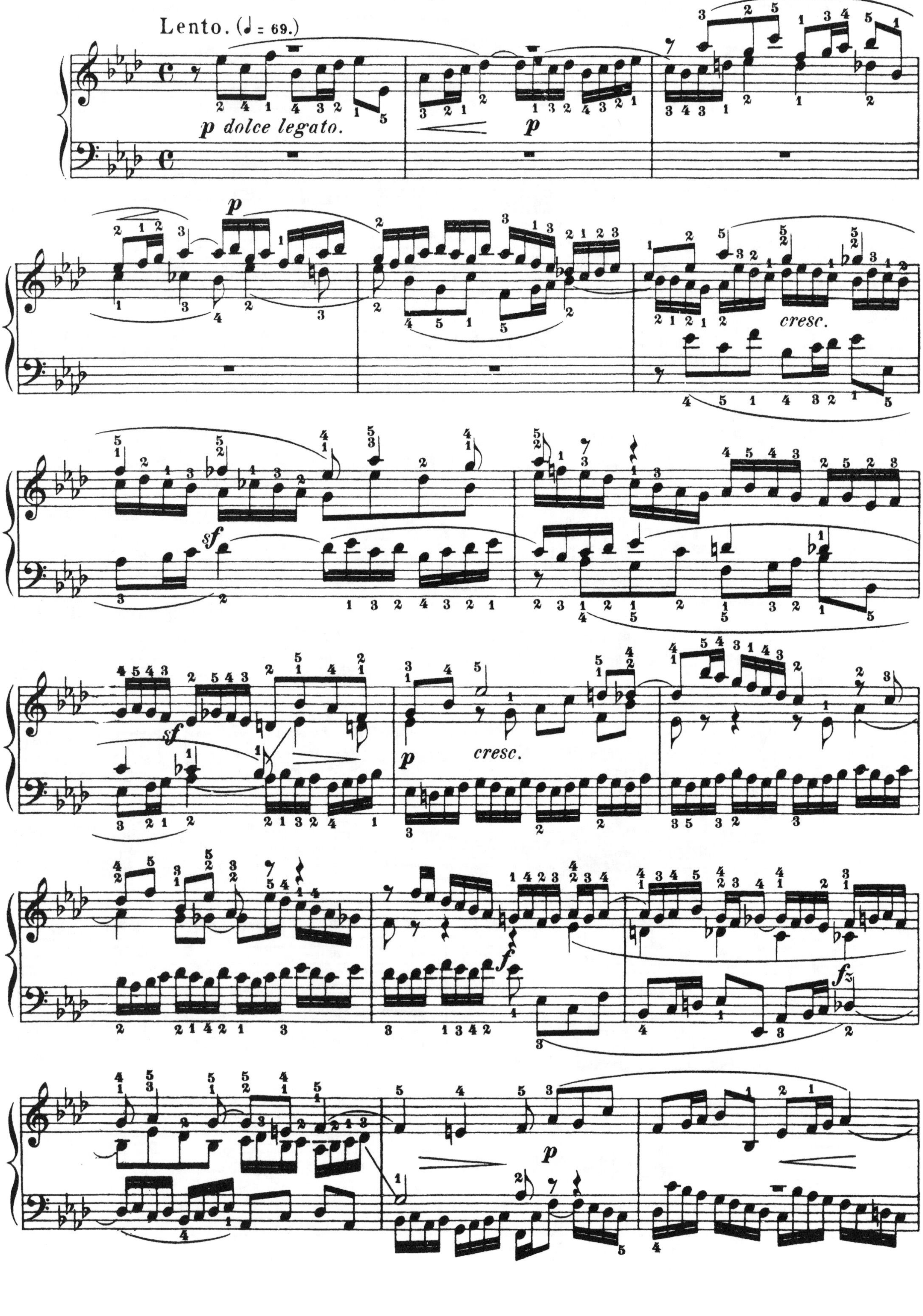

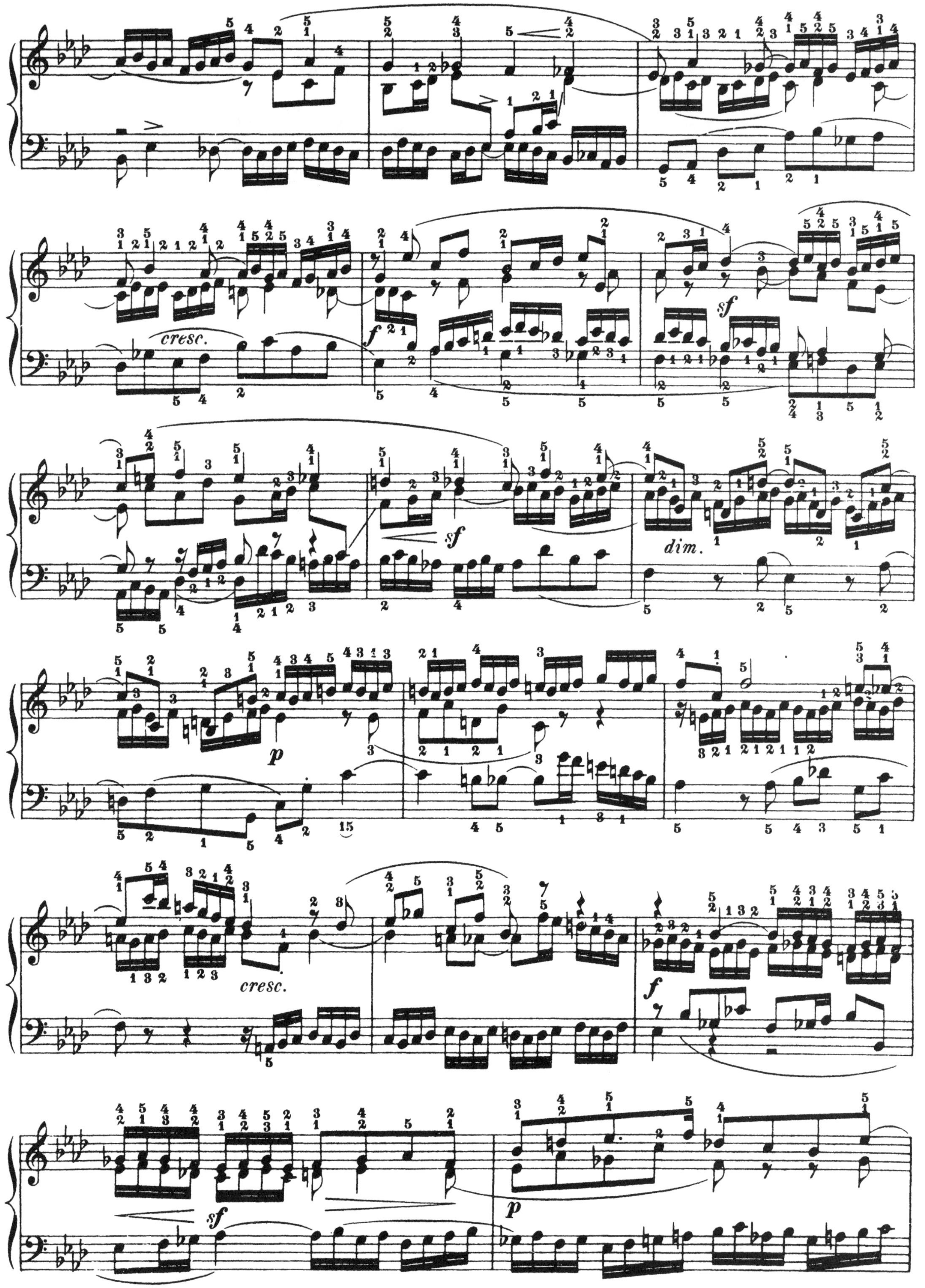
cresc.
f
sf
dim.
p
cresc.
f
sf
p

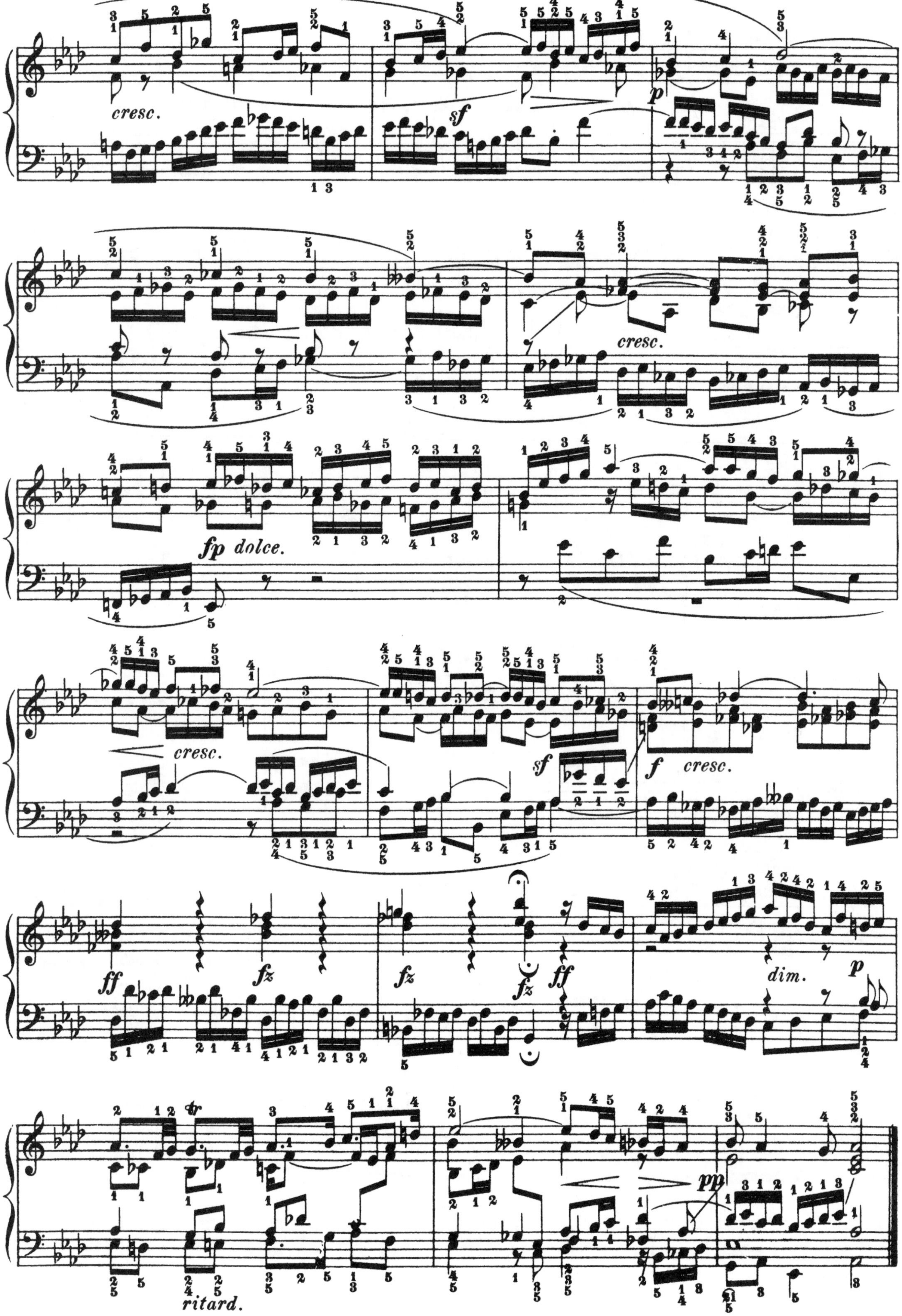
cresc.
sf
p
cresc.
fp dolce.
cresc.
sf
f
cresc.
ff
fz
fz
fz
ff
dim.
p
ritard.
pp

Preludio XVIII.

Allegro moderato. (♩ = 100.)

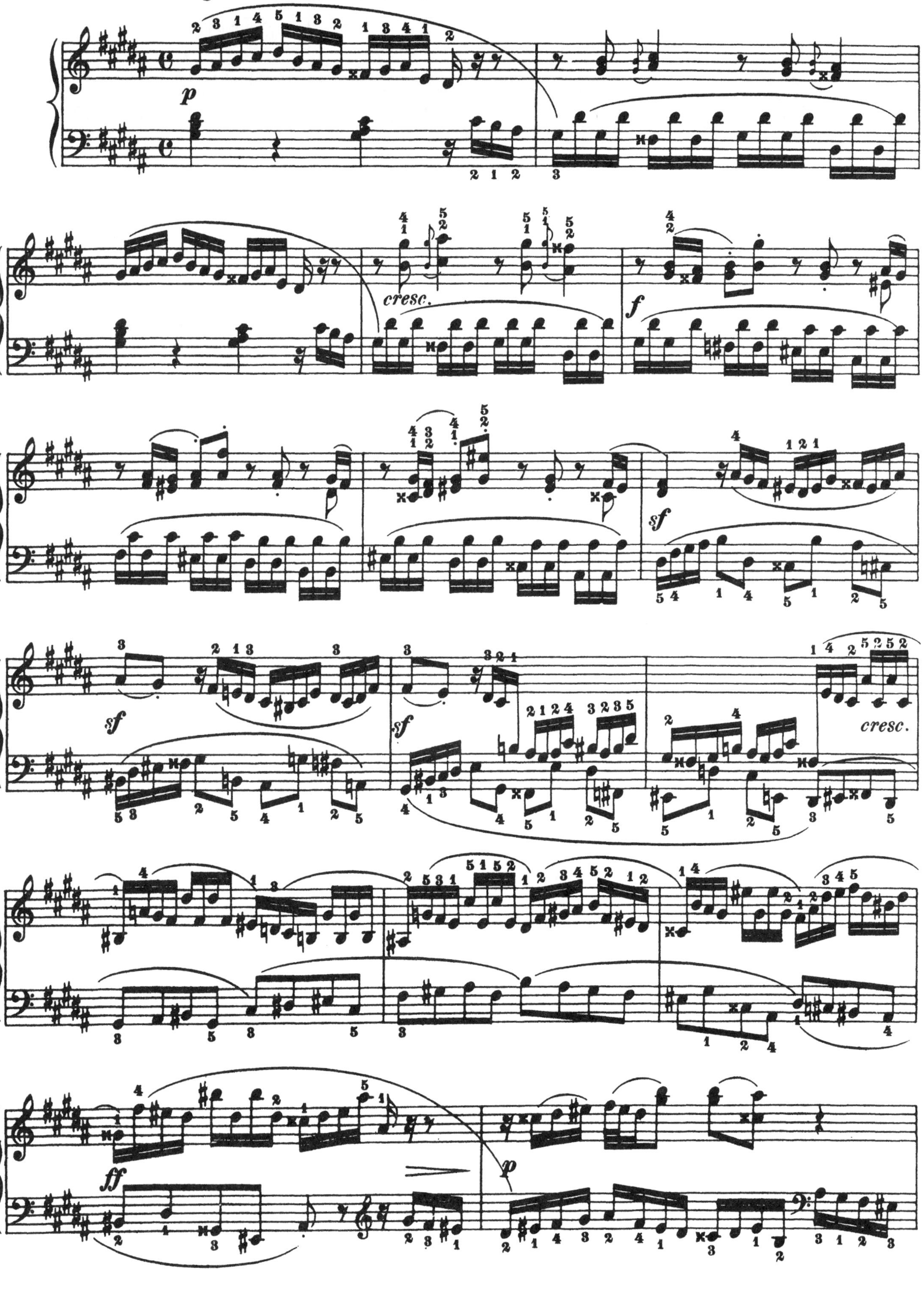

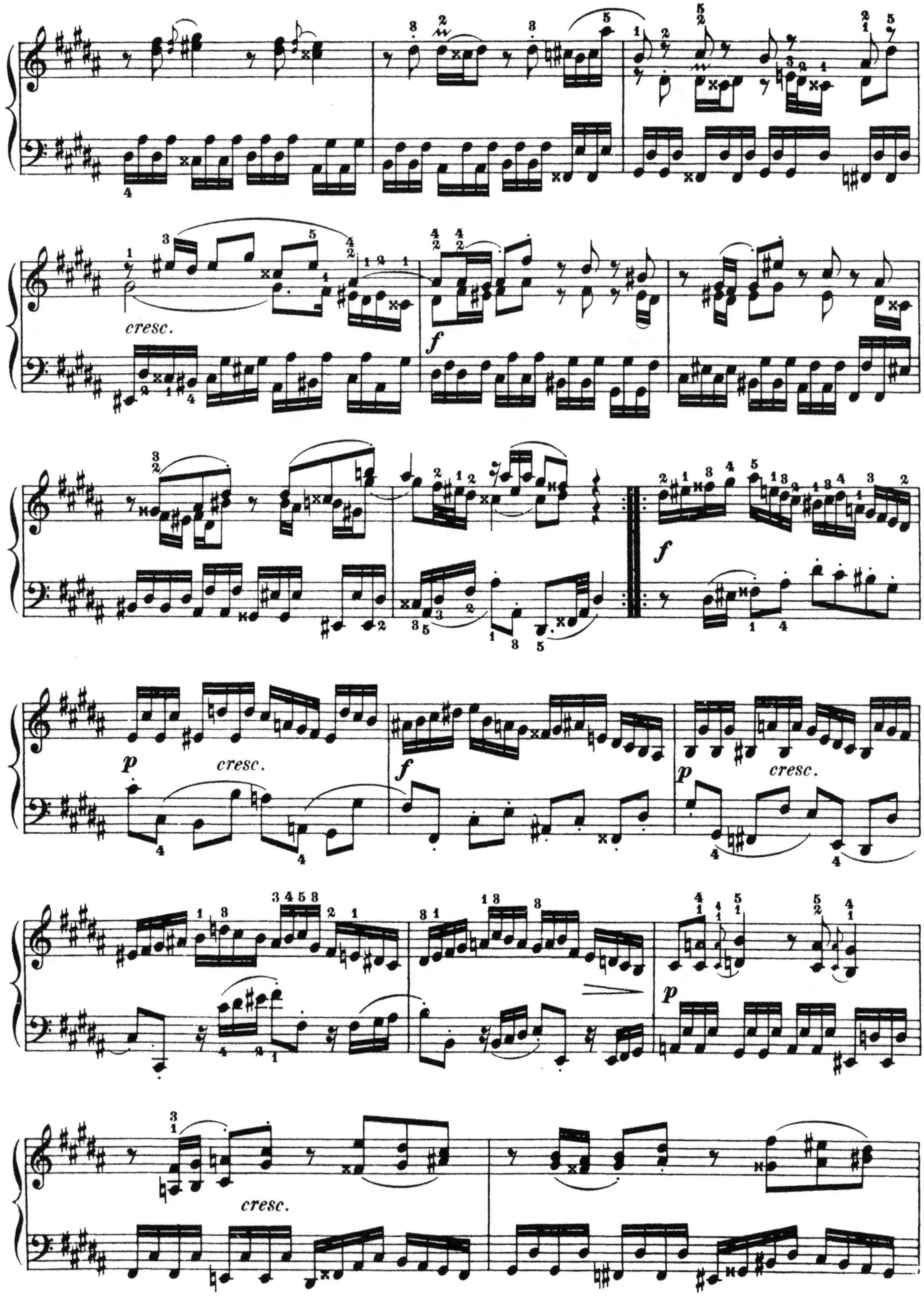
cresc.
f
f
p
cresc.
f
p
cresc.
p
cresc.

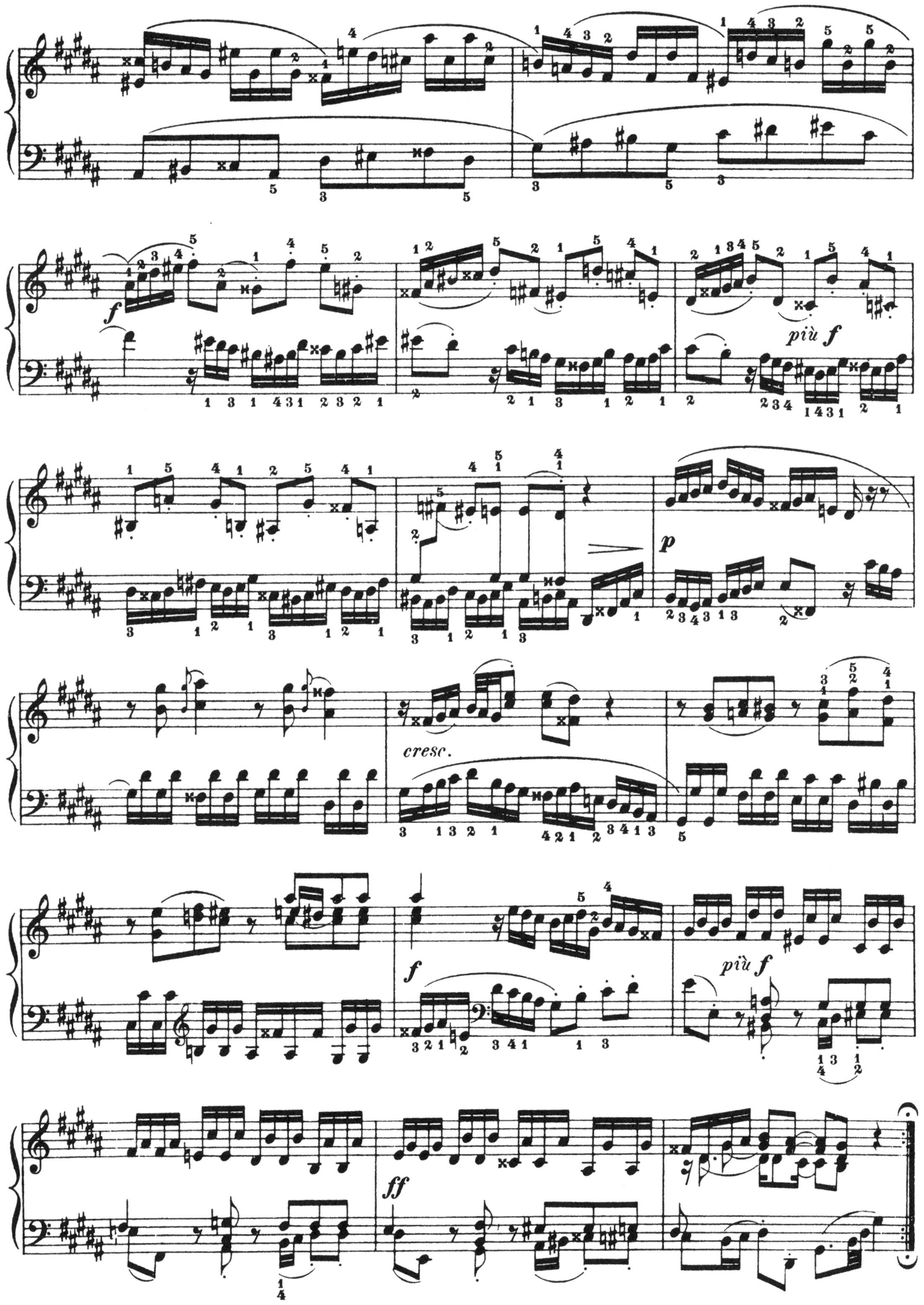
più f
p
cresc.
f
più f
ff

Fuga XVIII.

a 3 Voci.

Moderato e quieto. (♩. = 56.)

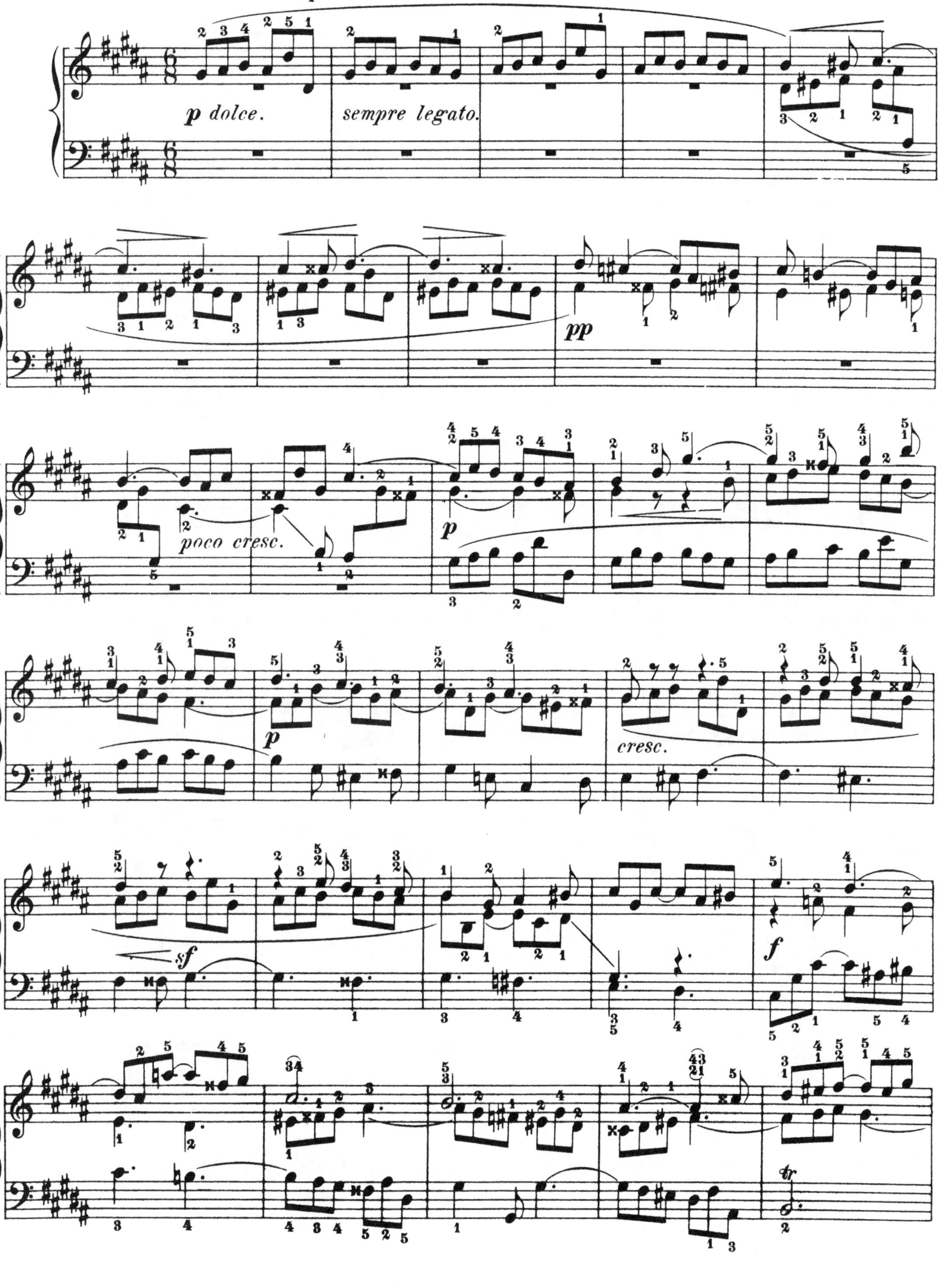

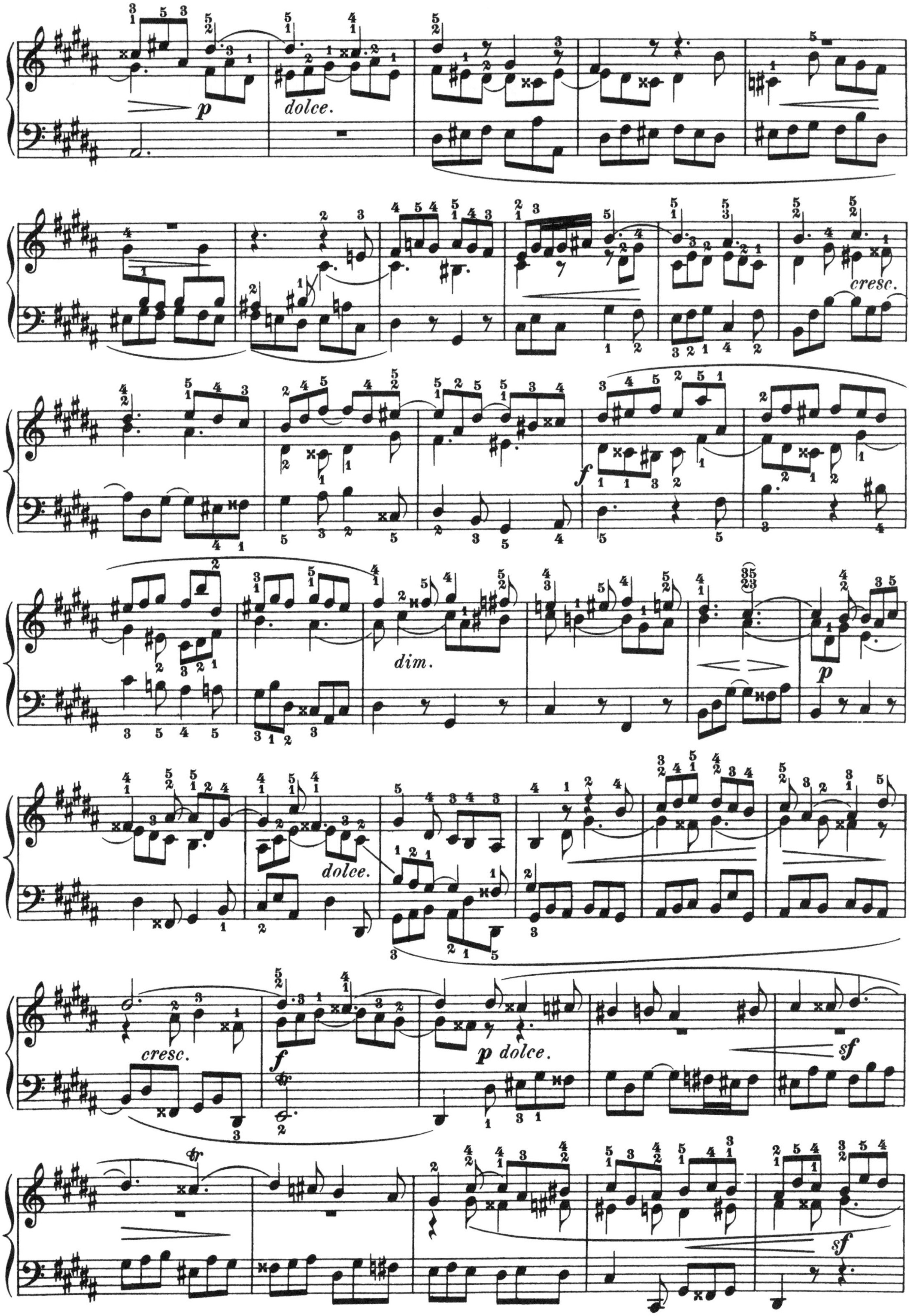
p
dolce.
cresc.
f
dim.
p
dolce.
cresc.
f
p dolce.
sf
sf

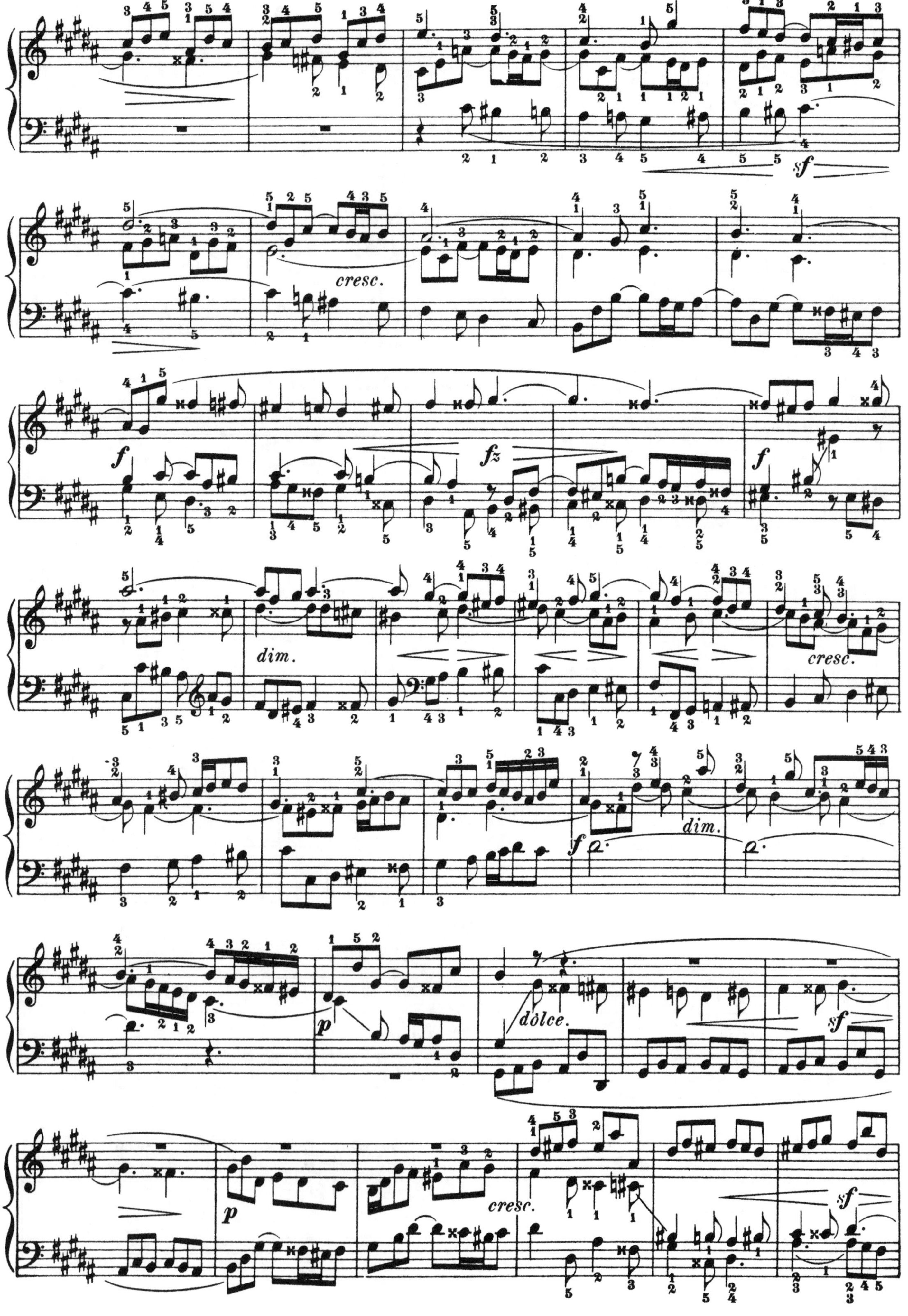
cresc.
dim.
cresc.
dim.
dolce.
cresc.

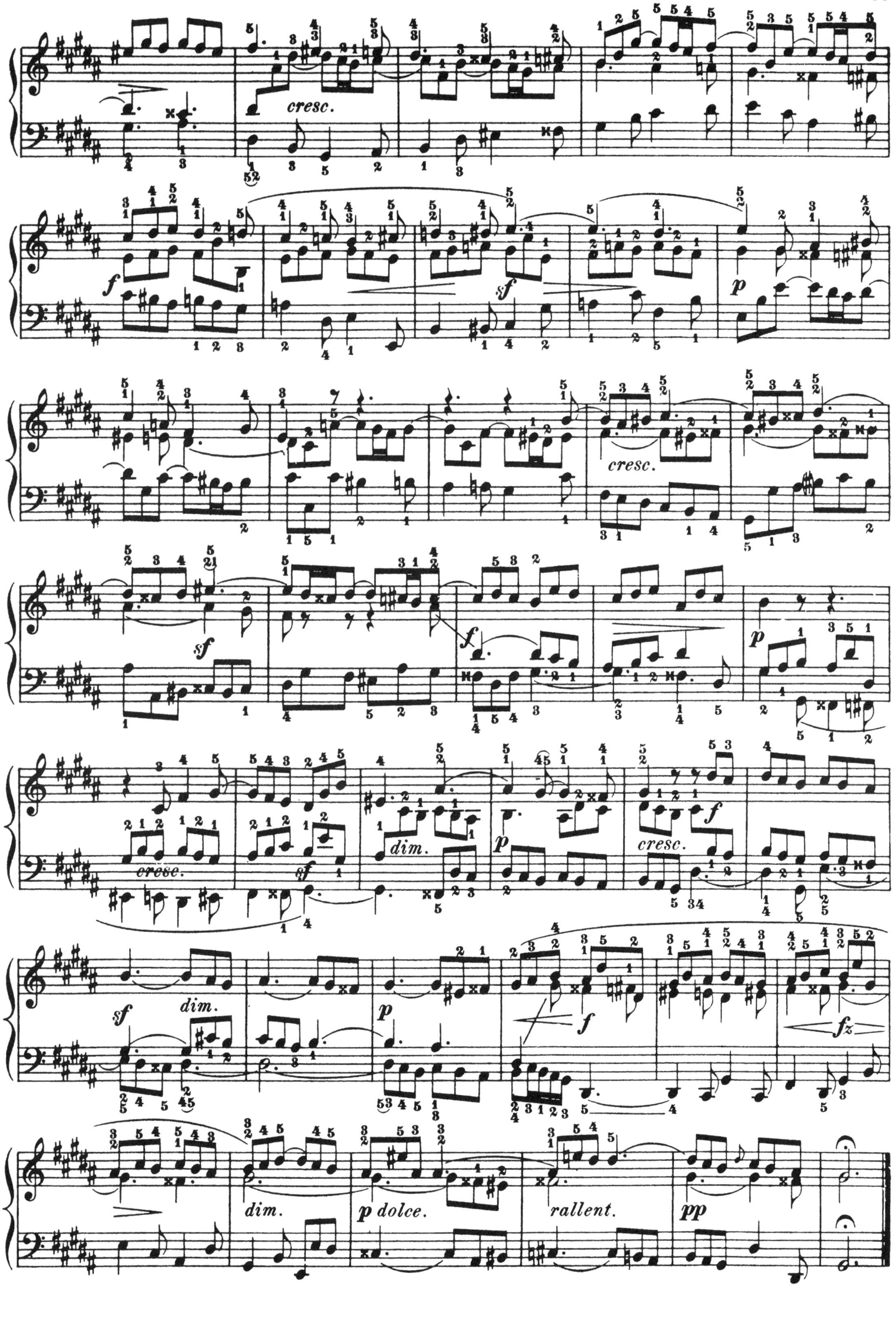
cresc.
f
sf
p
cresc.
sf
f
p
cresc.
sf
dim.
p
dim.
cresc.
f
sf
dim.
p
f
fz
dim.
p dolce.
rallent.
pp

Preludio XIX.

Allegretto vivace. (♩. = 88.)

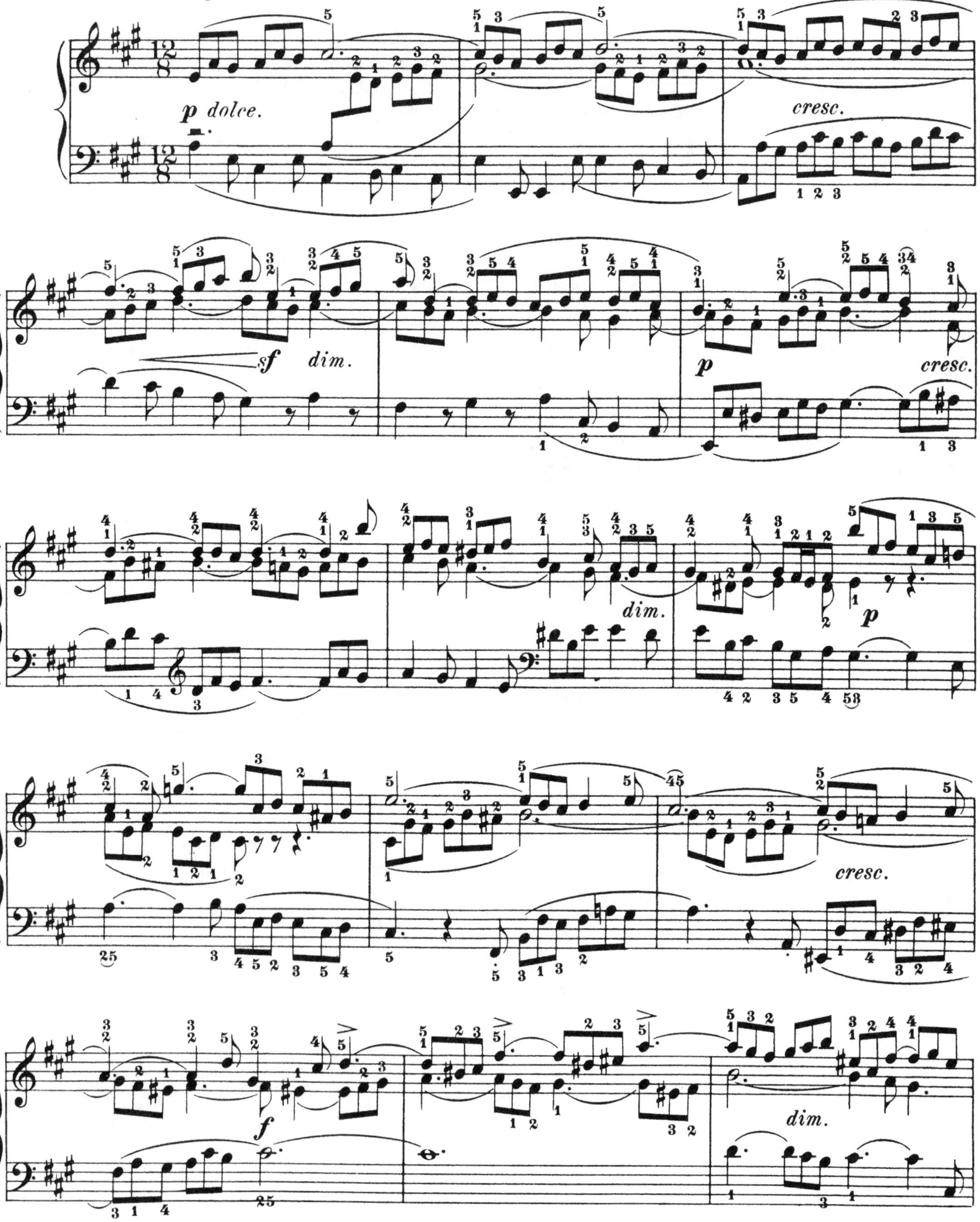

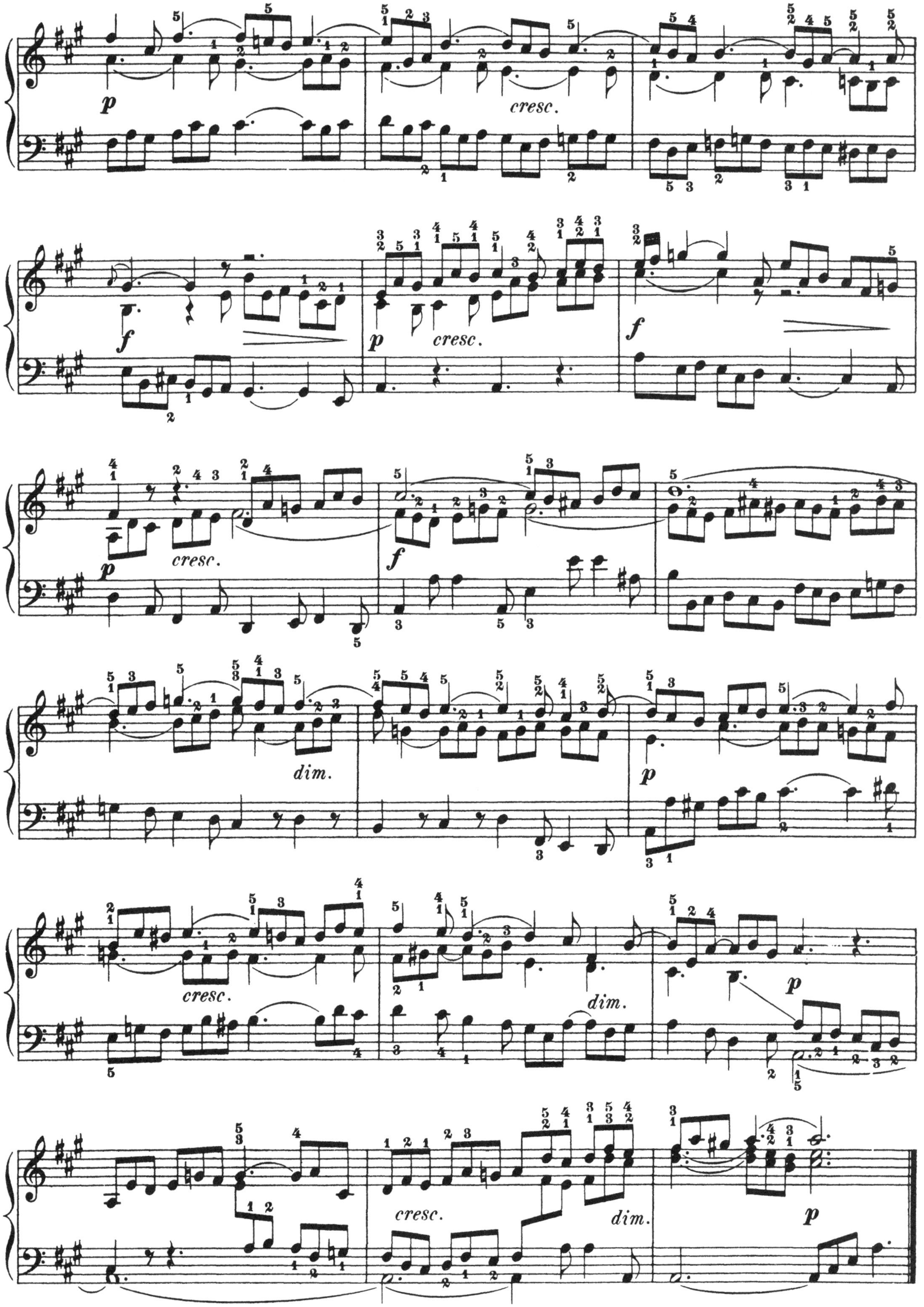
p
cresc.
f
p
cresc.
f
p
cresc.
f
dim.
p
cresc.
dim.
p
cresc.
dim.
p

Fuga XIX.

a 3 Voci.

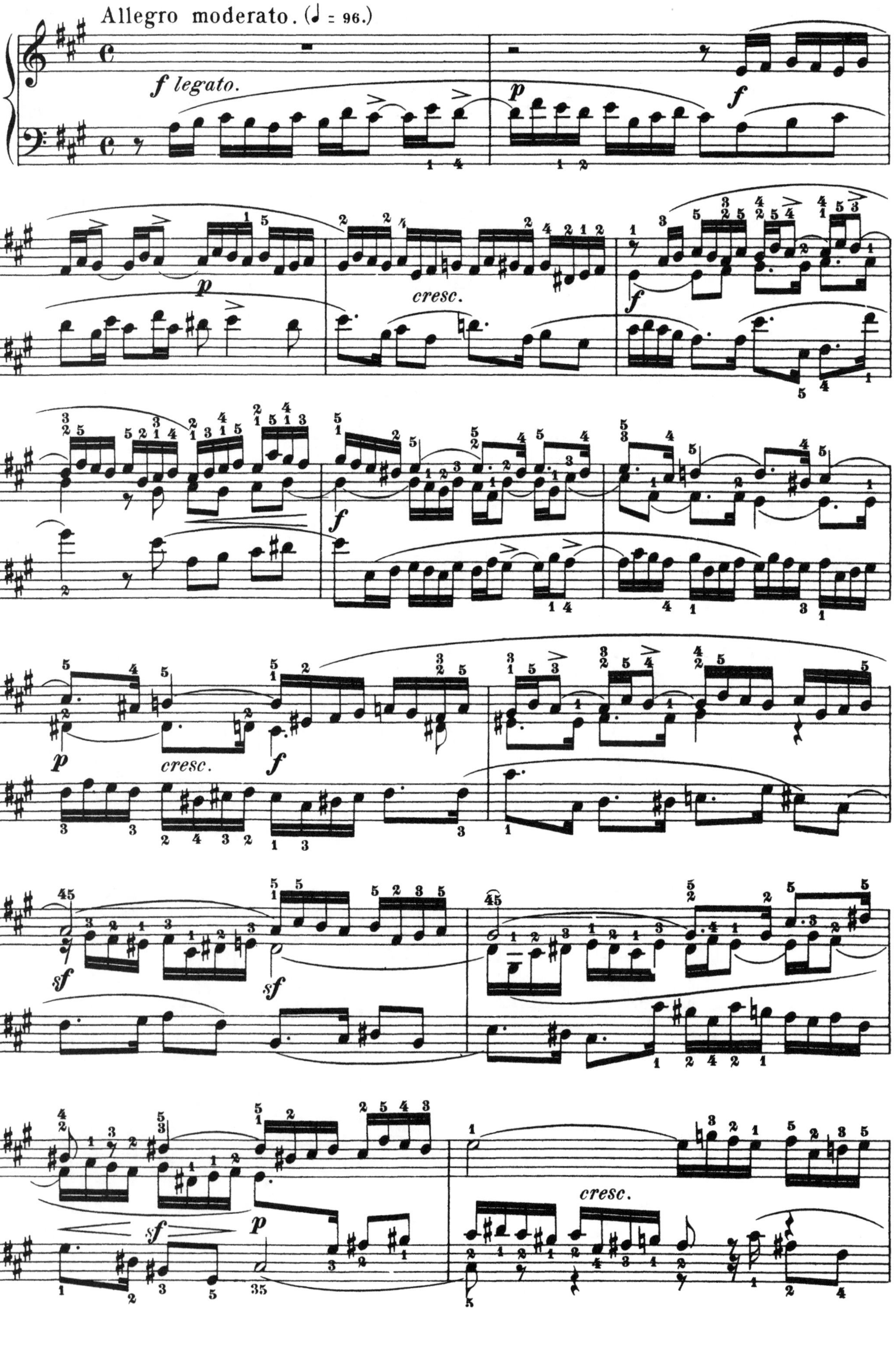

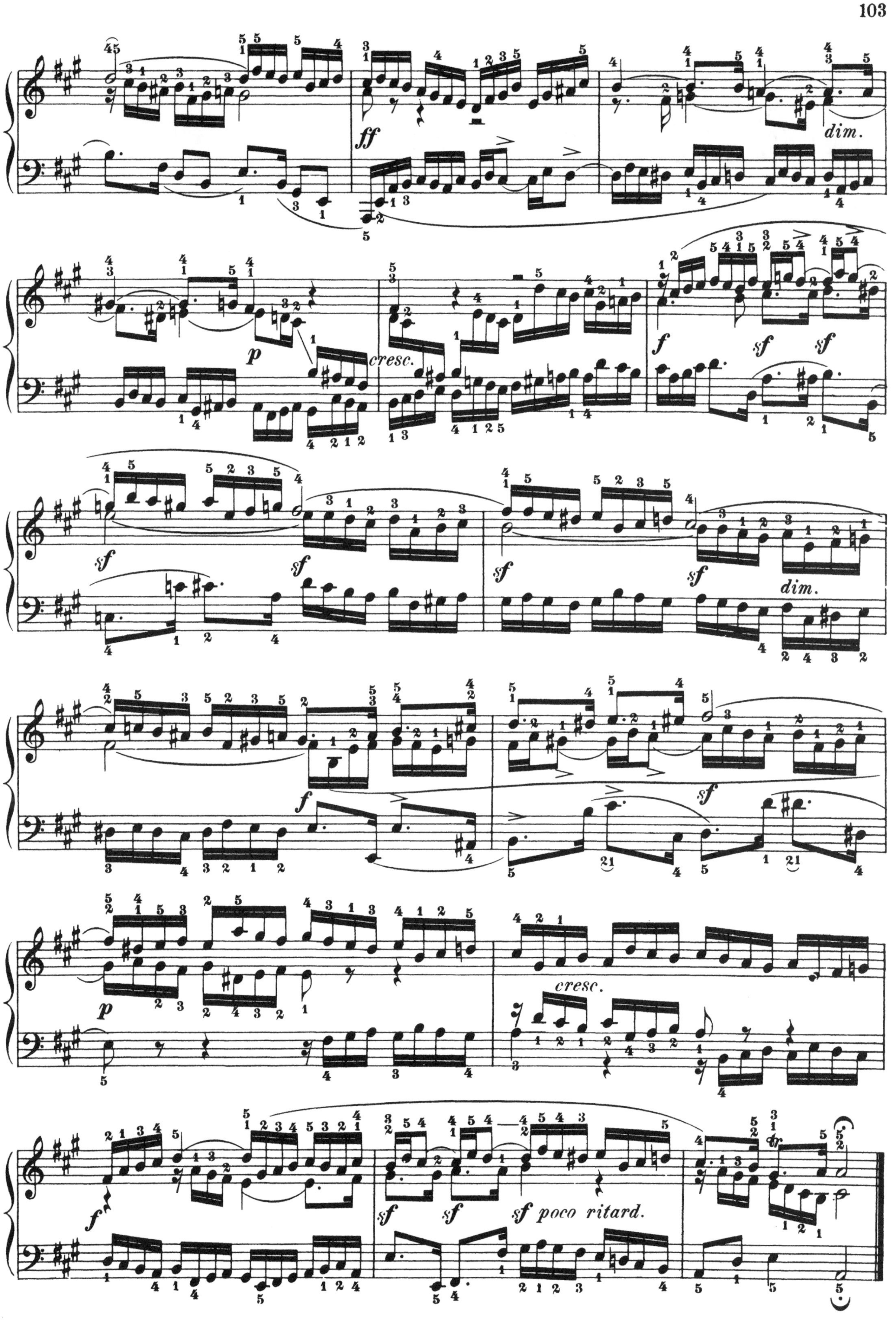
ff
dim.
p
cresc.
f
sf
sf
sf
sf
sf
sf
dim.
f
sf
p
cresc.
f
sf
sf
sf poco ritard.

Preludio XX.

Andante molto espressivo. (♪ = 92.)

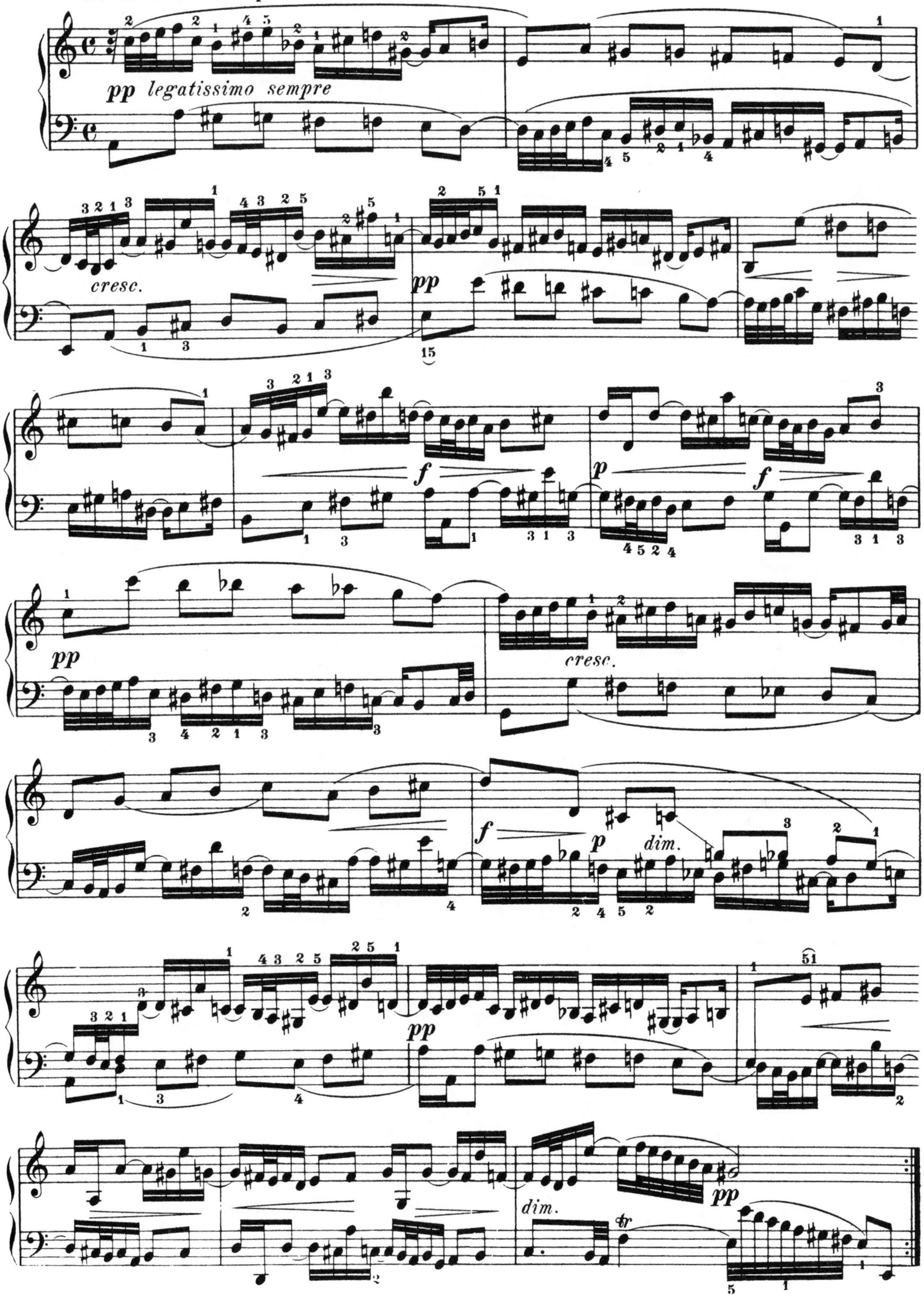

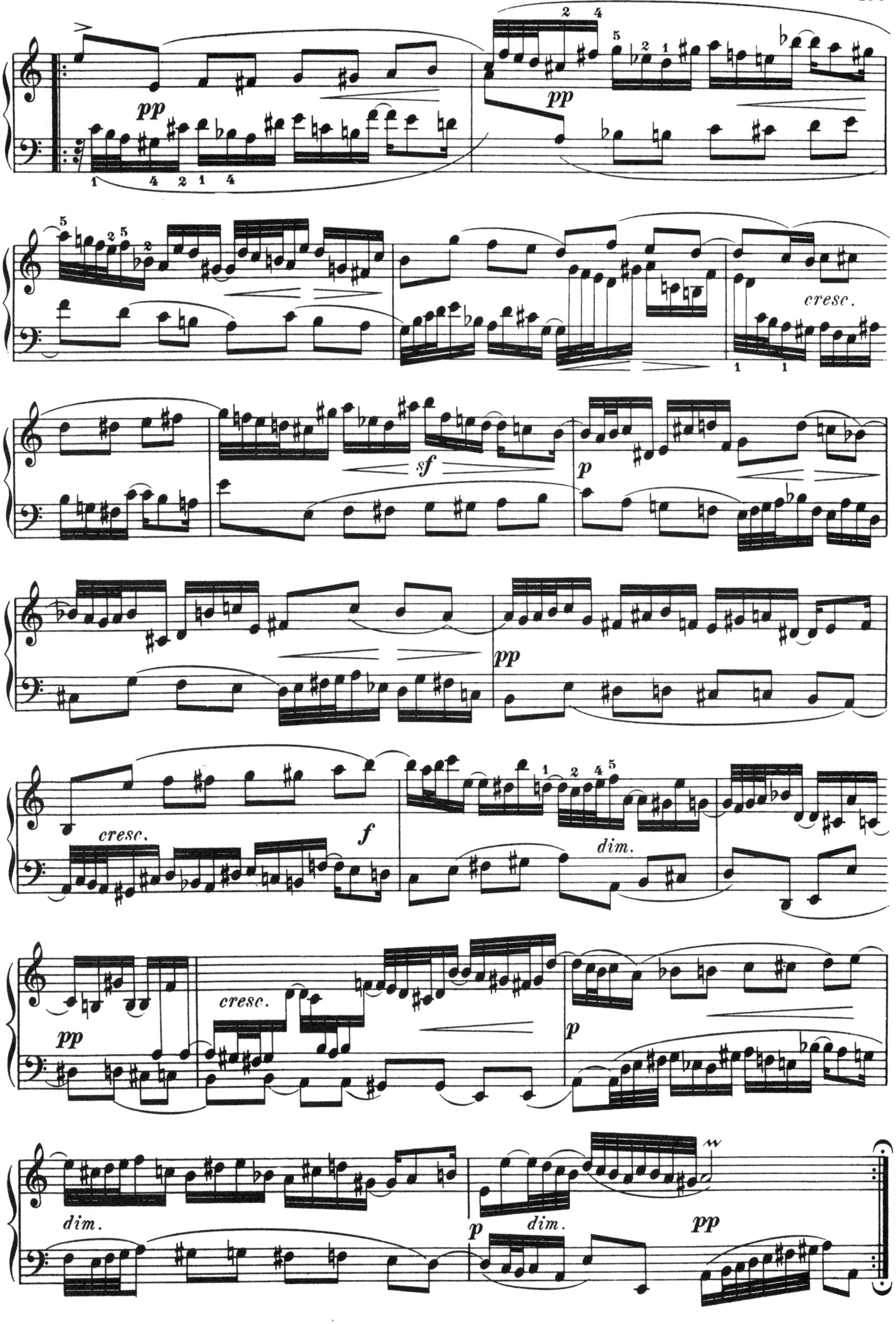
pp
cresc.
sf
p
pp
cresc.
f
dim.
pp
cresc.
p
dim.
p
dim.
pp

Fuga XX.

a 3 Voci.

Andante maestosso ed energico. (♩ = 66.)

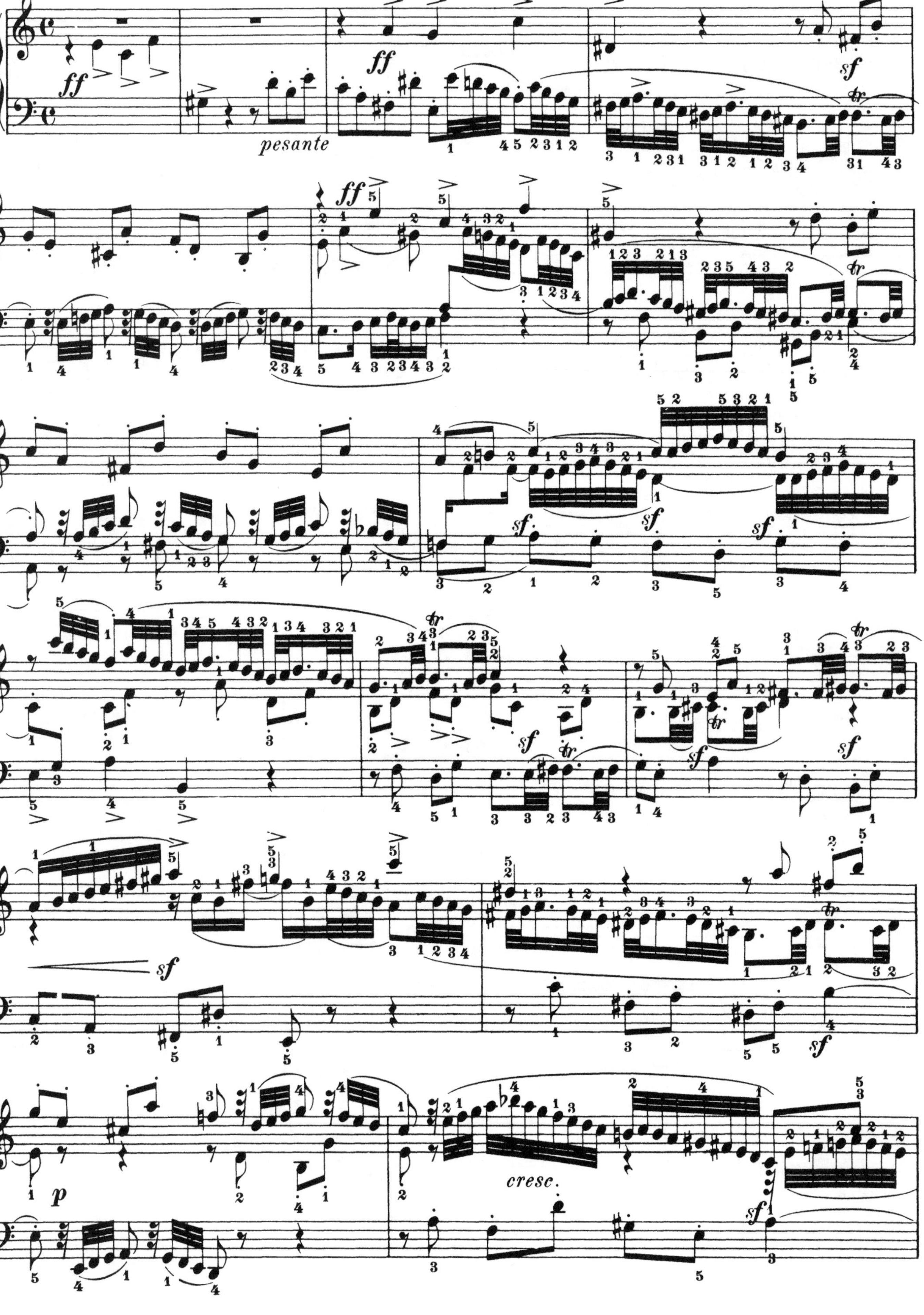

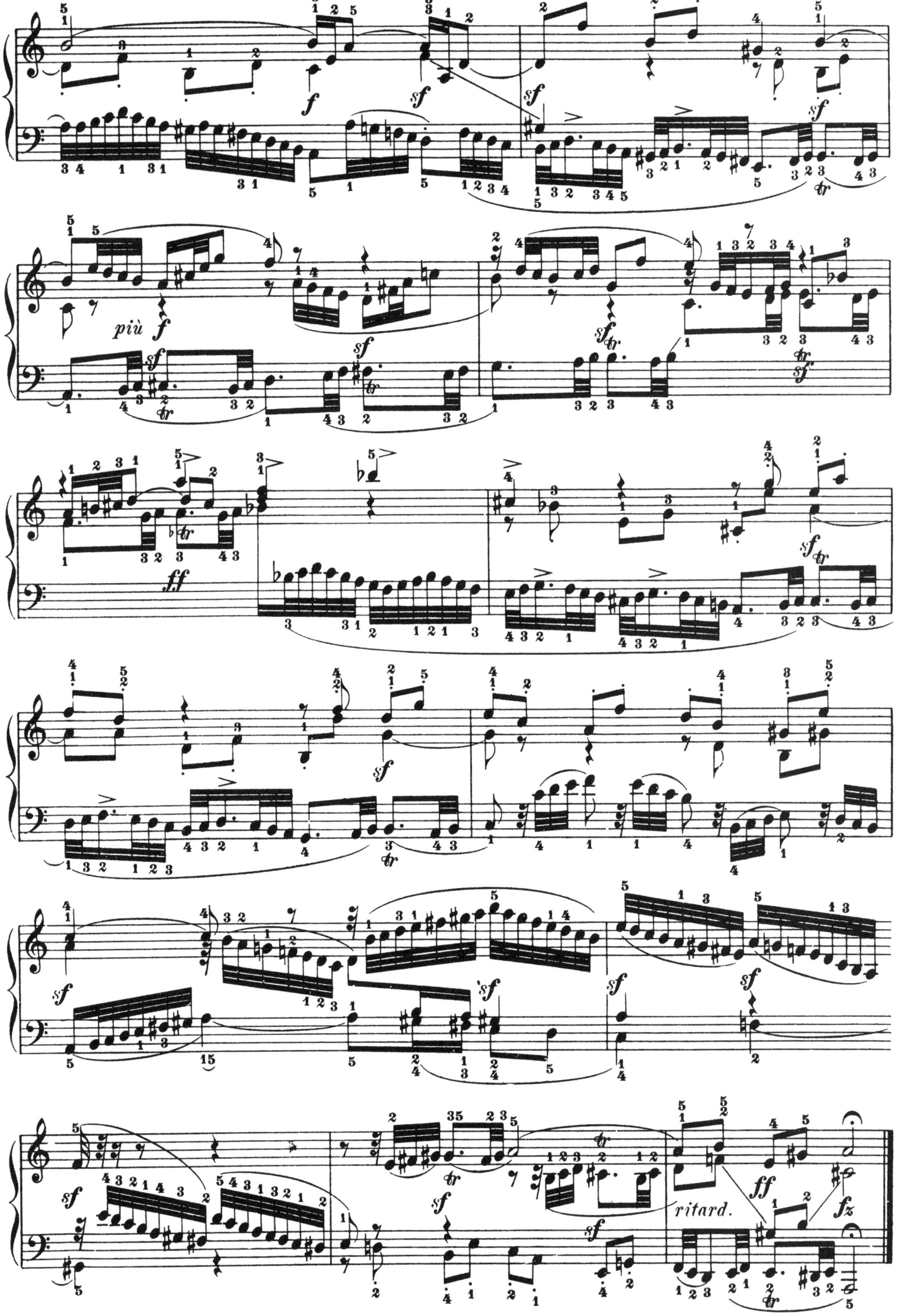
più
ritard.

Preludio XXI.

Vivace. (♪ = 116.)

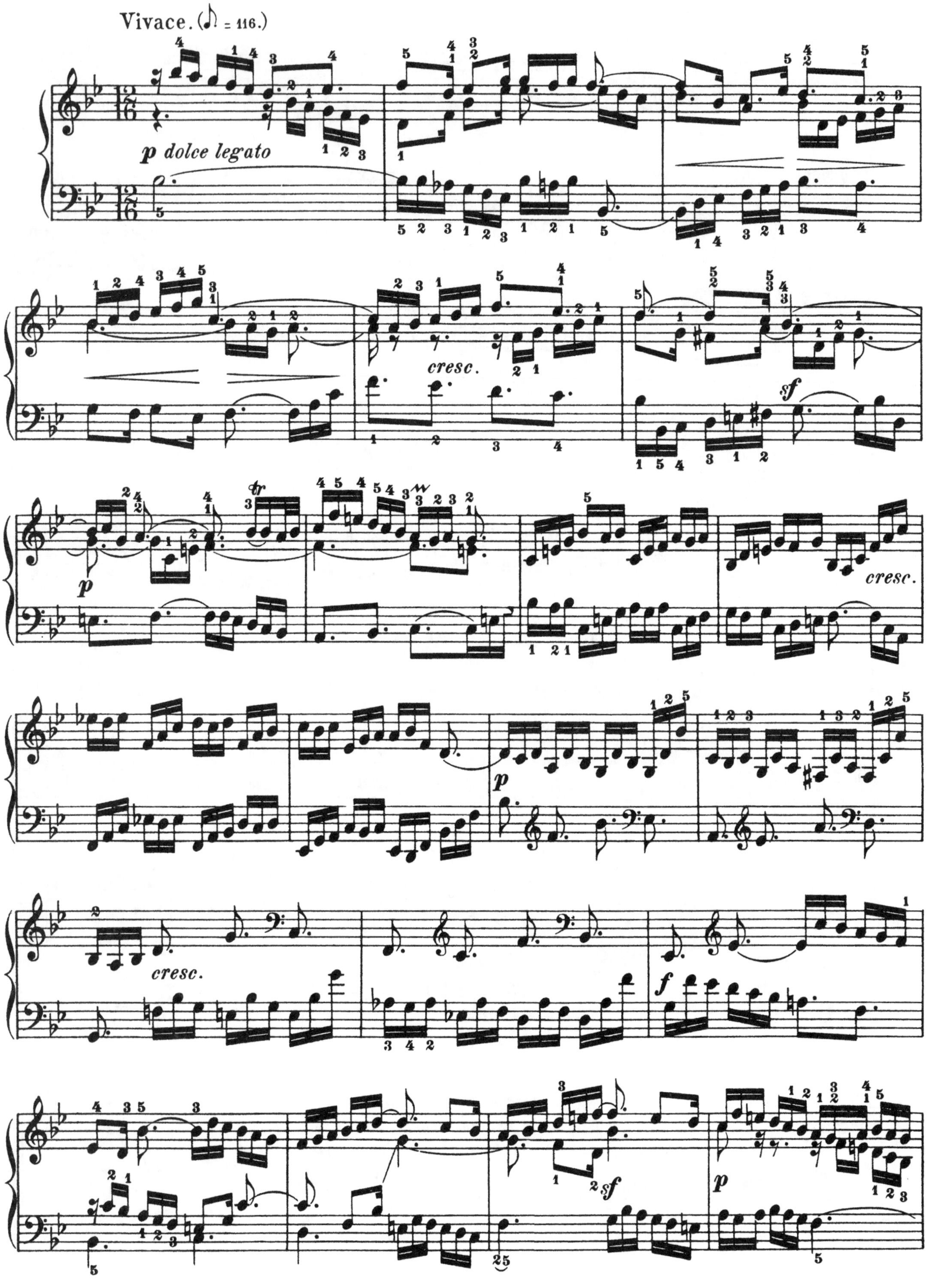

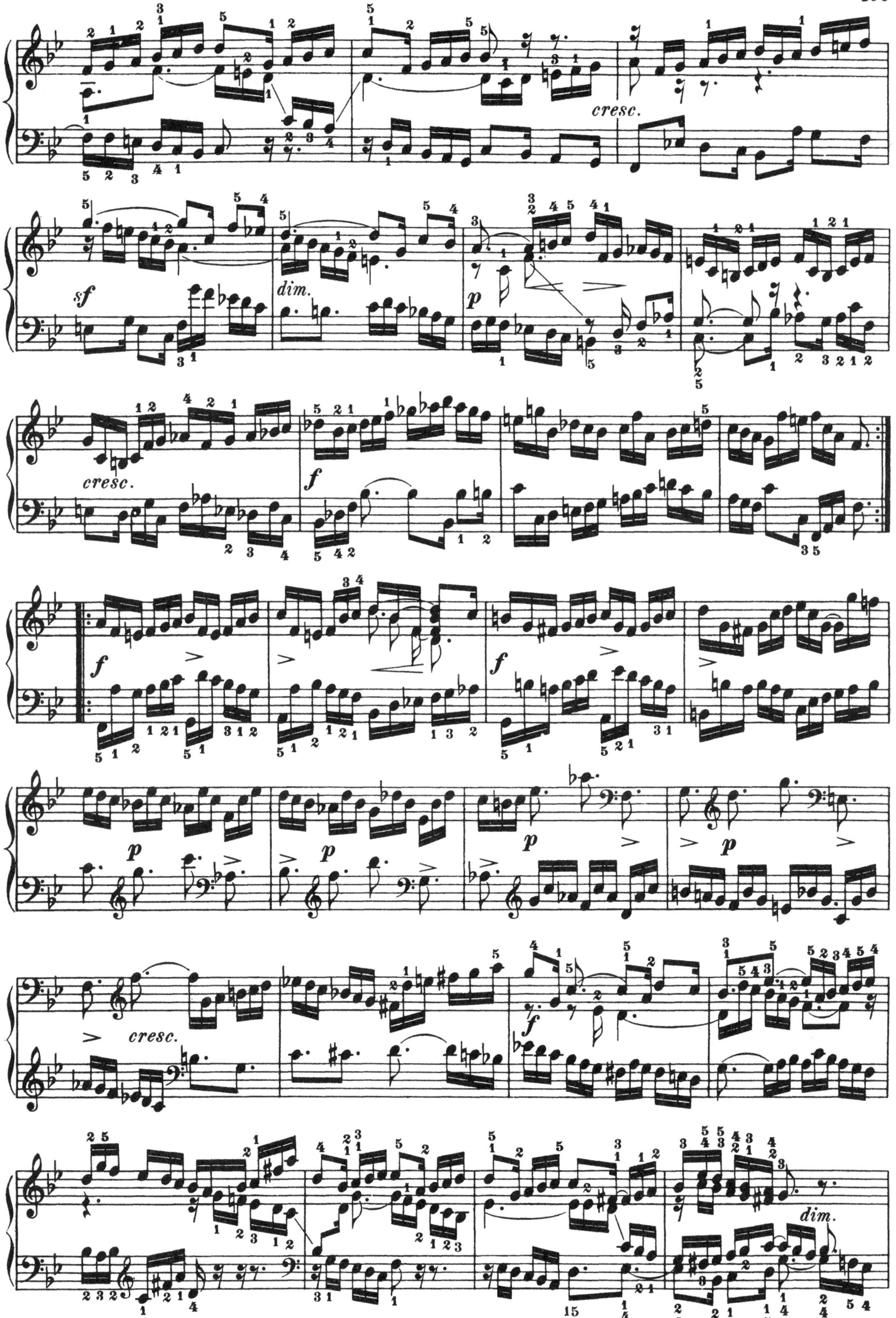
cresc.
sf
dim.
p
cresc.
f
f
f
p
p
p
p
cresc.
f
dim.

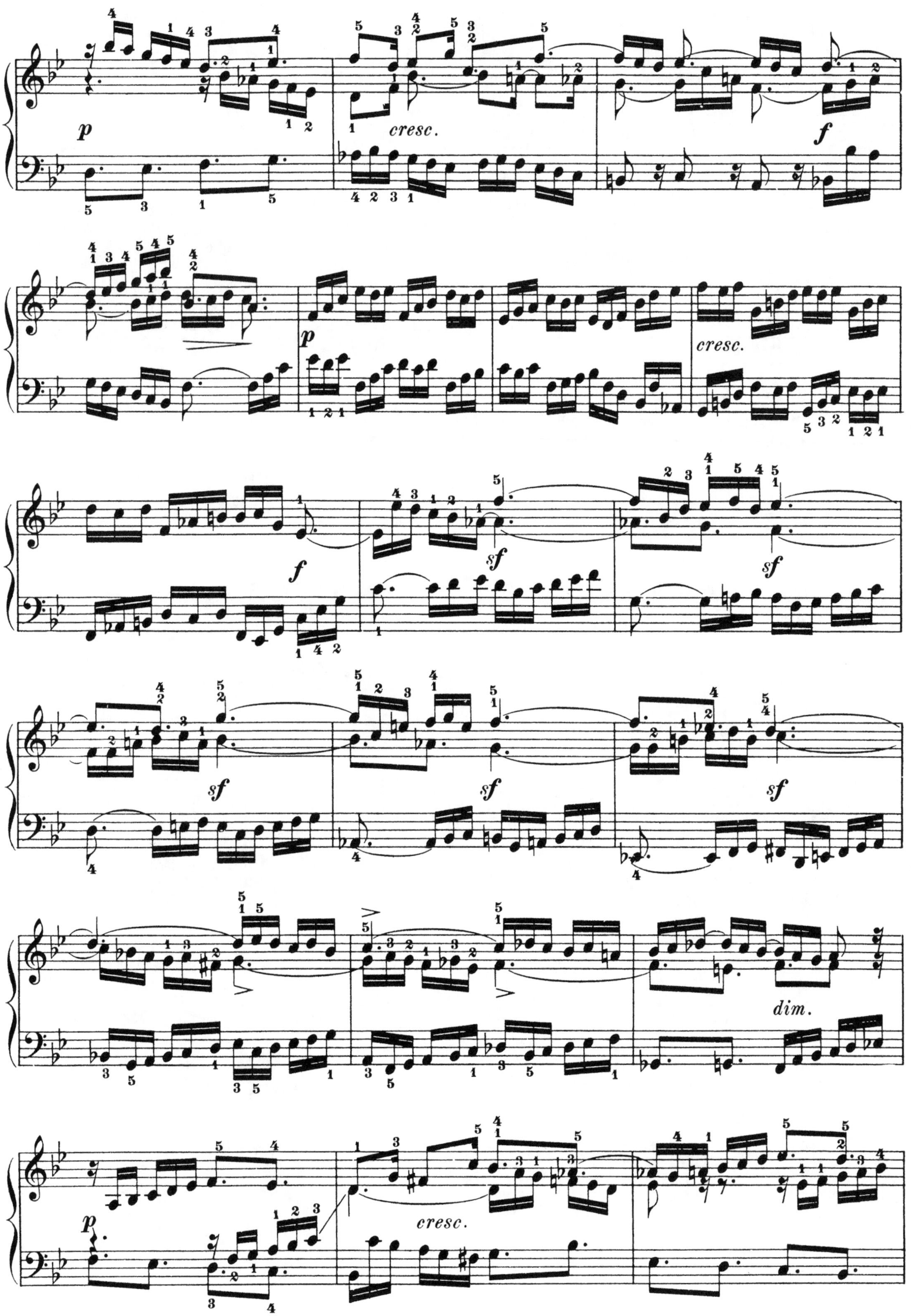
p
cresc.
f
p
cresc.
f
sf
sf
sf
sf
sf
dim.
p
cresc.

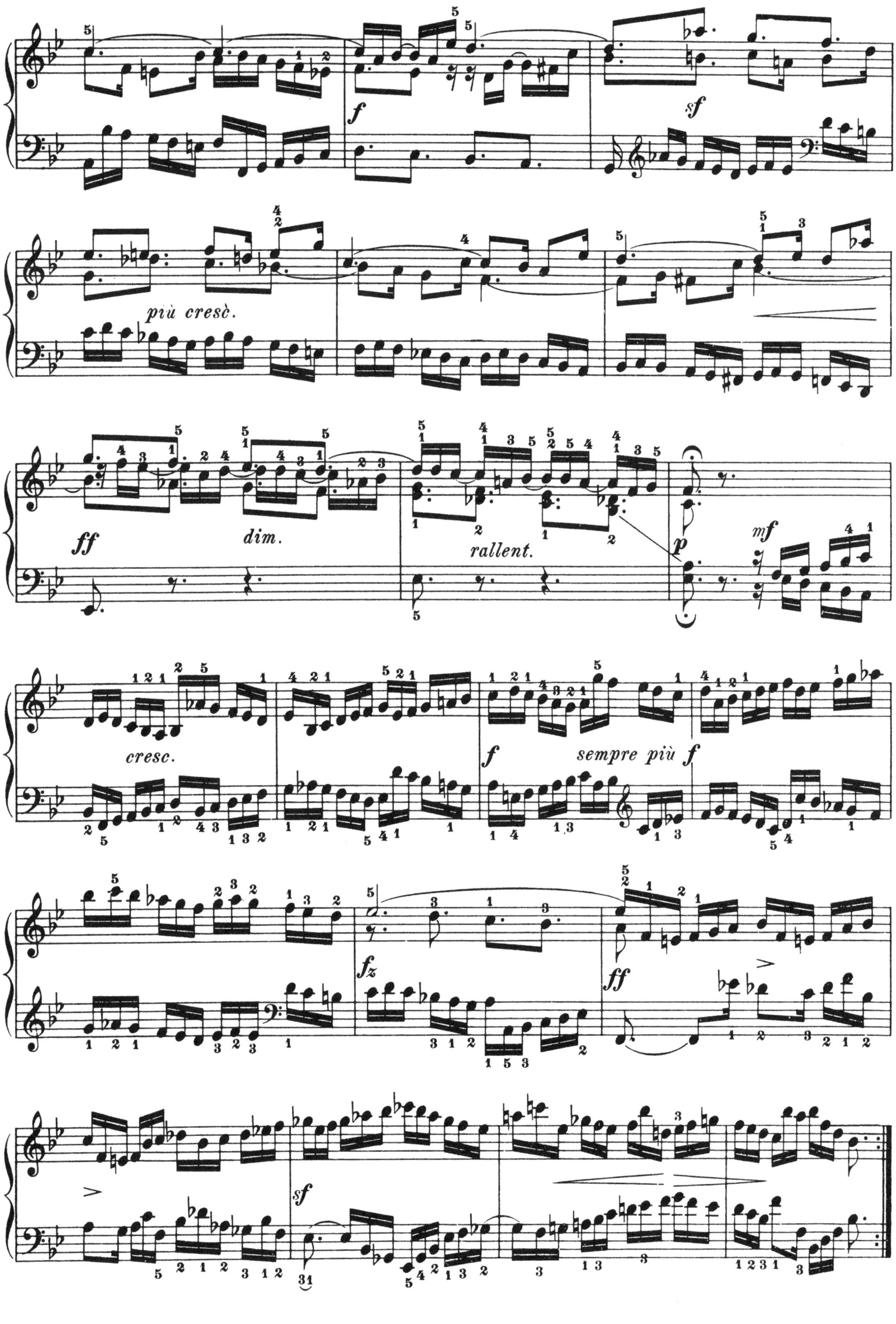
f
sf
più cresc.
ff
dim.
rallent.
p
mf
cresc.
f
sempre più f
fz
ff
sf

Fuga XXI.

a 3 Voci.

Allegretto vivace. (♩= 108.)

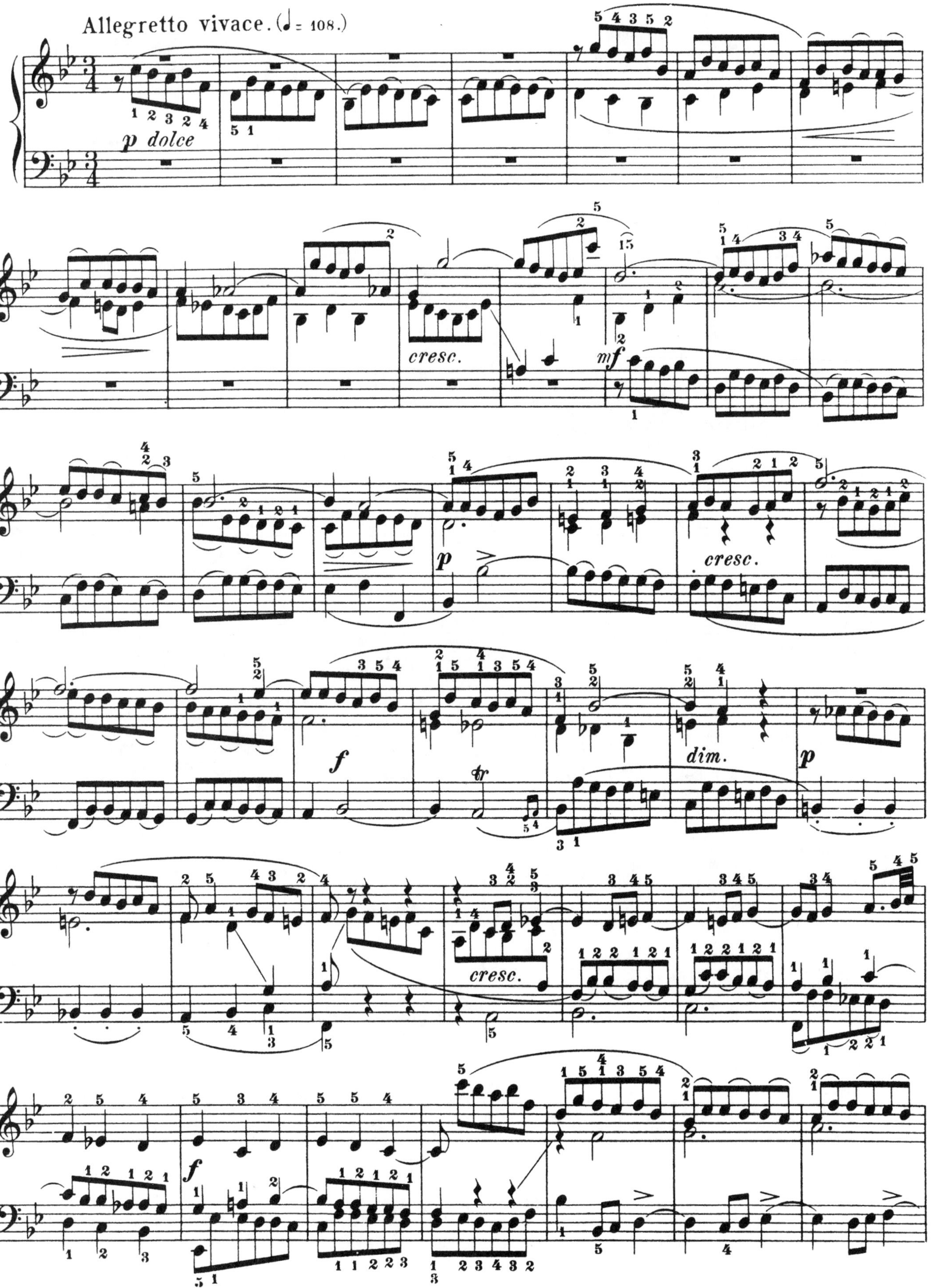

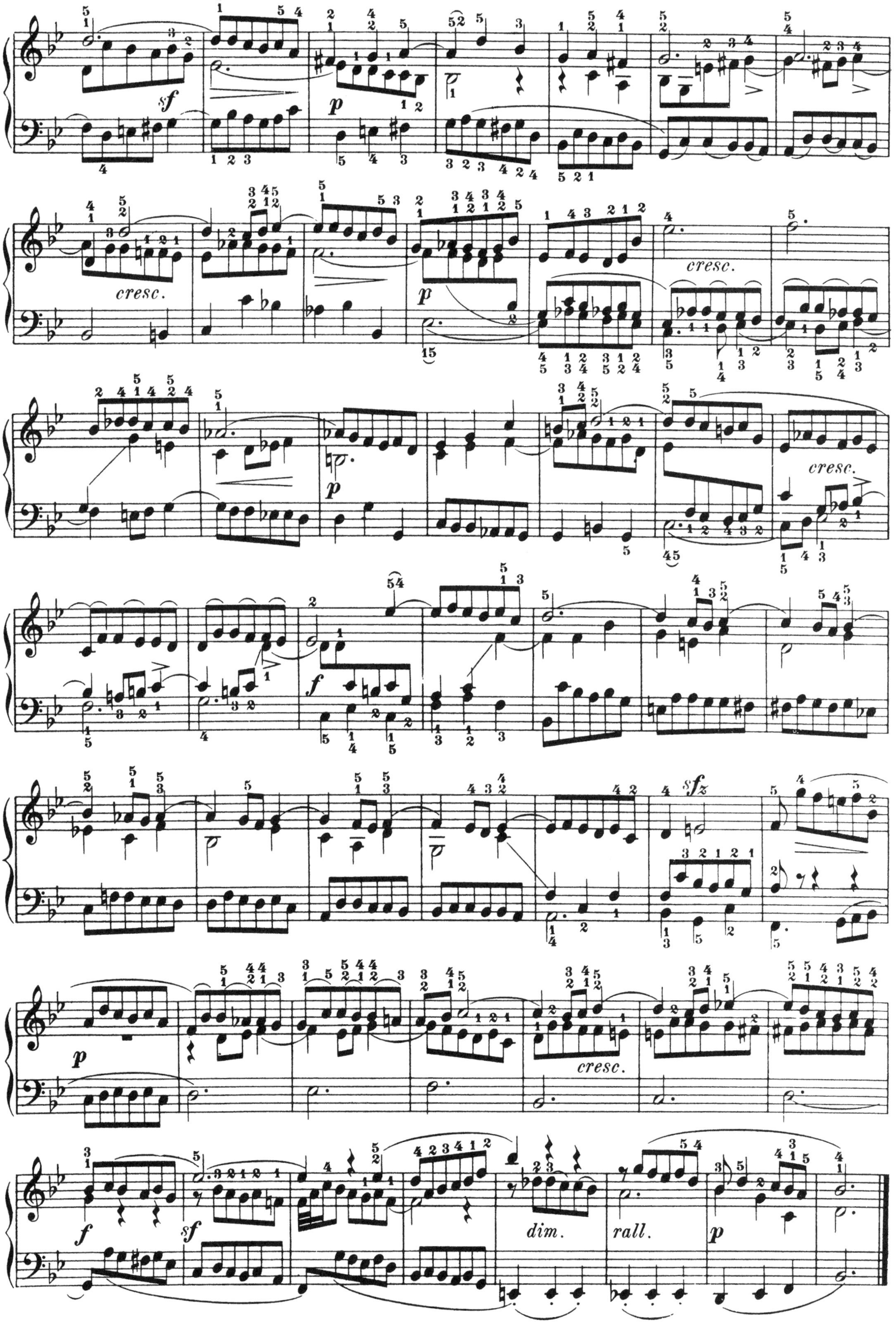
sf
p
cresc.
p
cresc.
p
cresc.
f
sfz
p
cresc.
f
sf
dim.
rall.
p

Preludio XXII.

Andante con moto. (𝅗𝅥 = 60.)

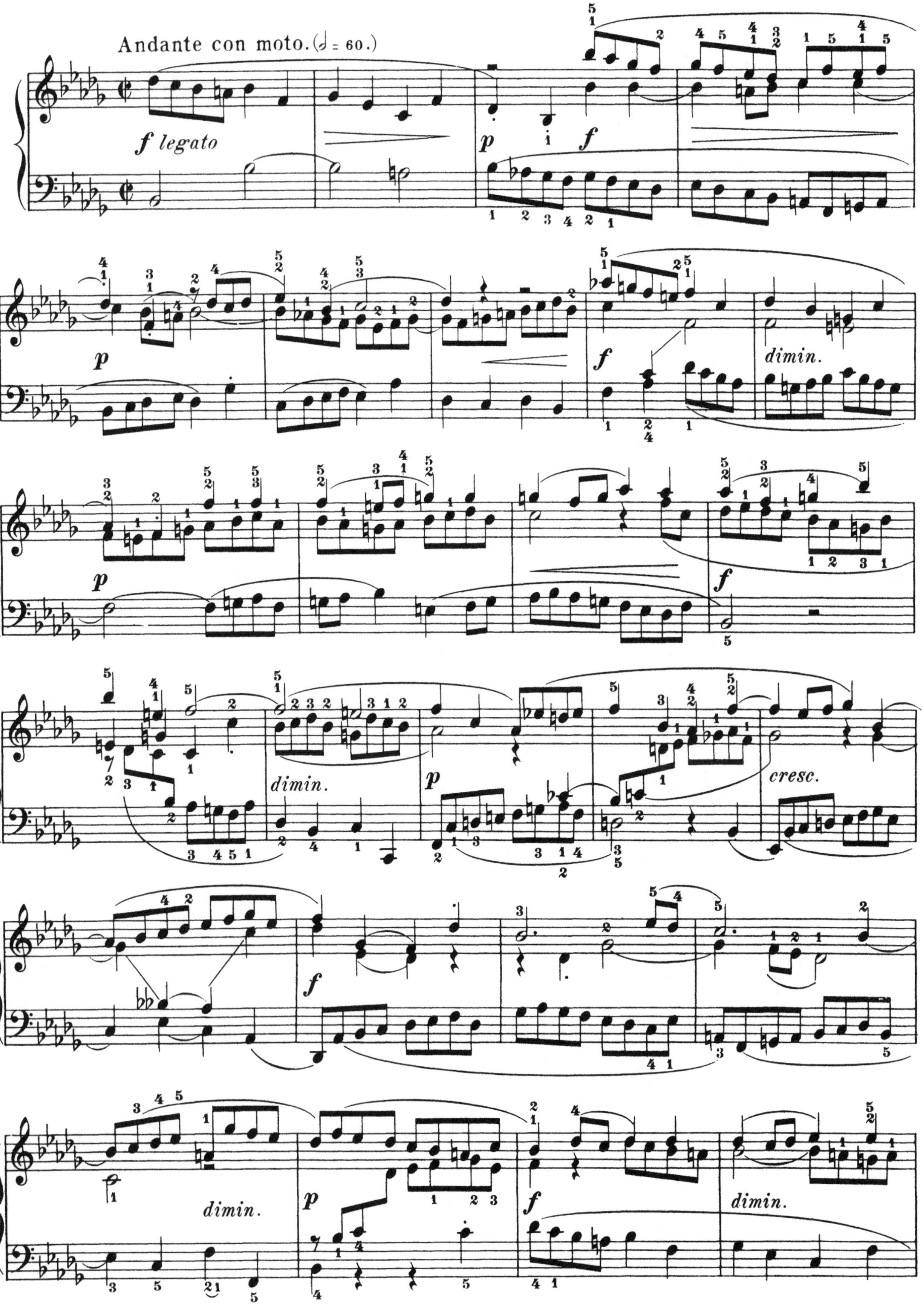

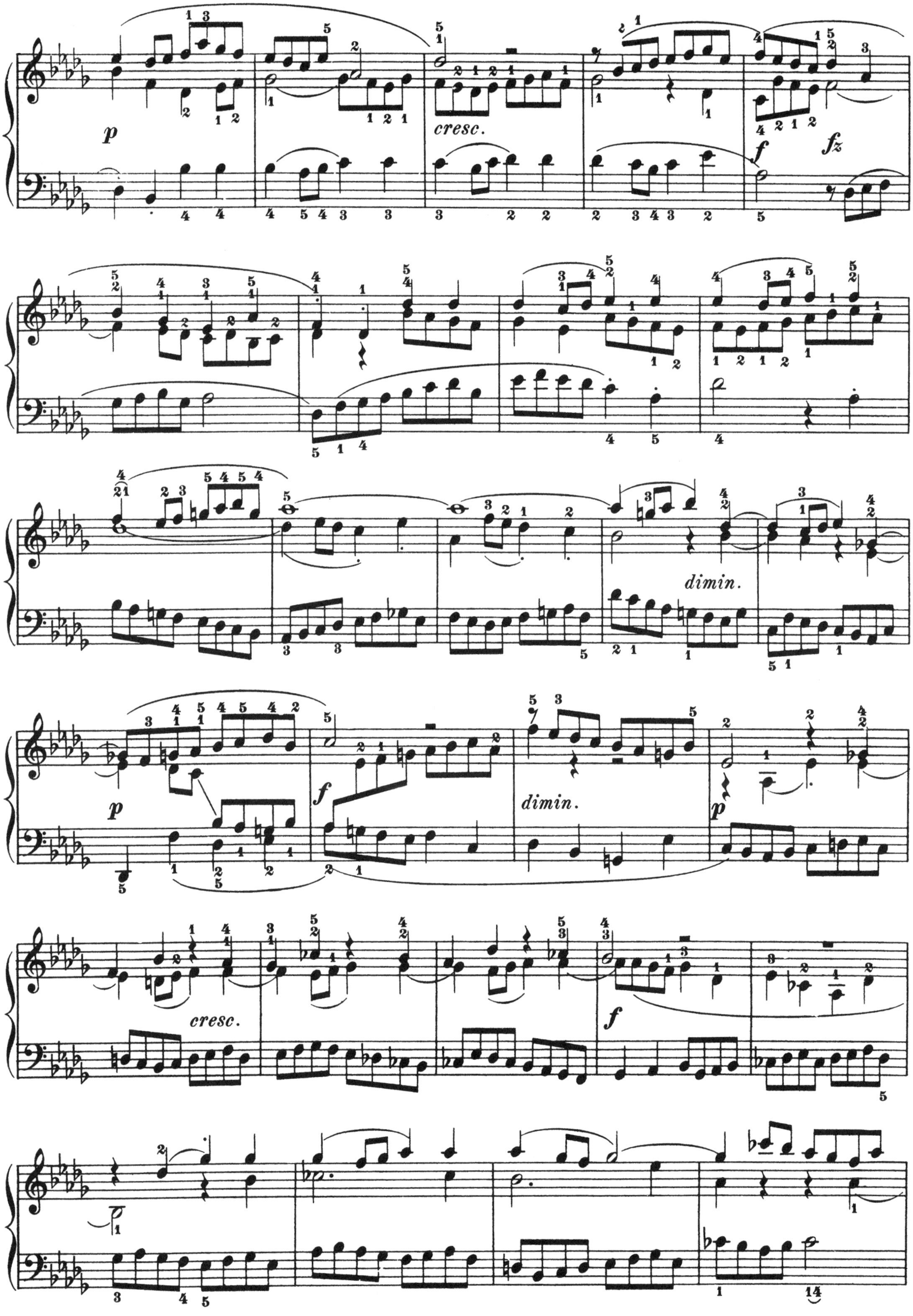
p
cresc.
f
fz
dimin.
p
f
dimin.
p
cresc.
f

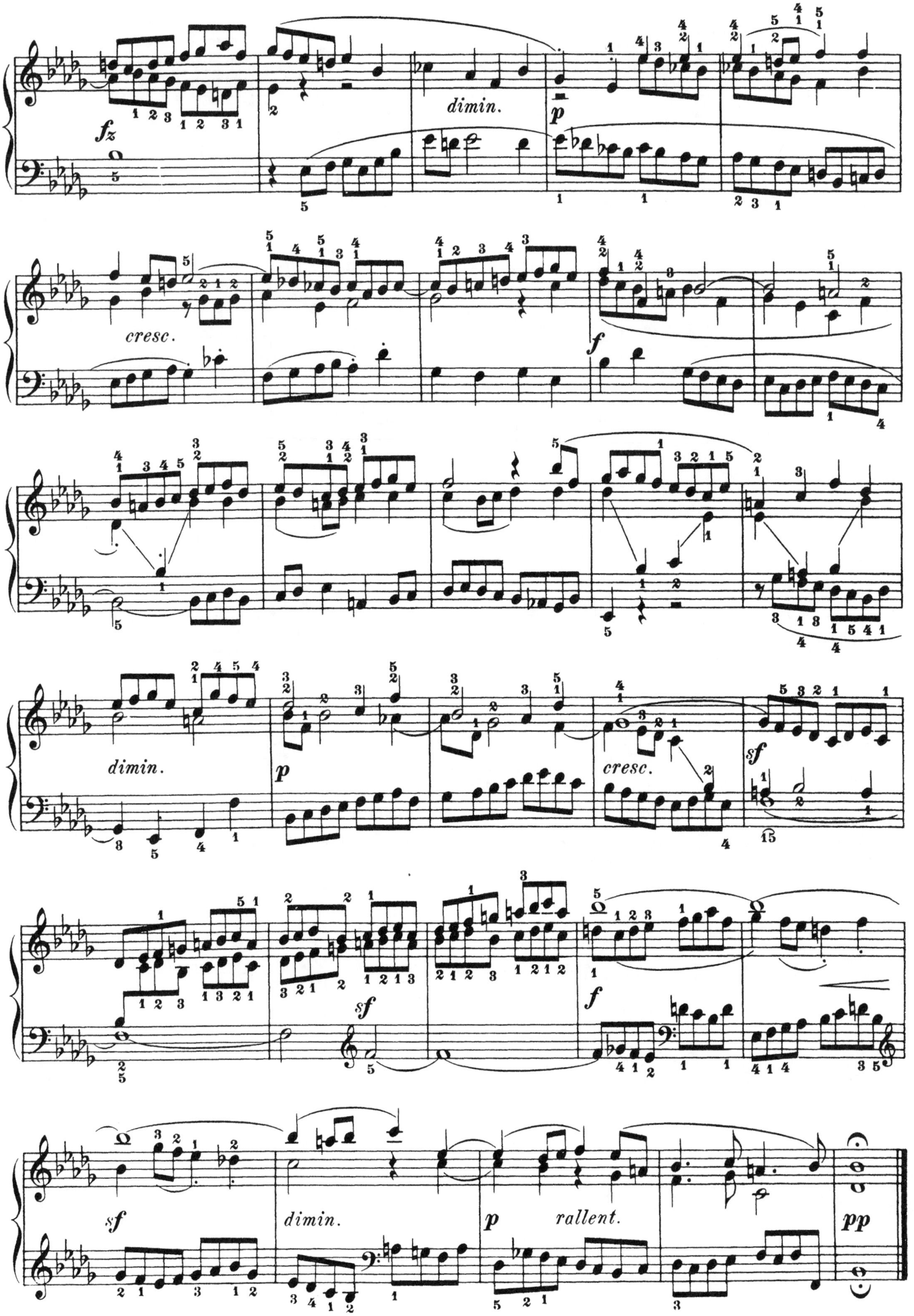
fz
dimin.
p
cresc.
f
dimin.
p
cresc.
sf
sf
f
sf
dimin.
p
rallent.
pp

Fuga XXII.

a 4 Voci.

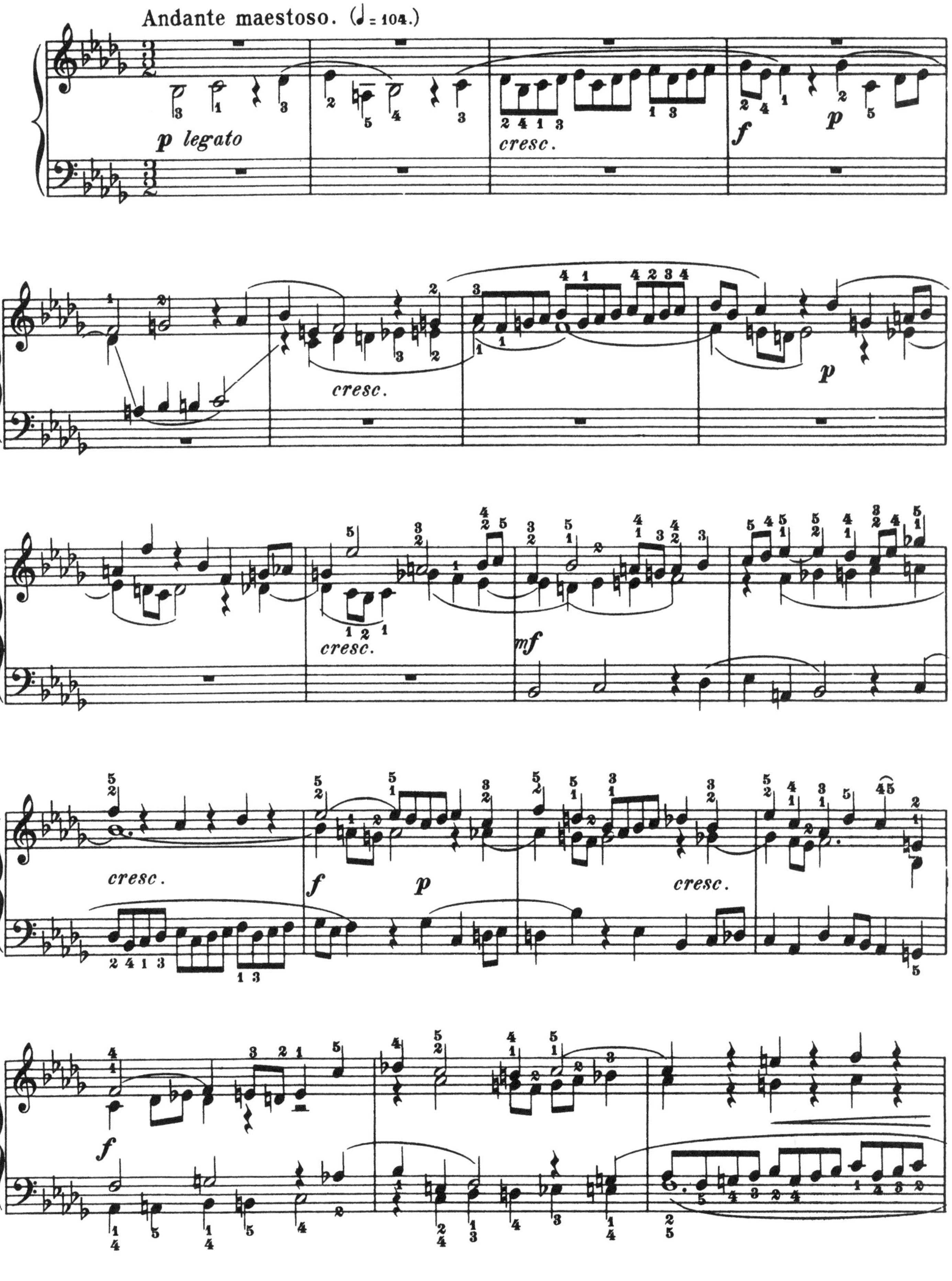

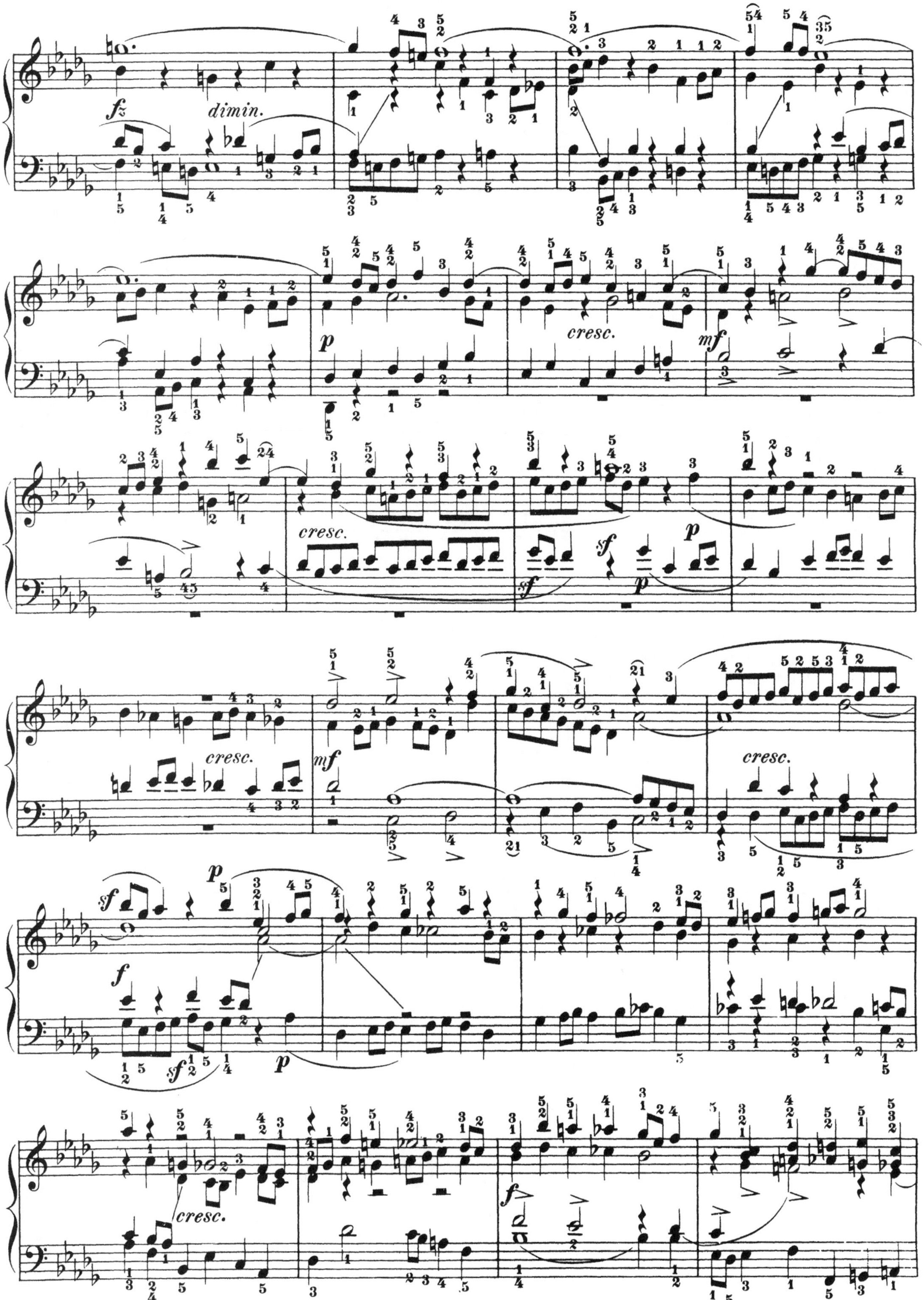
fz
dimin.
p
cresc.
mf
cresc.
sf
p
cresc.
mf
cresc.
sf
p
f
sf
p
cresc.
f

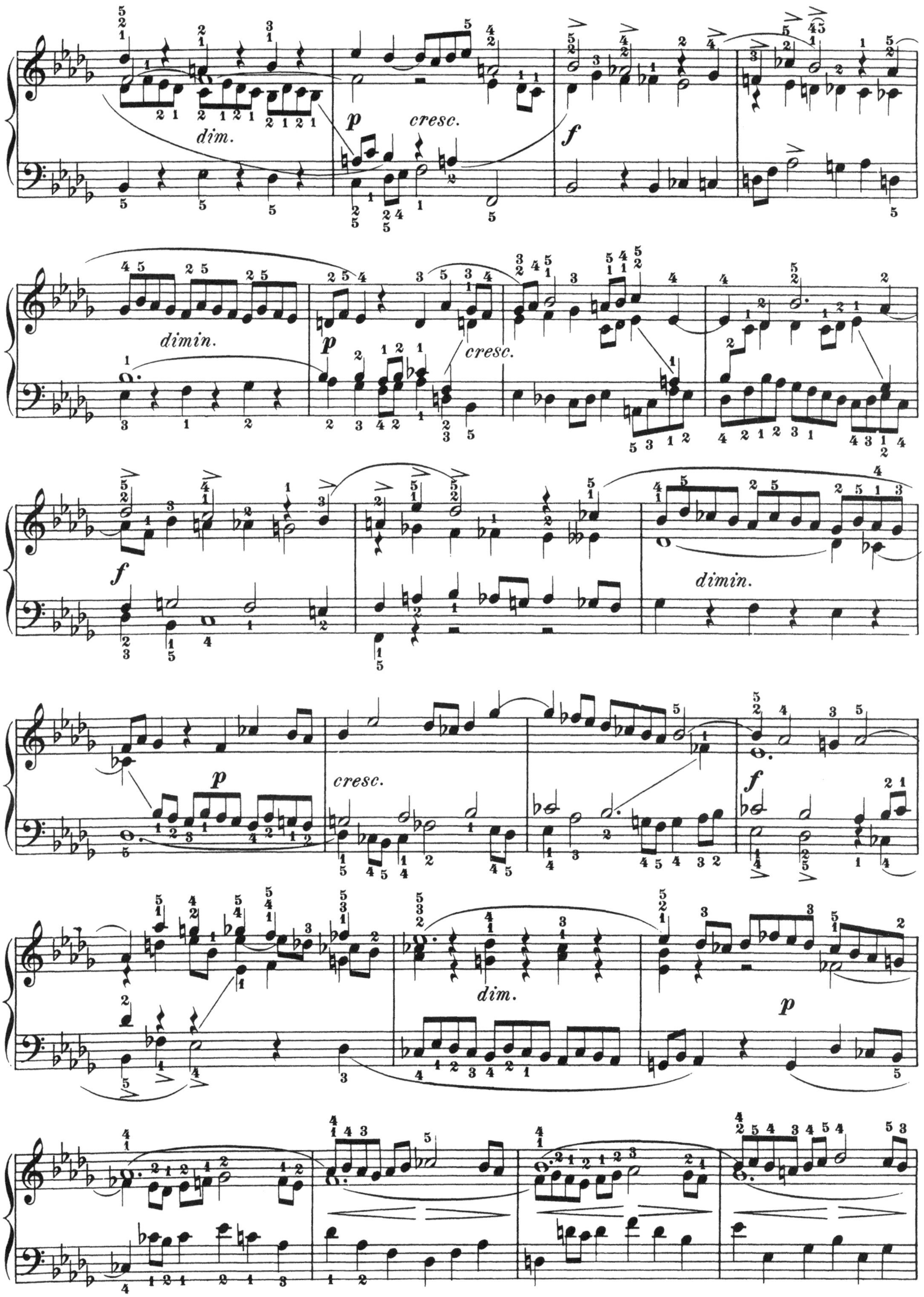
dim.
p
cresc.
f
dimin.
p
cresc.
f
dimin.
p
cresc.
f
dim.
p

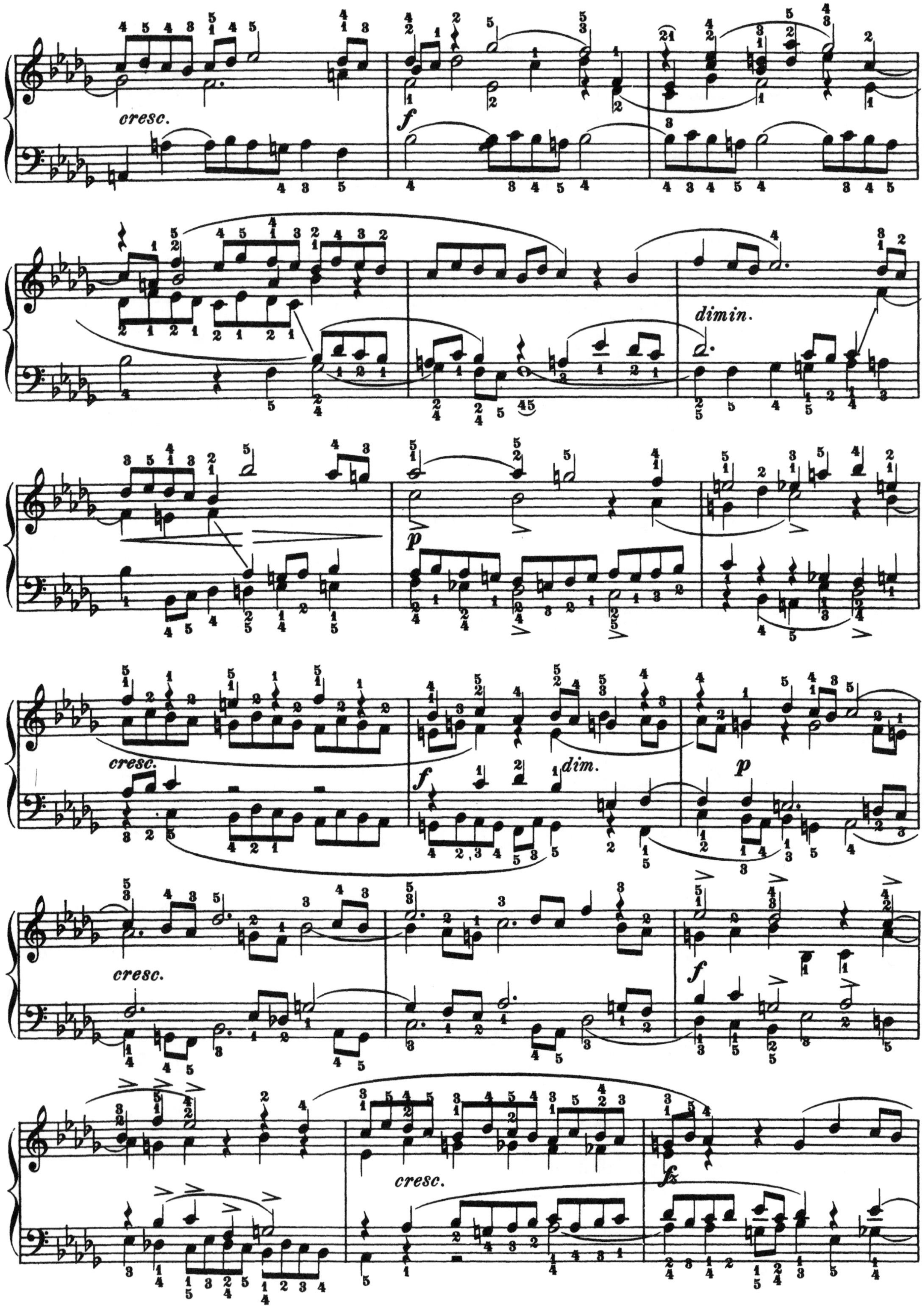
cresc.
f
dimin.
p
cresc.
f
dim.
p
cresc.
f
cresc.
fz

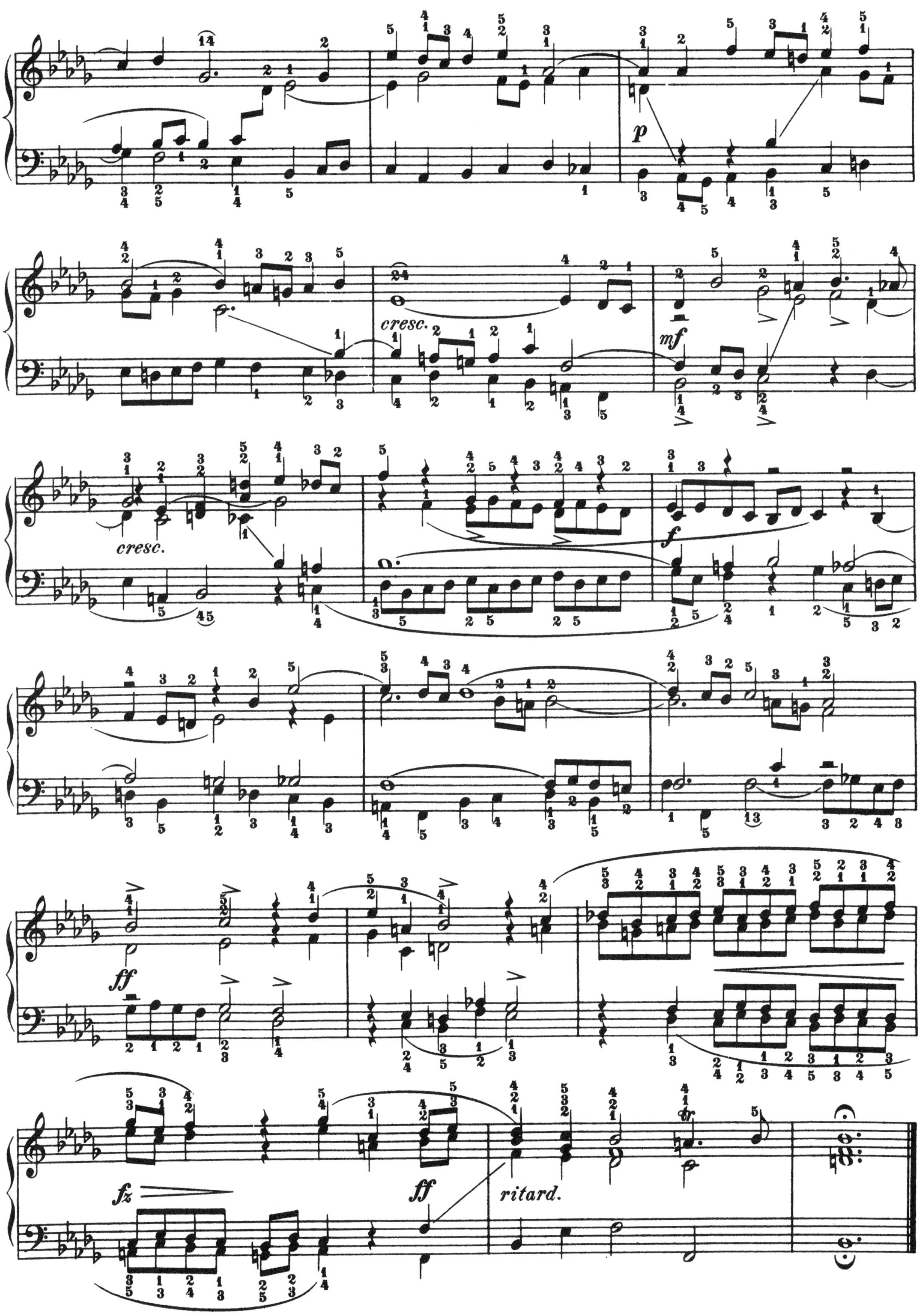
p
cresc.
mf
ff
fz
ritard.

Preludio XXIII.

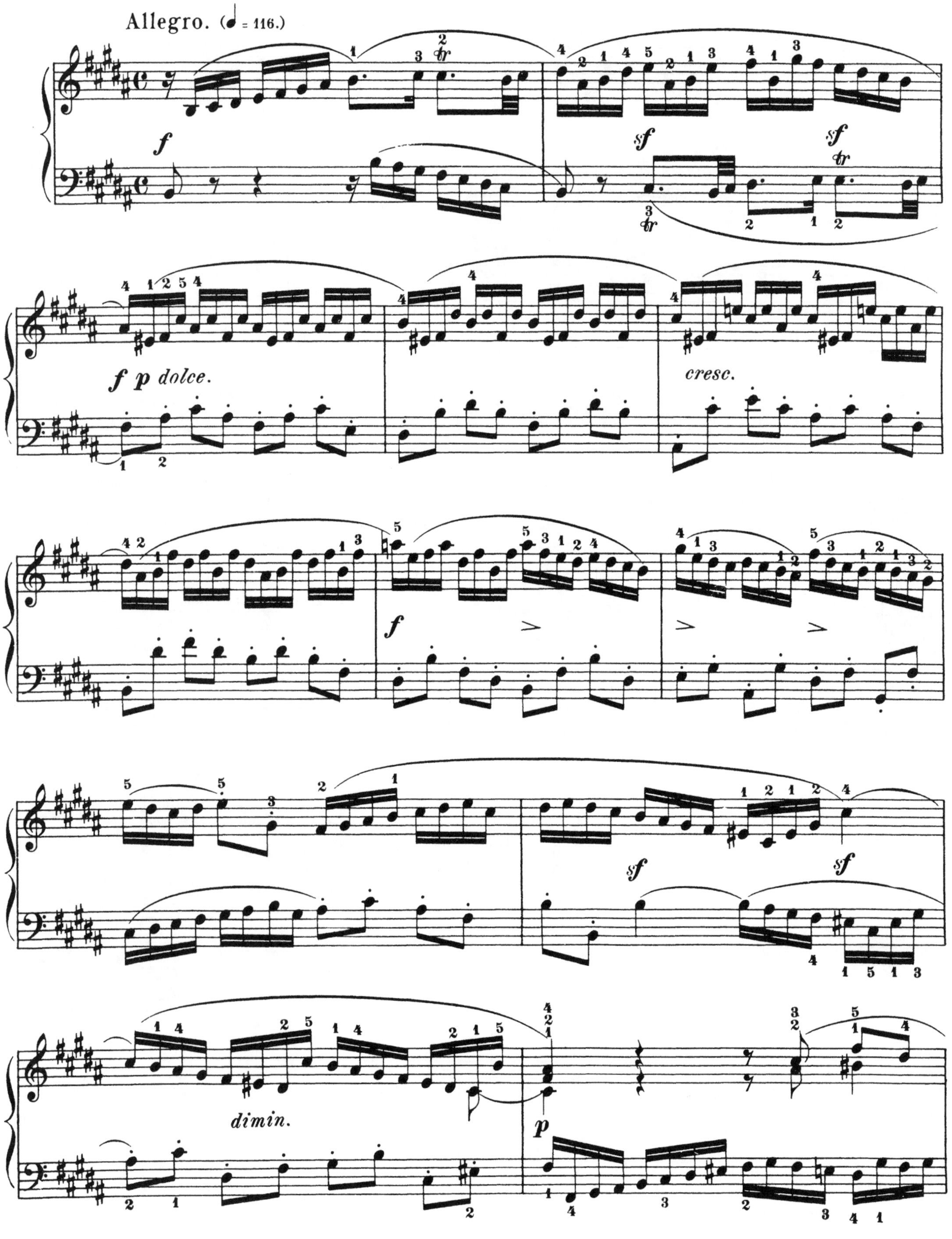

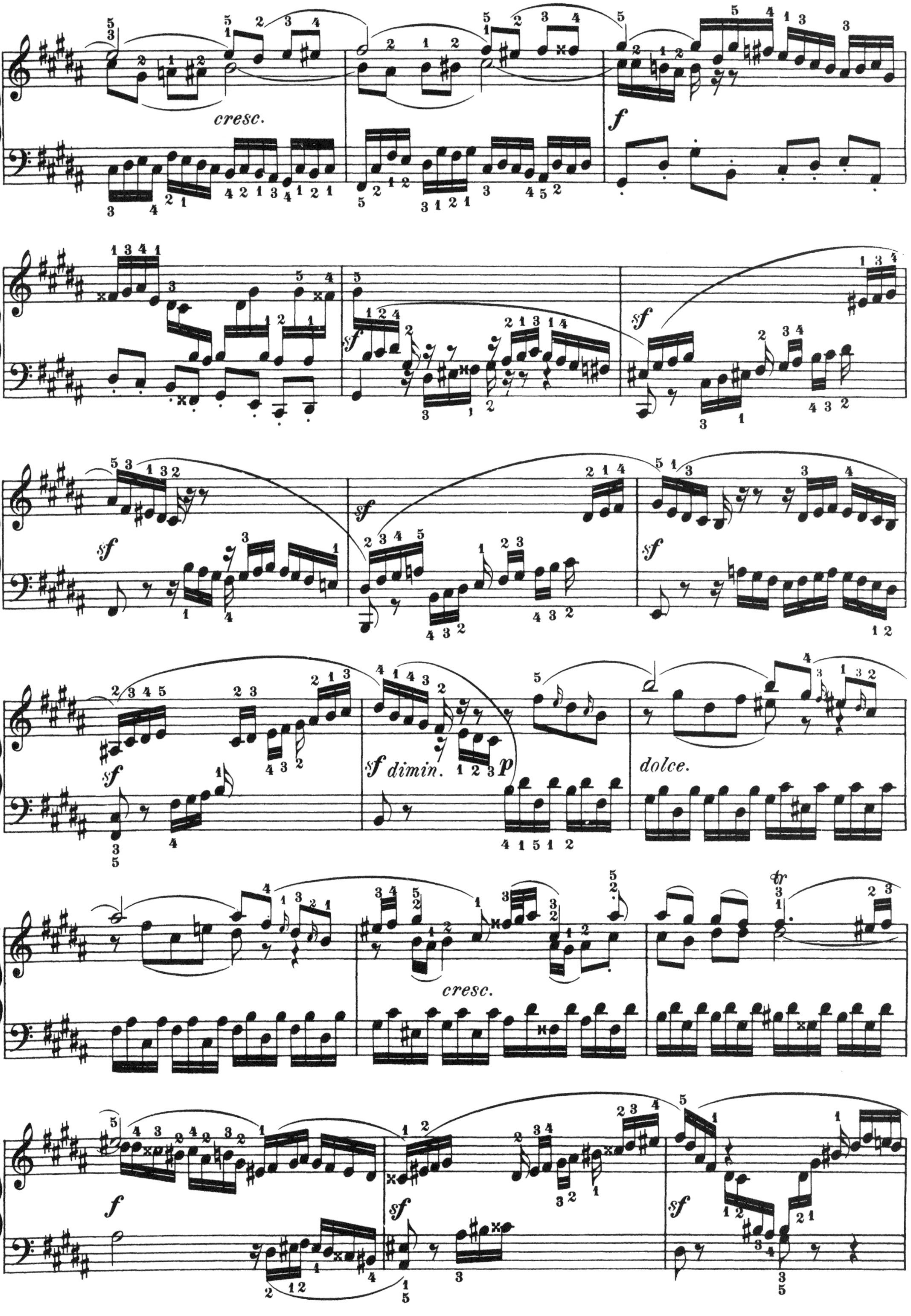

cresc.
f
sf
sf
sf
sf
sf
sf dimin.
p
dolce.
cresc.
f
sf
sf

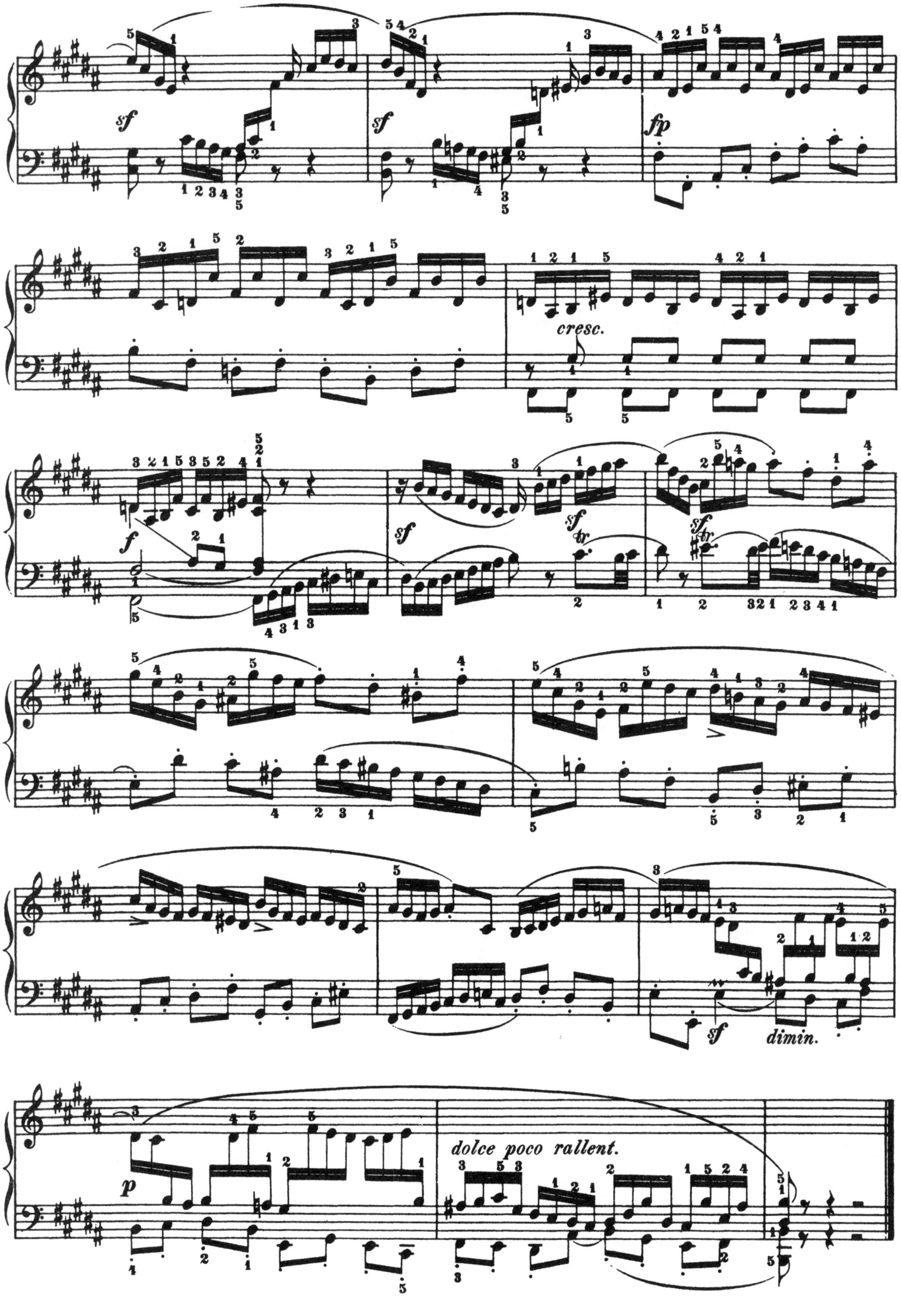
sf
sf
fp
cresc.
f
sf
sf
sf
sf
dimin.
p
dolce poco rallent.

Fuga XXIII.

a 4 Voci.

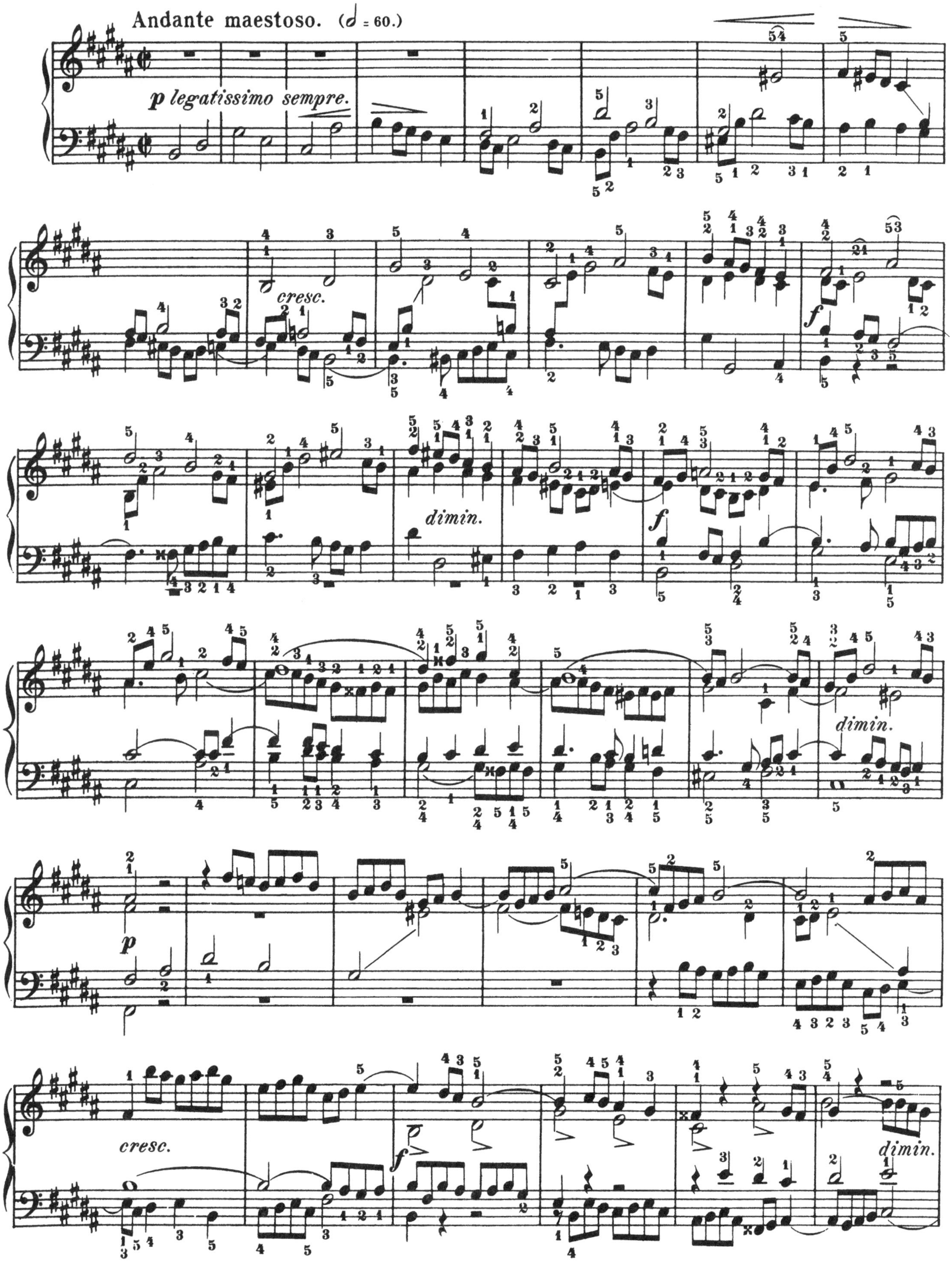

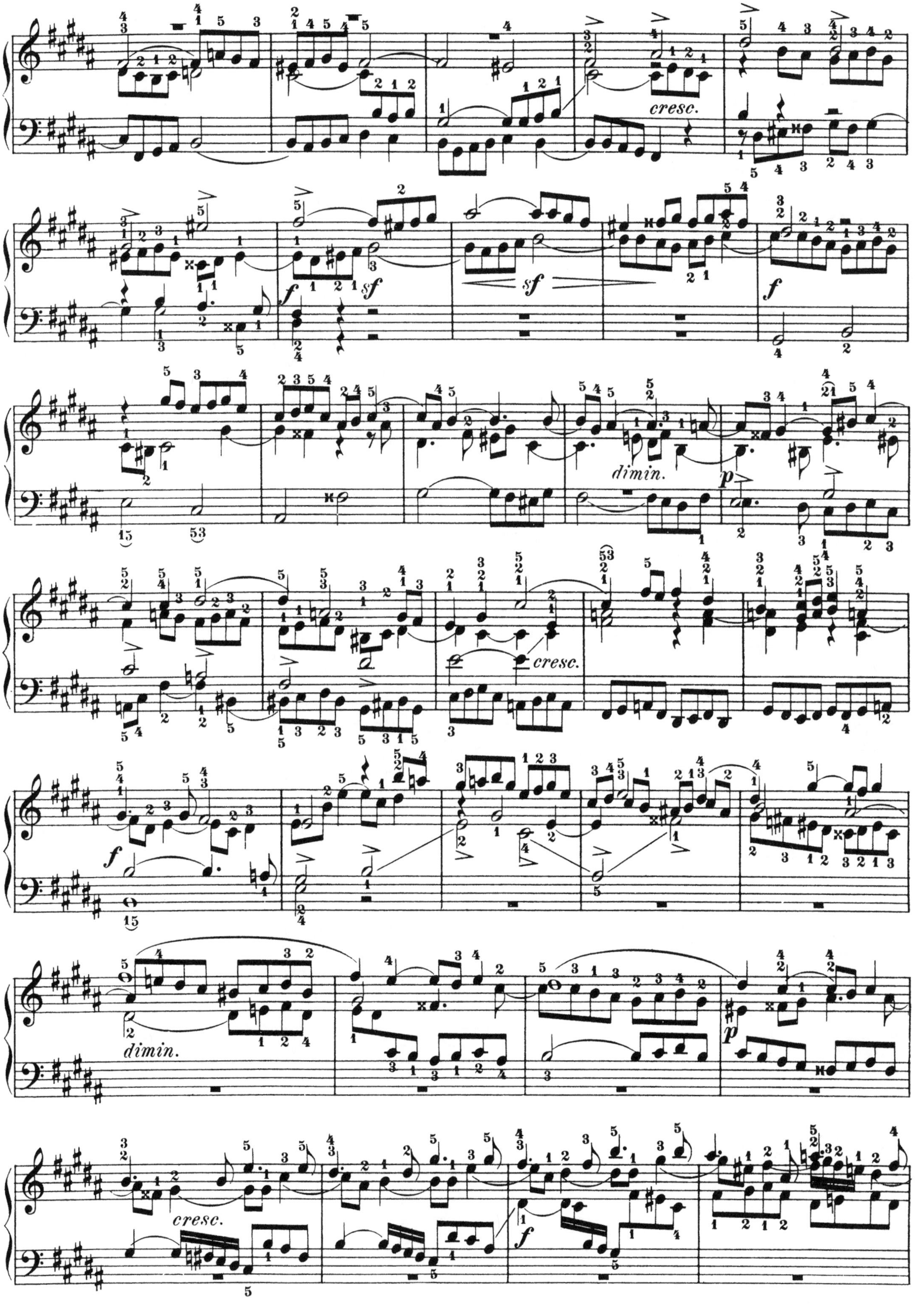
cresc.
sf
f
dimin.
p
cresc.
f
dimin.
p
cresc.
f

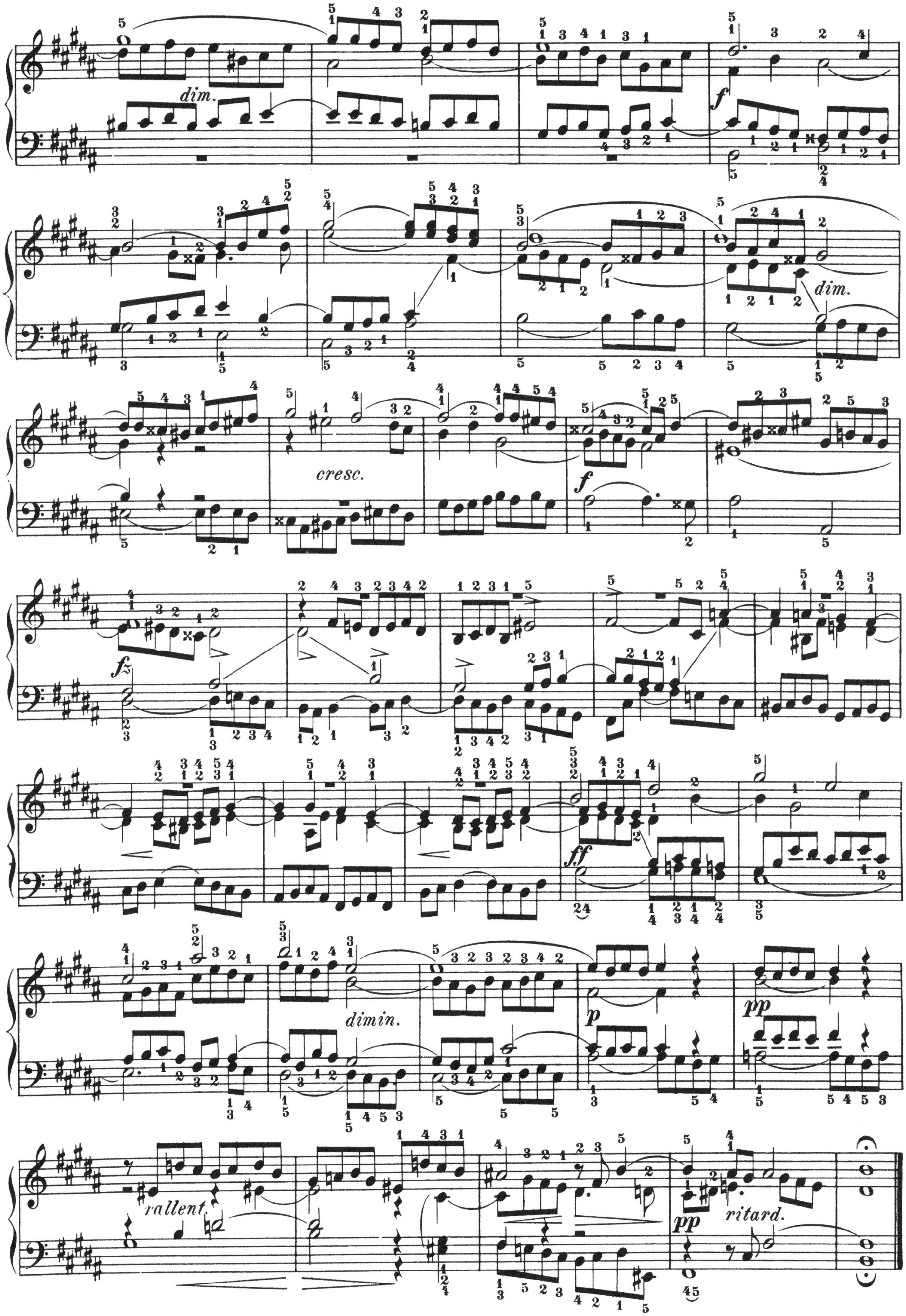
dim.
f
cresc.
f
fz
ff
dimin.
p
pp
rallent.
pp
ritard.

Preludio XXIV.

Allegro. (𝅗𝅥 = 80.)

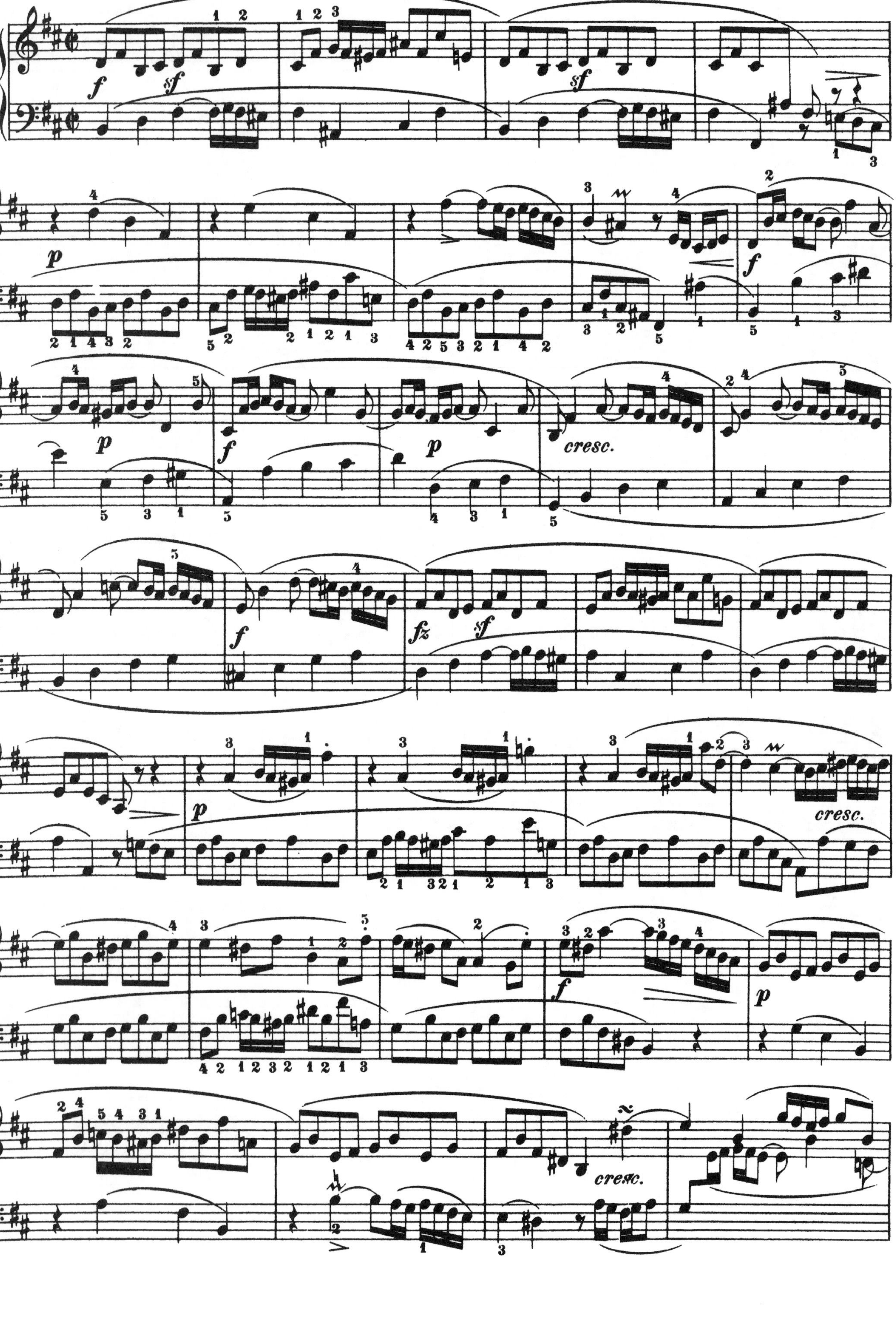

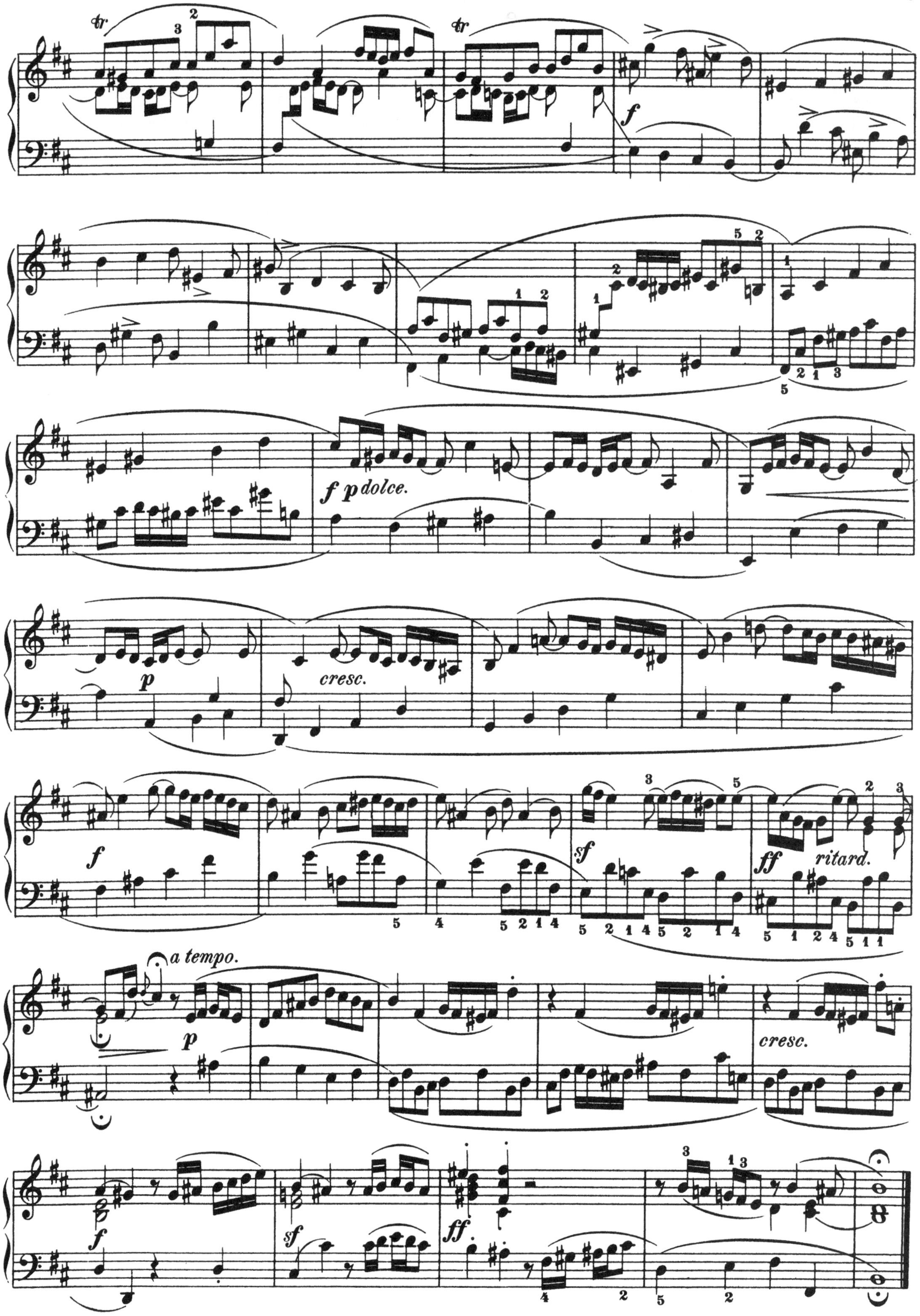
f
f p dolce.
p
cresc.
f
sf
ff
ritard.
a tempo.
p
cresc.
f
sf
ff

Fuga XXIV.

a 3 Voci.

Allegro vivace. (♩. = 76.)

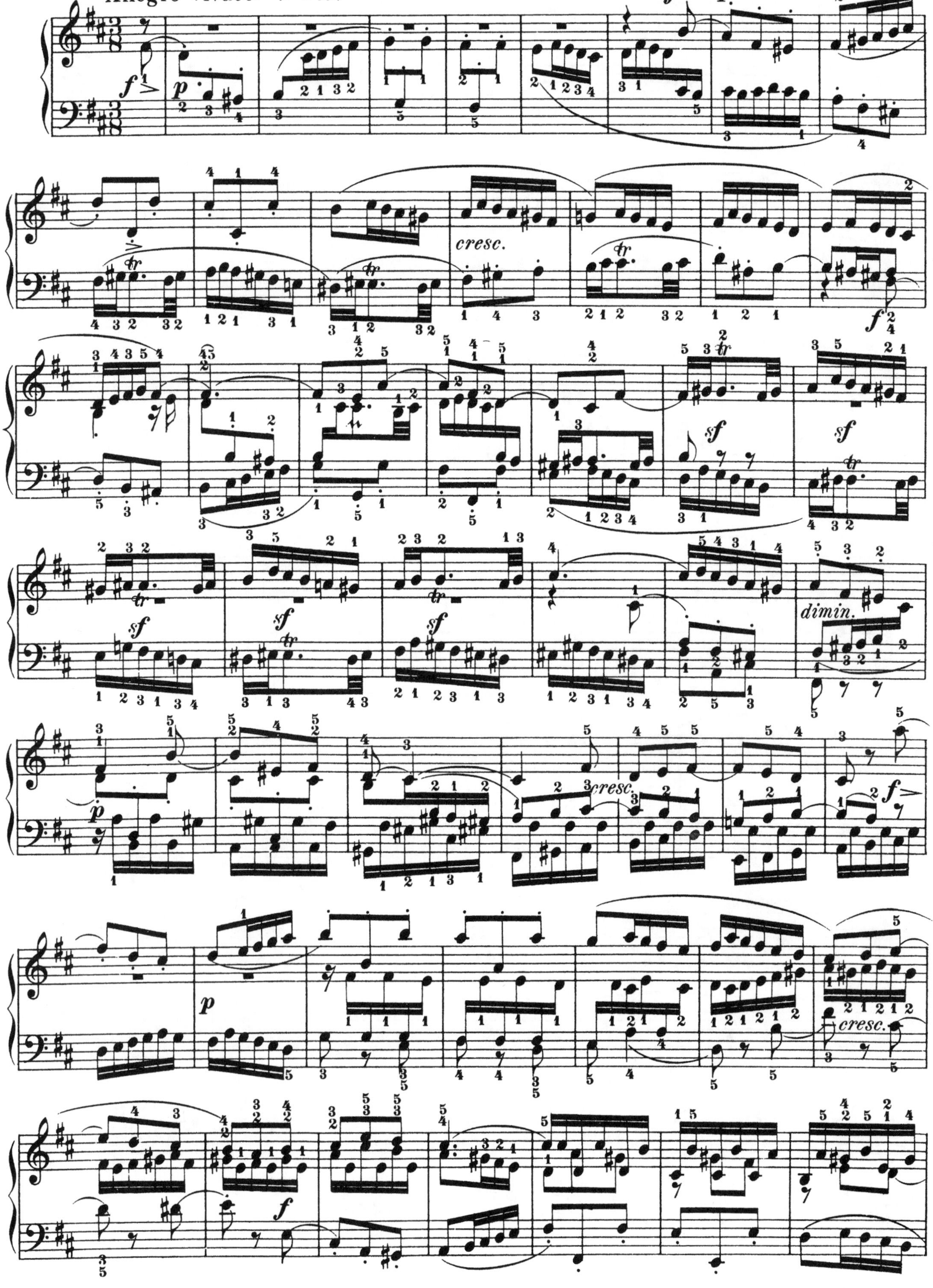